KT-173-921

Sharon Osbourne

EXTREME

MY AUTOBIOGRAPHY

Sharon Osbourne

with

Penelope Dening

TIME WARNER
BOOKS

TIME WARNER BOOKS

First published in Great Britain in October 2005 by Time Warner Books
Reprinted 2005 (eight times)

Copyright © Sharon Osbourne 2005

The moral right of the author has been asserted.

Permission to quote from 'It Was A Very Good Year'. Ervin Drake
© 1961. Renewed 1989 and assigned to Lindabet Music Corp.
Administered in the USA and Canada by the Songwriters' Guild
of America and the rest of the world by Memory Lane Music Ltd.
International copyright secured. Used with permission.
All rights reserved.

All rights reserved.
No part of this publication may be reproduced,
stored in a retrieval system, or transmitted, in any
form or by any means, without the prior
permission in writing of the publisher, nor be
otherwise circulated in any form of binding or
cover other than that in which it is published and
without a similar condition including this
condition being imposed on the subsequent purchaser.

A CIP catalogue record for this book
is available from the British Library.

Hardback ISBN 0 316 73131 5
C Format ISBN 0 316 73132 3

Typeset in Bembo by M Rules

Printed and bound in Great Britain by
Clays Ltd, St Ives plc

Time Warner Books
An imprint of
Time Warner Book Group UK
Brettenham House
Lancaster Place
London WC2E 7EN

www.twbg.co.uk

I dedicate this book to my darling husband Ozzy.
Thank you for being my partner and my
best friend and for changing my life for the better.
Thank you most especially for our babies.
My love for you is endless.

Acknowledgements

All the people at Time Warner who made this such a happy experience for me, especially Antonia Hodgson and Viv Redman.

Pepsy: without you I would never have been able to put my words onto paper. Thank you for making my book a reality. I've found a new friend.

Ian Willis: we have never met, but your wonderful book *American Rock 'n' Roll: The UK Tours 1956–72* unlocked the door to so many great memories.

My co-workers: I thank you for your loyalty. Lee Ali, Heather Bohn, Hardy Chandhok, Tony Dennis, John Fenton, Dave and Sharon Godman, Michael Guarracino, Kymberly Johnson, Dana Kiper, Dave Moscato, Marysia Murray, Dawn Odins, Dari Petrashvilli, Lynn Seager, Howard Smit, Claire Smith, Saba Teklehaymandt and Melinda Varga.

My loyal friends: there are not a lot of you, but you all know who you are. Thanks for always being there for me and even though I never call or write when I say I will, you accept me the way I am and I love you all for that.

Elton John and David Furnish: thank you for always being there with your friendship, guidance, love and, most of all, laughter. Puss loves you both.

Shelli and Irving Azoff: Shelli – you and I were separated at birth, but fortunately we found each other.

Colin, Mette, Michelle, Caspar, Jonathan, Fleur and Jake Newman: over the last thirty years we've all become one huge dysfunctional family together. What about the Newbournes? I thank you for always being there for us. Love you loads.

Gina, my dear niece: I love you and your gorgeous husband Dean and your divine babies Amelia and Ollie. Your love and support have been unconditional and I thank you.

My brother David: we've come a long way, haven't we? Thank you for your support throughout these last difficult years both through my cancer and with our father.

Jessica and Louis Osbourne: much love and respect. Your father and I are proud of you both.

And finally my children: Aimee, Kelly and Jack. Each of you has been a gift from God for me. How proud I am of your individuality, your wisdom and your passion.

Contents

Sharon Osbourne

Prologue

I am at the house, standing by the gate. Kelly is running across the courtyard, blonde hair bouncing around her little cherub face. She's like the golden angel on the Mormon Temple on Santa Monica Boulevard, and she's holding Jackie Boy by the hand, and I want to call out to them, and tell her to mind the fountain, that it's deeper than it looks, and that they shouldn't go sitting on the edge. And then Aimee is smiling up at me, pulling at my sleeve, wanting me to go with her, to show me something. And I feel so happy, and safe and calm. To know that the house is mine again; the same tall, tall palm trees, their trunks the colour of charcoal, and the creeper hung with the purple flowers, and everything like it used to be. I want to tell Dadda but I don't know where he is. So I watch my babies kneeling by the fountain, one at each corner of the cloverleaf, peering over the edge and listening to the water tumbling from one shell down to the next, and then to the next . . . but where is Dadda? He won't believe it when I tell him. I try calling out his name, but the tinkling of the fountain gets louder and louder, drowning everything else out . . .

. . . and then, like a cold liquid, like that cocktail of chemo trickling through my veins, I realise it's not the fountain I can hear, it's the fucking telephone. And I'm not even in California, but in Buckinghamshire in the kitchen at Welders, sharing the sofa with Minnie in front of a cold fire.

'I love you, Minnie,' I tell her, in my just-for-Minnie voice. And she opens her eyes and smiles. Nobody else believes me when I say she smiles, not even Ozzy who loves her nearly as much as I do. But she does: although she's a Pomeranian, Minnie has a mouth like a cat.

And now it's Beau's turn to give me a sloppy morning kiss. He's such a beautiful, beautiful dog. 'And so you should be,' I tell him, 'when I think of how much you cost.' Shitloads. Kelly, carried away in some charity auction. But, excuse me, Kel, a Labrador?

Kelly's problem is that she adores puppies and feels compelled to buy them. But as soon as they begin to shit and piss and smell, she's gone. Full-sized dogs just don't do it for her, and Beau is about as full-size as they come. So naturally, just like her other rejects, he came to live at Doheny in Beverly Hills. Unfortunately, sharing a shit-patch with a pack of midgets turned out to be not his idea of fun, nor theirs either, and when he went for Minnie one morning, I knew That Was It. It wasn't his fault, it was the situation. He's been in England ever since, where our 120-acre corner of English countryside seems to suit him very well. And now Minnie and he get on great. But he still needs somebody to love, so until we find him a new mummy or daddy, it has to be me. And I feel my eyes begin to prick.

What do other people do when their children leave home? Curled up on the sofa, the fire just a heap of ash with a few ends of half-charred wood sticking out, and no noise, no slamming doors, no rows, no arguments, no bickering, I feel cut off from everything I ever felt or ever thought I knew. Ozzy calls it our own Chinese Water Torture. A slow and painful and inevitable death of something that was once so vibrant and alive. And I think of my father sitting out the end of his life in his room above Hollywood Boulevard, listening to his Frank Sinatra records and wearing diapers. He's even got a picture of Sinatra on his bedside cabinet, a black and white ten-by-eight in a silver frame, with the famous signature slashed across the bottom. And at the top, 'To Don'. It sat on his office desk for years, there to impress, one of the props, like the cigars and the Rolls and the Rolex and the diamond cufflinks and the Mayfair address and the Savile Row suits. Don's friend, Ol' Blue Eyes . . .

He never even met him, let alone got him to sign a fucking photograph. He just forged it, framed it and there you are. Easy. 'No one hurt, eh, Sha?' No one hurt. In the end I think he even believed it himself. And now those nurses that feed him and wipe his arse probably believe it too. He loved all that connection with the mob, Joe Pagano, Charlie Kray and the rest of the two-bit hoods. He even liked to call himself the Godfather of Rock.

I thought I needed him. But I didn't.

And now it's my children who don't need me. They say they do, but it's all bullshit. I know it, they know it.

But I need them.

For months now I've been trying to get my office to print up a weekly schedule, with our names down the side, showing where each one of us is and what we're doing. Just to keep track. But Jack says it's me being controlling. And it scares the shit out of me, because that's what my father was all about. Control. But do they really want me phoning in the middle of the night because I don't know what fucking time it is wherever they happen to be? Right now Jack is in some jungle boot camp learning how to kick-box for a telly programme; Kelly is somewhere in the dance-music triangle of Miami–LA–New York, while Aimee is here with Ozzy and me in England. Can it be normal to have your children in three different continents? Is there anybody out there who can tell me what to do?

The only person who needs me now is my husband. He says I saved his life, but it's not true. He saved mine. If it wasn't for Ozzy, I'd have ended up in jail like my brother, like one of those crazed women in *Prisoner Cell Block H*. Or dead from an overdose of sleeping pills, looking for a way out.

And as I think of my husband, whom I love with all my heart, I realise he must still be asleep, and that it must be earlier than I thought, because by seven I know he'll be down here looking for me, worried that I'm not there beside him. He hates sleeping alone. But he needs his sleep so I tiptoed out and came down to the kitchen to read my script, hoping that the fire would still be alight. I put a couple of logs on but by the time it really got going I must have nodded off.

On normal days Ozzy always wakes first. Always, always. At Malibu, where the waves crash on the shore not ten yards from our beach house, the tide never seeming to go out or in more than a couple of yards, he'll wander onto the deck from our bedroom and stare at the ocean, watching for dolphins or whales dipping along the coast. In LA he'll put in the hours on his treadmill, working out in his gym and watching the History Channel at the same time, with the volume turned up way too high, his hearing shot from too many years on the road.

My husband has always been a morning person. Long before he and I got together, when I really didn't know him at all, I'd see him wandering hotel corridors or hovering in lobbies, while the rest of Black Sabbath would be totally out of it until way into the afternoon. And then they'd turn on him. Why was it always Ozzy's picture in this magazine or that magazine? Why was it always him they interviewed? Why not Tony or Geezer or Bill? Why not one of them? Possibly because he was the only one of you fuckers who was ever awake when it counted, I would tell them – though that was many years later. While the band were still unconscious, sleeping off whatever debauch they had perpetrated the previous night, their singer would be downstairs looking for people to talk to: musicians, journalists, girls, hotel staff, even me. He wasn't choosy. It was the company he wanted, though if anything else was on offer he wouldn't say no – one of the reasons his first marriage came to an end. One of the reasons he's always had such trouble keeping away from the bottle. A bar is the one place you can always find someone to talk to, if only the barman.

Now he just wanders around whatever house we happen to be in, humming melodies into a little tape recorder, talking to whoever is there at the time, playing his music at a hundred thousand decibels. Because once my husband is awake, that's it. He can never get back to sleep again. Never. Not like me. Sleep has always been my way out. My one escape. There were times when things got really bad that I'd take a couple of pills and not wake up for forty-eight hours. Ozzy says I would sleep through a nuclear explosion. But I love my bed. Love, love, love my bed. Which is where I'd be now if I didn't think I'd wake my husband with my cold feet.

Tucking them under me, I stare at the clock on the dresser, which says 6.45, trying to remember if it's the one that works. Beau looks at me, his head cocked to one side, and I realise I should let him out.

The sound of the sofa leg scraping on the floor is enough to set off a yawn of excitement, and his paws scuffle on the tiles as he scampers from side to side, and his great tail is going like a metronome. I slop sleepily across the room, turn the key and open the back door, and he's off, slurping noisily from the fountain on his way. And the sound of the water breaks my dream. The fountain. I was back at the Howard Hughes house. I hardly ever dream, but when I do it's always that. I was back at the Howard Hughes house, and it was mine again.

'And you, Minnie – do you want to go out too?'

She looks up at the sound of my just-for-Minnie voice.

Only if my mummy's going too, she says. In fact, I didn't need to ask her. Minnie never leaves my side unless she's forced to.

As I settle back under the blanket on the sofa, I notice that the clock is still showing 6.45. At the last count there were eleven in this kitchen, and only one of them goes, and now I know it isn't this one. It's not that the others are broken, it's because they never get wound. Anyway, a kitchen full of ticking clocks would drive me, and everybody else, insane. Like most things I own, I buy them for what they look like, because I'm a magpie and I like to be surrounded by beautiful things. So I have clutter on every table, chest of drawers, shelf, wall, you name it, in every room in each one of our three houses. And I'm always adding to it: pictures, photographs in silver frames, dolls, golliwogs, angels, books, boxes, lamps, chandeliers. I have more chandeliers than most people have light bulbs. And as I look round the kitchen, with its tiles of medieval musicians with their instruments, like tiny figures in a Bruegel painting, and the dresser and my blue and white china, my mind goes back to the kitchen where I grew up, the Brixton basement with its lino, its fifties glass-fronted cabinet, its miserable coal fire that was the only form of heat. And how everything in that house, apart from my father, was always dirty. And how I thought that everybody lived like we did; that arguments were only ever settled by a fist in the face, that bailiffs were as likely to be outside the front door as milkmen. That smashing a light bulb into your brother's ear was a perfectly reasonable way to behave. That all fathers had guns. It was only when I got to be about twelve and went to stay at my best friend Posy's house for the first time that I discovered other people's lives weren't like that.

I woke in the middle of the night with what I thought was diarrhoea – ever since the operation to remove my cancer it's either been one thing or the other. All or nothing. Story of my life.

So I crept out of bed and ran to my bathroom, but this time it was nothing more than old-fashioned butterflies in the tummy, because, after three days of intense one-to-one rehearsals with the director, it's crunch time for my acting career: the first full-cast read-through of *The Vagina Monologues*, and I know it's key, which is why I'm down here going over my lines for the hundred and seventeenth time.

I have never done anything remotely like this before. The audience might be buying their tickets to see that motormouth Sharon Osbourne in the flesh, but Jenny Eclair and Diane Parish don't give a shit about who I am. They've probably never even seen *The Osbournes* or *The X-Factor* and must be wondering what the hell they've let themselves in for. The last time I set foot on a West End stage was forty years ago in panto: *Cinderella* at the London Palladium, with Cliff Richard as Buttons, me as a mouse.

All I want is to not let anybody down, not the cast, not the audience, not the director, but especially not Aimee, who's been so patient with me these last few days: getting my breathing right, my phrasing right, all that technical theatre stuff she knows about. And finally, of course, the gentlemen of the press will be just gagging for me to fall flat on my arse. But when I think who's done it before: Kate Winslet, Glenn Close, Sharon Stone . . . I've got my work cut out. No autocues, no retakes, just me, the audience and the words.

And that's what I must learn to trust in, Irina Brown the director says. The words. Let them work for me. And she's right. The testimony of these women is so powerful that the more you look into each character, the easier it gets. Though 'easier' here is a question of degree. Right from the start she made it clear that the crib cards we're allowed to take with us on stage are for emergencies only, and by the time the show opens we will all need to have every line by heart. If not, she says, we'll be short-changing the women whose emotions and lives we are borrowing. And they deserve better than that. And of course she's right.

At the beginning, I honestly didn't think I could do it. But I'm getting there, by just reading the script over and over and watching the Eve Ensler video, the woman who wrote it and who performed it originally as a one-woman show. And, like I used to tell it to my *X-Factor* kids, success is as much to do with hard work as raw talent. I know I have as much raw talent as a fucking lobster, but at least I'm working hard and am now comfortable with what I have to do.

This isn't the first time I've been approached to do *The Vagina Monologues.* A theatre company in Chicago contacted me in early autumn 2002 and I remember feeling totally overawed. I mean, what did they want with me? Although I've been called a drama queen by my family for years, I'm no actress. *The Osbournes* might have played like a comedy, but it was totally unscripted, the shape of each episode only emerging at the editing stage. No lines, no rehearsals, no retakes, no nothing. But if those people in Chicago thought I could do it, perhaps I could. What did I know?

Throughout all my years with Ozzy, I had never been in the limelight. People in the music industry knew who I was, but that was it. As far as the world (and I) was concerned, I was a wife, a mother and a business woman. But with *The Osbournes* all that changed. And after I was diagnosed with cancer, I had this need, an obsession you might even say, to experience everything and anything. Time was too precious to waste and I wanted to take in as much of life as I could before it was too late. It wasn't like I saw my future in the theatre; although I'd spent years as a child moving from one stage school to another, I couldn't sing and I couldn't act. However, after all I'd come through, and the brave women I'd met on the way, I didn't want to say no. But Ozzy put his foot down. I was only two months into my chemo and was still really, really sick.

So when early in 2005 a production company in London approached me, it was as if fate was giving me a second chance. I had survived Simon Cowell, and was ready for another challenge. Another experience. Why stand still? And when Aimee agreed to do it with me, mother and daughter on stage together, it seemed like destiny.

Since the moment she decided not to be involved with *The Osbournes* – perfectly understandable when you're eighteen and would be embarrassed at your family even if they were entirely normal – there's been an inevitable separation. Not an estrangement, but on a practical level our lives were just so different. I mean, by the time we were six months into the show she wasn't even living at home. So the fact that she and I would be spending six weeks working together was something very precious indeed.

However, two months ago, in February, Aimee discovered two lumps in her breast. When I heard the news I literally could not speak. It was as if every cell in my body was closing down. She's twenty-one. I wanted to scream, to wail, to howl. To tear up every plant in the garden that dared go on living. But how could I do that to Ozzy after all he had been through with me? In fact, I had to do all I could to calm *him* down. Aimee, of course, was as dignified as she always is.

Lumps at her age, I told him, are usually benign, and the chances of them being cancerous were very remote. But it was as if I had been taken over by somebody else's voice. Inside I was fucking terrified. The idea that cancer only hits people of forty-plus is a crock of shit. It's like an epidemic out there. And more and more young people are coming down with it. While I accept that I'm only a layman, because of the work I do with the hospital now, I'm talking to patients all the time. One that I see regularly is a young woman whose lump in her breast turned out to be malignant. It was removed. Then she developed a lump in the back of her neck, and then her spine. And then she called me the other day to tell me it's now in her bones. She's twenty-four.

In Aimee's case an ultrasound was done immediately, but apparently it's difficult to make a firm diagnosis at her young age, so they decided to remove her lumps anyway. Thank God they turned out to be benign. We didn't celebrate. How can you celebrate something like that? It would be like tempting fate. The best thing, the only thing, was to try and forget it, like a bad dream, and get on with our lives.

This wasn't as difficult as it sounds, because the next week or so was insane. The Oscars were in town and I'd been asked to front them for Sky. Then, only four days later, there were the Australian MTV Awards in Sydney that we were hosting as a family. Kelly was going to be performing there with her band, so there were rehearsals, accommodation and the rest of it to fix. At the same time she was busy doing the video for her first single from her new album. It's unbelievable that you have three and a half or four minutes of a song and it takes two days of constant filming and it's like they're shooting *War and Peace*. And if that wasn't enough, the very last episode of *The Osbournes* would soon be screening and a final 'special' had been planned with Dr Phil, the family counselling guru discovered by Oprah. Then there was the tenth Ozzfest to organise; this year will be the twelfth consecutive summer we have been on the road. Merchandising to agree, other bands to firm up (we only have twenty-one . . .), schedules to organise, stage design to finalise. Of course, I've got a whole team of people doing the day-to-day, but ultimately all decisions are made by me and it's been that way for the last thirty years.

About a week into the mayhem came the call from the clinic. Although, as we already knew, Aimee's tumours were clear of cancer, the cells around them were 'a little unusual', they said. She would need radiation, but first she needed to build up her strength as her blood count was too low to start treatment immediately. Naturally I panicked. To me radiation is as terrifying as chemo. But it was just a precaution, they repeated. Like removing the lumps. Just a precaution.

We talked about cancelling *The Vagina Monologues*. But Aimee saw the show for what it was. A real opportunity. A showcase for her. It might be years before a chance to work on something serious came along again. This was already my second chance. And she felt fine, she said. She'd been overworking, writing and recording her own album, staying up late and all the rest of the shit, but now she was clear and planning to spend a month in Australia after the MTV Awards, which would give her a real rest.

Then, last night, just as Ozzy and I were about to leave to record *The Parkinson Show* – to promote Ozzy's new boxed set and *The Vagina Monologues* – there was a call from Irina. Aimee needed to get herself to a doctor, she said. 'This child is so tired that I cannot work with her, and if nothing is done, she's never going to make the show.'

I know Aimee's tired, but I still think it's just the combination of jet lag – flying from Australia to England really takes it out of you – and first-night nerves. Aimee's like Ozzy: a fucking nightmare for anyone around him before he goes on stage, but once he smells the audience, he's on fire.

I called our doctor in Harley Street and got Aimee an immediate appointment. When she got out and called us, we were already on the set with Michael, but we spoke as soon as I got back to the dressing room. The doctor had taken some blood tests, she said. He'd get the results to her as soon as possible. She didn't seem that worried, and we talked about Stephen Fry who'd been on with us.

I went to look in on her just now on my way downstairs. Back in her old bedroom in the attic under the sloping roof. Fast asleep.

It was Ozzy who found the fax, on his way down to find me. Wandering around.

Aimee is seriously ill. Her doctor says it's amazing that she'd been able to do anything at all. As for the radiation related to the breast tissue, there is no way anyone will touch her in the state she's in. We should contact her oncologist immediately and also begin the process of building up her immune system. She just needs complete bed rest of at least six weeks combined with high doses of selected vitamins via a drip.

We were in the kitchen. Aimee was crying and finding it hard to breathe, her breath coming in gasps, her Ventolin in her hand. Ozzy was sitting on the sofa beside her, holding his head in his hands. The fire was roaring, spitting and hissing. I couldn't believe that I hadn't seen it coming. And suddenly I couldn't cope with it any more.

'Don't worry, baby,' I said, cradling her head in my shoulder. 'We'll get you back to California to the doctors who know you.'

I didn't think about the consequences. All I knew was that this was the right thing to do. Nothing else mattered. With Kelly and Jack, I had all too often put work first. Not that I realised it at the time. My problem, they now say, is that I didn't know how to say no. It all came out when Ozzy and I went to the family sessions at rehab. I had been there so many times before with Ozzy. But seeing your own children like that, so distressed, so humiliated, so desperate, is beyond any pain I have ever known.

I knew that, whatever they said, it would be hard to hear, and I prepared myself for the worst. And, to give them their due, they didn't milk the situation. They just told it us like it was: their father was a drunk and their mother wasn't there for them.

It was unbearable. I didn't cry. They would only have been tears for me. Selfish tears asking what had I done to deserve this when I needed all my strength for them. And I swore then I would never let that happen again. Never. This time I was saying no.

I put Aimee to bed and she fell asleep almost instantly although it had barely gone nine. We decided that Saba, our housekeeper from LA who had come over to England to be our dresser on the show, would take her back to California. Ozzy and I would fly back as soon as I'd sorted everything out this end. As for *The Vagina Monologues*, we had had only three days' rehearsal and we hadn't even met the other members of the cast. There were plenty of proper actresses out there who had done it before, professional enough to step in at short notice. I was sure everybody would understand.

But I was wrong. No sooner was it on the news that Sharon Osbourne and her daughter had pulled out than rumours started circulating on the internet. Another Osbourne kid who'd fallen victim to drugs. So that was why we made the decision to go public. Originally, we had just said 'medical reasons', as I hadn't wanted to make the details of Aimee's health general knowledge – it was nobody's fucking business, and I hadn't the right. But in the end Aimee made the decision for me.

In later days people would ask me why I needed to go back with her. Why couldn't I have stayed in London and fulfilled my commitment? I have only one commitment, I told them, and that's to my children.

In March 2005 we were hosting the Australian MTV Awards in Sydney, and a TV executive had invited us to his home to have dinner one evening.

So we get there and the house is lovely, and it's a lovely spread, and lovely people, and I'm beside the hostess, and she's laid out this beautiful supper for us. And then she turns to me and says, 'You're a Jew, aren't you?'

I was completely dumbstruck. To me, it was like saying, 'So you like a bit of dick up the arse, don't you?' It's that extreme. It's like saying, 'Do you like to give head then?' You would never, ever ask anybody that question. And I'd just met this woman and I'd just been saying to her, 'Nice shrimp,' and then she goes, 'You're a Jew, aren't you?'

And I said, 'Yes, I am.'

And when I went away I thought, Why did I say 'Yes, I am' when I'm not? Technically in Judaism to be a Jew you have to be born of a Jewish mother. My mother was an Irish Catholic. But I was so taken aback by what she said, and I found it so offensive, it was like, 'Yes, I fucking am, and what are you going to do about it?' If she had said, 'So you're black?' I'd have said, 'Yes, I fucking am, and proud of it.'

1

Brixton

Memory is a strange thing, and since starting this book I have discovered that people's memories of the same event can be very, very different. What follows, therefore, is only my memory of what happened in my life. I cannot say this is how it happened. I can only say this is how it seemed to me at the time.

My earliest memory is of sitting on a wooden chair, watching some girls going through their dance routines in fishnet tights and silver shoes. I can't have been much more than two, but far from this being unusual, it was everyday life for me.

The church hall where my father would always do these rehearsals is no longer there, though the church still is, and the house where we lived – 68 Angell Road – has become one of a row of townhouse-style council flats.

The area has changed too. There's an edge of danger to it now, which wasn't the case back then. In the fifties and early sixties, Brixton was where all the variety artists lived, comedians, singers, ventriloquists, acrobats. Entertainers. Pre-TV, variety was the only entertainment there was for ordinary people, and with the Brixton Empress and the Camberwell Palace being less than a mile away, Brixton was the hub. Over the road from us were the fire-eater and a juggler. A dog act, a man called Reg, lived in a caravan in a bombsite behind our road and I used to play with his little girl.

Our house was large and old, with six steps leading up from the pavement, and pillars on either side. At one time it must have been quite grand, but by the fifties the plaster was peeling off, and once you got inside everywhere was dingy and draughty and damp.

Before I was born in 1952, my mother ran it as a theatrical digs, a boarding house for artists who needed a place to stay when they were working in town. And that was how she met my father. He took a room for the week in 1950, and six weeks later they were married.

Looking back, it's hard to see what they saw in each other – she didn't own the house, it was rented, and belonged to a chart-topping honky-tonk piano player called Winifred Atwell. And although my mother was obviously nice to look at – at least my father must have thought so – she was ten years older than him and divorced with two children. Her name was Hope Shaw (Mr Shaw had been a band leader and had fucked off to Canada with somebody else) but she was always called Paddy because of her Irish background, though my father would often call her Paddler because he thought it sounded more Jewish.

Maybe my father saw her as being a bit bohemian, because he himself had come from this very strict Jewish background, very *frum* as they say in Yiddish, while my mother was the polar opposite: an Irish Catholic and a former dancer.

My father's family were Russian Jews who had arrived in Manchester around the time of the First World War. He was born Harry Levy, but changed it to Don Arden when he decided to make a career in show business. With such an obviously Jewish name he'd get nowhere, he said, and he'd had his fill of anti-Semitism in the army during the war. I don't know where he got it from – perhaps from Elizabeth Arden, the make-up line – but it did what he wanted. It's a name that says nothing about who you are or where you come from. A blank canvas.

My father was a singer, and although popular with audiences he was always in trouble with management. Things came to a head one night when he had a fight with a stage manager who had called him a Jew-boy. It ended with them both rolling around the stage kicking the shit out of each other and the other guy falling into the orchestra pit. Not only was he told to pack his things and get out, Don Arden was banned from performing in any venue owned by Moss Empires for two years and, as these people had a virtual monopoly in variety theatres, this was like a death sentence for his career. (They owned fifty of them, so artists would be under permanent contract, moving around the country playing one town a week.)

In order to make enough money to survive, he began packaging whole shows, which he'd then tour around independent theatres where his name still held good. He continued to perform, topping the bill with his own act – not only singing but doing impressions of American stars like Bing Crosby and Al Jolson that people knew from films – but also compèring the rest of the show: a comic, puppet act, dancers, whatever. He was like a one-man band. He did so well that when the ban was lifted he never went back to simply performing.

My father didn't dare tell his family he was married until 1951 when my brother David was born. Even then, as he expected, his mother went insane and only finally agreed to meet my mother when I came along. Sally, as everybody called my grandmother, was herself divorced from my grandfather, so maybe he thought she'd be sympathetic – in fact I later found out that she'd been dumped in very similar circumstances to my mother – but she never really accepted having a *shiksa* as a daughter-in-law, and that went for my father's sister, my auntie Eileen, as well.

I can't remember a time when there wasn't turmoil within the family: fights between his mother and my mother, between his sister and my mother. And then, back in Brixton, there was my half-sister Dixie: always some drama with her. And different sorts of problems with my half-brother Richard. In fact, my father detested both his stepchildren, who by the time I was born were fifteen and ten respectively. According to him, Richard was always a *dimp* and a *schmuck* and Dixie was always a tart. But I was very close to them when I was growing up. With both my parents involved in the business, they relied on Richard to babysit and Dixie to cook and make my clothes.

The house in Angell Road was always overflowing with people. Not just us: my parents and me, David and Richard (Dixie had been sent away to school – my father got rid of her as soon as he could) but, to bring in extra money when it was needed, they continued to rent out rooms, mainly to other artists. In the basement next to the kitchen there was a permanent lodger, a young man called Nigel Heathhorn, who lived there until we moved. He had been orphaned during the war and put in the care of my mother by the bank that acted as his legal guardians. I never really knew what he did, but he used to spend money like water. My father had a record player he'd bought at Boots, and Nigel would buy all these classical records and stand there conducting them with a baton while admiring his reflection in the window. He even got hold of a proper film projector, 35mm, and would rent out films from Wallace Heaton in Victoria and show them on the back wall of the garden, with a sheet pinned up for a screen, and everyone in the street would be hanging out of their windows watching.

Apart from Nigel, the only people who ever came into our

house were artists or people connected with that world. The first room on the right when you came in was used as the office, and behind that was the sitting room which opened onto the conservatory, and this was where friends and business associates were entertained. My mother's pride and glory was a bar that she bought at the Ideal Home Exhibition in Earl's Court, made out of wine barrels cut in half, which was stuck in the corner of every home they ever owned. There was a bit you lifted up to go behind, and there was a corner shelf for the miniatures. And I can picture my mother there now, leaning on that bar, a gin in one hand and a cigarette in the other.

School was about half an hour's walk up Brixton Hill but we usually took the bus from the end of our road. It was a preparatory school called Clermont, and the owner and only teacher was Miss Mayhew, a survivor from the *Titanic*. It was tiny, never more than thirty children, and we did our work in two rooms at the front. Our playground was the garden.

I was five when I started. David, being eighteen months older than me, had gone the previous year. My mother took us for the first week, to show me how to do the bus, but then we were on our own, rain or shine, sometimes with a packed lunch, usually not. My mother was never an early morning person. I'd go to my parents' bedroom to ask for a shilling for my lunch and she and my father would both be still sleeping and it was like: 'For fuck's sake, Sharon, can't you see your mum's sleeping?'

Even when I was older and could make my own sandwiches, half the time there was no bread in the bin. So we'd buy a bag of chips from the chippie, or pick up a packet of crisps from the corner shop. In the summer, we might walk to the café in Brockwell Park, an old building that seemed very grand in the middle of all that green and trees, and it was on top of a hill, so you could see right over London and David would watch the birds.

Brixton then was a good place for kids to grow up. It was a poor part of London, which meant it was cheap. There were the market arcades under the railway line full of little stalls, like the pie and mash shop with its metal trough of jellied eels that they would chop up, which made me gag but fascinated me at the same time. And then there were the Indian shops with saris hung up outside the little entrances, all those amazing colours and strange foreign smells.

Just up from the market was Woolworth's where, as well as spending any money we might have, my brother and I would go stealing for sweets. My role was to go up and ask for something, and when the assistant went looking for it David would stuff his pockets with anything he could find: play cigarettes, blackjacks, fruit salads, flying saucers.

The other place we stole from was a tiny sweet shop that was the only building still standing on the bombsite behind our house, at the end of an alley. The lady who ran it was very old so taking anything was easy: flying saucers, sherbet dips and Jubblies, a pyramid of iced orange that you used to squeeze.

In those days my brother was very industrious in trying to find ways of making money. When it was Guy Fawkes night he used to dress me up, put me in an old-fashioned pram with big wheels, stick me outside the pub and I'd be penny-for-the-guy. My father was a Black and White Minstrel for a while, on the hit TV show that was broadcast on Saturday nights. It would never be allowed now. In America it's called black face, exactly what Al Jolson did, and it was probably the high spot of my father's singing career – so there was always plenty of greasepaint hanging around the house. David would black me up, then find a bit of black cloth to drape me in, shove on an old hat and push me along to the pub and we'd get all the Irish drunks as they came out.

Those were the good days. Bad days were when I'd be put in

the coalhole, which was like a horrible underground cupboard off Nigel's bedroom. Coal still got stored in there – delivered down a chute from the street – and whenever my brother or I misbehaved, my parents would lock us in there for what seemed like for ever, but was probably only an hour or an hour and a half. It was horrible. And the worst thing was the spiders, and scufflings that David said were rats.

My grandmother, Nana, lived in Prestwich, a smart suburb of Manchester, and I absolutely adored her. She's probably the only woman I ever met who was bald, and to hide it she had this terrible wrap-around hairdo, a real Bobby Charlton, except hers would wrap around twice. When we were out – Nana was a big one for afternoon tea at the Midland Hotel – she wore hats to cover it up. Hats with matching gloves and matching handbag. Everyone wore hats in those days, if you were a lady. There were other things she taught me about being a lady, like using rosewater and witch hazel on your skin and not sitting on the lavatory seat when you were out because you could catch things. Unspecified things, but which later I discovered included babies when you didn't want them. So she showed me how to cover the seat with overlapping sheets of shiny Bronco and then try to sit down quick before they fluttered away.

Whenever my parents were on tour in the north, they'd take us out of school and leave us with her. They didn't give a shit about the academic side of life. But the atmosphere between my mother and Nana was terrible, and until my parents left the house it was like walking on eggshells, so I couldn't wait for them to leave.

Being with Nana made me feel warm and safe. She was motherly. She would cook for me. She would tuck me up in bed. And she was very house proud and would scrub the front step every day. Everything in that house was scrubbed and cleaned till it shone.

She couldn't have been more different from my other grand-mother, who unfortunately I saw more of because she lived not far from us in Clapham, just off Wandsworth Common. She'd been a dancer like my mother, and again like my mother she now ran a theatrical digs. Dolly O'Shea had long white hair that she wore down to her shoulders, curled under and tied with a huge red satin bow, and she always had dark red lipstick, like Bette Davis in *Whatever Happened to Baby Jane?*, that went over the lines of her mouth, and I never saw her without a fag hang-ing out of her mouth. She was incredibly ugly and had the biggest nose I have ever seen. A real Fagin nose. She frightened me and she stank, stank of her fanny and BO, and her flat stank of fried food. She adored my brother – she even paid for him to go to stage school at the beginning – but she hated me. If she'd been Chinese she'd have been the sort of person who had the girls put out to die.

And I remember so clearly clinging onto the banisters in Angell Road when my dad said we had to go and see her, and me saying, 'Please don't make me! Please, please let me stay home!' And then he would whack me over the knuckles so I'd let go of the banister and then he'd drag me into the car.

My father was soon going further afield with his tours, mostly to American air bases in Germany. There were four in Frankfurt alone, each one of them full of bored GIs waiting to be enter-tained. We never stayed on the bases themselves, but sometimes we'd be allowed in to watch the show. He could keep the fuck-ing show; what I wanted was the PX, the general store with all the American magazines and comics, *Batman* and *Superman*. But the best thing was the food, milkshakes and burgers – there was nothing like that in fifties Brixton. But usually at night they'd leave us back in the boarding house or hotel, where my brother and I would run riot, breaking into the kitchens, playing around with the lifts and generally causing havoc.

The other thing I remember about Germany was Christmas. My father had a partner called Gisela Gumpher who had a house in the Black Forest where we spent two Christmases running. In Angell Road we never had what you could call a proper Christmas, and so this was my first experience of what fun and how happy a family-type Christmas could be, and I never forgot it.

Religion was never a big deal in our house. My father used his religion only when it suited him, like speaking Yiddish. As a lot of other people in the business were Jewish, it was a way of keeping some people in and other people out – perhaps even my mother. Though, having been brought up with it, I understood everything.

Being Jewish, he told me, was something to be proud of, and he gave me a pair of Star of David earrings and a little Star of David to put round my neck. I had no idea really what it meant, it was just a necklace as far as I was concerned. But one day when my brother and I were coming home from playing in the park, some kids began to taunt us, calling us Dirty Jews. I hurled myself on them, and suddenly David was there too, punching and kicking and scratching, till they were the ones backing off. It didn't affect me. They could just as well have said I was an alien or a Dalek for all the difference it made. That was just how it was.

As for my mother, she never mentioned religion, never wore a cross, never went near a priest. But Kath McMurray, whom she had known since they worked in the same dance troupe before the war and who was one of her few real friends, was very Catholic. As Teresa, her daughter, was a friend of mine, I'd sometimes go round to their church with her, and wait while she went into the confessional box, dilly-dallying around until she came out. My parents' line was that we were 'cosmopolitan'. And it was 'whatever you want to do'. It was the same with any other kind of prejudice. Being in the business and living in Brixton made us colour blind. There were no feelings about being gay, black, nothing.

In 1960 my father experienced the nearest thing he would get to a religious conversion. It was called rock and roll. In the January he had compèred a tour where Gene Vincent was topping the bill, and seeing the effect Gene was having on teenagers he decided that was the way to go, and within a year, promoter Don Arden had succeeded in bringing over Gene Vincent. From then on it was like Angell Road was on speed. Gene was England's first real rock god, wearing black leather instead of a suit, and with sell-out performances and screaming girls he was soon my father's first cash cow. The support bands would change, but Gene would always be the crowd puller and he was part of our lives for nearly five years.

And then it was just a roller coaster: Brenda Lee, Connie Francis, Little Richard, Jerry Lee Lewis – he arrived just a few days after his three-year-old son had drowned. In Cardiff he caused a riot when he played 'A Whole Lot Of Shakin' Goin' On'. And then in Mitcham, just down the road from us, he ended up destroying his piano – the first time anybody had done anything like that.

But the one I will never forget is Sam Cooke. I thought he was the most handsome man I had ever seen in my life, and he smelled fantastic and he wore these tight black high-waisted matador trousers on stage, and whenever he'd see me he would kiss me and I knew I would blush every single time, because I was so much in love with him. I was nine, and I would go and sit in the audience when he performed and I never did that with anybody else. But after that tour I never saw him again: he was shot dead in 1964.

I remember one night being taken to Victoria Station, because my mum and dad were seeing off Bill Haley on the midnight train to Europe. My father used to wave all the artists off – as the promoter he had to make sure everyone was on the train and accounted for – then he would go and join them a couple of days later. He'd always be there for the Big Welcome, and then there'd be the Big Wave Off, although I don't think this kind of thing was that unusual in those days, because everything was far more courteous. Now the only place you'll get a promoter coming to the airport to meet you is Japan.

Gene Vincent and the rest of them might have been getting girls weeping and screaming in the aisles, but to me they were just people my father worked with. These artists just happened to be musicians, as opposed to ventriloquists or comedians. Some of them were arseholes, some of them were nice – just like everybody else.

One problem my father hadn't foreseen with bringing over Americans was that they had to be paid up front, and when you're talking about a whole tour, and these people were being paid over £1,000 a week, that was a lot. Fifty per cent of the entire fee had to go to the William Morris Agency in New York before the artist even left America, and then the balance would have to be handed to them personally every night, in cash, and some even wanted that in advance. A year or two later I remember being on the road with my dad with Little Richard and Chuck Berry and them literally refusing to play. It was like, 'Yeah. We go on, but we get the money first.'

My father lived a cash-only existence. Although he carried around a chequebook twice the normal size, it didn't matter what size it was, or how many noughts were on it – you could have filled it with fucking noughts – nobody wanted anybody's cheque. Not in rock and roll. It had to be notes.

Carrying so much cash on him was the reason my father gave for employing the 'heavies', as they were called, who

would be 'handy' in difficult situations. They'd start out as driv-
ers and if all went well he would bring them into the company
as tour managers. These heavies would come from the fringes
of show business, always recommended by somebody who
knew somebody. The first one I really remember was Peter
Grant, mainly because he would pick David and me up from
school on days he had nothing else on. He began his career as
a bouncer in the 2i's club in Soho (where people like Cliff
Richard and Adam Faith had started out) and then was a stunt
double and bit-part player in films, or at least that was what he
used to tell us. His first job for my father was driving Gene
Vincent, and then he progressed to tour managing. With all the
things he had going on, my father couldn't handle everything
himself any more.

Once, when my parents were on tour somewhere we couldn't
go, we had to stay six weeks with Dolly in her flat in Elsynge
Road. As this was too far for us to go to our usual school, we
were put into one just by Clapham Junction, and I hated it.
Unlike Clermont, which was an ordinary house, this was a great
Victorian redbrick building with echoing rooms that rang with
the sound of desks banging and bells. There were about a hundred people in every class, and I didn't know anybody. As for the
playground, it was more like a battleground. The first thing I did
was tell them my father was a policeman. I couldn't possibly have
explained what he really did – it was far too embarrassing. The
last thing you want as a child is to stand out. And I stood out
enough anyway, because I wasn't at school regularly, because my
parents didn't participate in school life at all.

We never mixed with anybody who wasn't connected with
the industry, other than kids at school, and we weren't even
supposed to bring them back home. By now both rooms on
the ground floor were used as offices and there was always some
drama going on. Gene Vincent was always drunk and he'd

regularly be waving a gun around. Or someone had done something against my father, and he'd be threatening to kill the bastards. Violence was never far away from my father. From as early as I can remember people were frightened of him. Although he was quite a small man in terms of his height, because of the singing training he'd done as a boy in the synagogue, he had this barrel chest he was so proud of and he'd take anybody on.

In the early sixties my father had got involved with the Star Club in Hamburg; later he became a partner with Manfred Weissleder. The Star Club is famous for being where the Beatles first made their name. John Lennon idolised Gene Vincent and, knowing his connection with my father, asked Don if he would manage them, and my father said no. It was like 'English rock and roll? Don't make me laugh.' The Beatles were just copycats, he said. They wouldn't last. He was only interested in Americans and so he continued to bring them over: Carl Perkins, Brian Hyland, Brenda Lee, Little Eva, who was only five years older than me. But tastes in music had changed and he lost money hand over fist.

Apart from artists, the only other regular visitors to Angell Road were bailiffs and process servers, although they were never allowed past the front door. My brother said he could tell who it was by the knock. I couldn't. But it was me they sent to open it, because I was small for my age and the idea was they'd feel sorry for me. And yet once you saw them, standing on the step, you knew who they were by their lack of expression and way they were dressed. It was like a uniform: the raincoat, the trilby hat. It was born in you to know. And it was like, Oh God, so the TV's going back again to Granada, or DER, because he's not paid the instalments, or they're coming for the furniture because something's not been paid for. Or else it was the car. Sometimes we had a car, sometimes we didn't.

My father never believed in saving for a rainy day. So when the coffers were full, he'd be throwing money around, buying my mother jewellery and fur coats, taking us to the Talk of the Town in Leicester Square for a slap-up meal and Judy Garland, but then I'd overhear them talking and he'd be saying things like, 'Christ, Pads, ten grand. Where am I going to get that from?' And so the jewels would go down the pawnshop, until eventually she learnt to hide them where he couldn't find them.

It was as if my brother and I had two lives. There was the one at home, with the writs and the threats and the shouting down the phone. Then there was the street life, the park life, the skipping off school and going to the cinema life. David would buy one ticket and once inside he'd go straight to the emergency exit and let me in. We had it down to a fine art. It was an easy come, easy go kind of existence. We did what we wanted, and nobody seemed to care one way or the other.

When we were younger we'd go to Saturday matinées at the Ritzy – this was official and our mum would give us the money. But when David decided it was too babyish for him, we moved on to dancing at the Locarno. We'd put on our best clothes – in my case a party frock and silver sandals – and take the bus up to Streatham. I couldn't have been more than ten, if that; officially you had to be older, but my brother was a practised liar by then. I can't remember it being a problem. It was magical in there – everyone in their best, and dancing under a spinning mirror ball, and I have loved mirror balls ever since. But it could also be a bit strange, dancing to something like 'The Loco-motion' by Little Eva and thinking, I know her.

---

20 April 2005, 10.00 a.m.
Doheny Road, Beverly Hills

A knock at my bedroom door.

'Sharon?'

'Yeseeee . . .'

'Are you decent?'

'Of course not, Mikey. I make it a point to be positively IN-decent.'

In steps Michael Guarracino, who has been with me fourteen years. He hesitates. I pull my dressing gown round me, and he blushes as if I had just flashed my tits. Michael is the straight man to my comic. He never says fuck or shit or arse or prick, or even willy, but then neither is he fazed by anything that happens here. Except possibly yesterday. Two days ago I had a colonic irrigation (don't even go there) and Ozzy was complaining to anybody who would listen how he'd been kept awake by my blasting away throughout the night. 'Put it this way,' he said, 'if I'd have lit a match the whole of Beverly Hills would have gone up, and there were twenty-five dead pigeons on the balcony!' When it was Michael's turn to hear the story, he turned white.

'Are you telling me you've never heard your wife fart?' Ozzy said, his eyes stretched in amazement. At which point Michael decided he had an urgent phone call to make and went out. Probably to be sick. He is the perfect antidote to my wilder side.

In his hand he's holding a pile of papers, emails and faxes and documents. Things he was working on yesterday, things that came in from London overnight. Things he wants me to read and sign and make decisions on. Things in all likelihood I don't feel like doing.

'So what delicious naughtiness have you for me this morning?' I say, shifting Minnie onto my lap.

He hands me a pile of papers half an inch thick.

'Do you know what you want to do about this, Sharon?'

I look at the top sheet.

Yes. I know what I want to do. I want to weep, weep, weep.

It's a writ, or as Michael calls it, a claim. Same fucking thing. *The Vagina Monologues*. Monologues Ltd are suing me for £260,000. It comes as no surprise.

'So, Sharon, what do you want me to do about this?'

'Throw it on the pile with the rest of them.'

Outside the window the dogs are going crazy. It's Jennifer come to take them for their morning walk.

'You want some of your special tea, Sharon?' Saba is from Sudan, and I swear she is graced with a sixth sense. I turn on the bath, take the most expensive bath oil I have. Pour it in. All of it. I light the most expensive candle I have to hand. Brand new, in its own special pot. FAAABulous. Burning money is about the only way I know to feel good about myself.

2

Mayfair

In early 1964 we moved to 71 Berkeley House, Hay Hill, Mayfair. It was a move designed to show that Don Arden was going up in the world. But going from Brixton to Mayfair in one leap was like going from Woolworth's to Tiffany's with just a credit card in your pocket and nothing to back it up but a job stacking shelves.

My father was all about show. He loved that thing of having important-looking offices and lots of staff. And he loved the fact that he could have an apartment in Mayfair and a Rolls-Royce.

I would far rather have stayed where we were. Because the previous term, just before I turned eleven, I had started at Italia Conti, a stage school run by a rather wonderful woman, very beautiful, very theatrical and very dignified. It was just ten minutes' walk from Angell Road, whereas now I'd have to go miles. For the first time in my life I had a real friend, Posy Kurpiel. Like me she had an unusual background, coming from Romania originally, and for most of her life her family had lived in a caravan in the West Country, but they had recently got themselves a home in the Elephant and Castle. David was also at Conti's, though only just. When he'd reached eleven, he'd somehow got a place at King's College Wimbledon, but had been expelled for fighting and playing truant when Dolly took him to the dog tracks in Wandsworth for a spot of greyhound racing.

I had always known I was going to be a dancer – my mother had been a dancer, her mother had been a dancer, so it was like it was in the blood. In fact, I was dancing even before I started normal school. This was classical ballet. My teacher was called Biddy Pinchard and I went there once a week and I absolutely adored her. I loved it all: the barre-work, the ritual, the little performances, the clothes. Dixie would make my tutus and my outfits and every so often there would be a trip up to the West End for some new ballet shoes, which came from Freed's in St Martin's Lane.

But after the move to Hay Hill, I hardly saw Dixie; she had married somebody my parents hated so I hadn't even gone to the wedding. We were still living in Brixton then, and I'll never forget my mother yelling, 'You're not going! Do you hear me? Not going', and me pulling the blankets over my head and crying my eyes out, because of course Dixie had asked me to be her bridesmaid. So it was Butlin's for the weekend instead. Fucking Butlin's in Margate.

I'd been too young even to begin to understand the tense relationship between my mother and Dixie at that time: 'Every boy your sister brings back here falls in love with me, and she can't stand the fact that they prefer my company to hers,' my mother told me once when Dixie had stormed out. And then when Dixie did marry it was: 'You know why she married him, don't you? Because he was the only one who didn't fall for me.'

'She'll be back,' she said, after the wedding. 'You'll see, when she needs money, she'll be back. They always come back.'

I still managed to keep in touch, and when Dixie got a job at the Royal Opera House in Covent Garden as a bookkeeper, she would get me tickets for the ballet when she could, and I absolutely loved it. I only stopped going after I married. Ozzy and ballet do not mix.

It was around this time that I got to know Dorothy Solomon. The Solomons had an apartment on Park Lane, only a few minutes' walk away from us in Hay Hill. They were friends of my father's – Phil Solomon managed the Bachelors, who were a very big singing act out of Dublin, and about the only non-pop artists who consistently topped the charts in the sixties.

In many ways you could say that she changed my life. It was Dorothy who introduced me to luxury. Everything about her was glamorous. From the way her clothes moved, to the rustle and the feel of the silk and the cashmere that she wore. And when I sat next to her, just to breathe in the smell that surrounded her was like entering paradise. When I asked her about it, she told me it was a perfume called Intimate and she gave me a bottle of Youth Dew by Estée Lauder as a gift. I had this feeling that there was a lot more out there than I knew about.

Her husband was a big-time gambler and racehorse owner. Their apartment on Park Lane overlooked Hyde Park and was full of beautiful paintings and antique furniture and chandeliers and shiny polished floors. And I used to love going there, just to be able to sit and move around in those surroundings. But the centre of it all was Dorothy, who looked and dressed like the ladies in the magazines I used to read. And that was the right word for her. She was a lady. Her clothes weren't made by the dressmaker across the street, like my mother's. They were couture, and she would have a Gucci handbag, and her jewellery and her nails and her hair were always done.

My mother's hair was never done; nothing was ever done. Only when she had to go out somewhere with my father did she make an effort. Otherwise she was a wreck. Yet she was lovely. She had classic Irish looks, red hair, pale skin and pale eyes. Not warm eyes – hers were like Fox's Glacier Mints. It wasn't like she didn't have the money. My father would have given her anything – part of that thing about showing how well he was doing. He did anyway, things like jewellery and fur coats, but they were never really her. I sometimes wonder what my life would have been like if I had bonded with my mother. I loved her because she was my mother, but I didn't like her because she embarrassed me, just as I now embarrass my kids.

I hated the way she kept our house, moving the dust around, shoving stuff under beds, into cupboards, clothes not washed before they were put away. It wasn't about having grand things, it wasn't about having expensive paintings on the wall like at Dorothy Solomon's. It was like at my nana's house: about nice towels, fresh tea towels, a clean fridge with food in it.

Shampoo didn't exist in our house. I would wash my hair with Fairy Liquid. The leftover soap in the basin would be cracked and slimy at the same time. You could never find a hairbrush that wasn't covered in dog hairs. We'd run out of toothpaste. There'd be no toilet paper. There was no attempt to make anything nice. In my bedroom, for example, there was a chest of drawers, a wardrobe, a bed and that's all. My only decoration was a picture of a little ballet dancer that Dixie had embroidered and framed when I was about five or six, and I used to have it hanging very close to my face so I could see it when I was in bed.

In Brixton, our next-door neighbour had done the washing, but once we moved to Mayfair you did it yourself. We didn't own anything like a washing machine. I used to just fill the bath, lay my uniform in it, add the washing powder and then use my hand as a brush. For the rest, I'd go to the launderette. Mayfair, of course, didn't run to launderettes, so I'd take the tube to Earl's Court from Green Park, and then sit there watching it go round and round.

The whole thing was insane. Here we were, living in Mayfair, but I'd have to go to the hall porter and ask to use his phone because ours was cut off. He had a flat at the other end of our floor, so I used to give his number to my friends, and he'd come knocking on the door and say, 'Miss Arden, there's a call for you.'

His name was Mr Watts and he looked like something from *Upstairs, Downstairs*. And he had the typical thing of the black tailcoat, pinstriped trousers and the dirty collar and cuffs. He was a nice, friendly old boy and one of his sidelines, to get a bit of extra cash, was making breakfast for people in the building. So when I used to go into his place in the morning to get or make a phone call, there he'd be frying up the greasiest food for Sir Whoever-it-was and Lady This One. Then from ten o'clock onwards he'd be down in his cubbyhole by the front door taking deliveries and keeping the riff-raff out.

In fact, the Mayfair apartment, for all its smart address, was actually smaller than Angell Road. We'd go up in a huge lift with two sets of iron gates that you had to physically close before it would start to move, rattling and clanking its way up to the seventh floor. But we had only three bedrooms: my brothers shared one, my mother and father had the master bedroom, and I had this little tiny box room. The only real improvement was that for the first time we did have two bathrooms.

My father had seen rock and roll as a licence to make money, but it wasn't, and turnover isn't income, and if he earned £4,000

one week, he'd spend £5,000, and then we'd be back in the shit.
And the phone would be cut off, and the light would be cut off,
and the water would be cut off, and the cars would literally
come and go. The timing of the move to Hay Hill had been
about as bad as it could have been. Beatlemania had arrived and
blown everything else out of the water. So he tried to bring in
artists the Beatles said had influenced them, like Chuck Berry,
Bo Diddly and the Everly Brothers. Phil and Don were just
lovely to me and my brother. They always found time to talk to
us, made us welcome backstage and always remembered our
names. You could tell that they had been brought up really well.
They were a total contrast to the Rolling Stones, who my father
put in as support and who weren't at all what I'd been used to.
Unlike the Everlys, they weren't interested in being nice to a
twelve-year-old girl and I remember feeling quite intimidated.
The Everlys also toured with Manfred Mann and they didn't like
my brother and me being backstage either. When they saw us in
the wings, I remember them saying, What the fuck is this? Is
there a children's party backstage?

In London they all mostly did well, but nowhere else and this
was when my father began having real cash-flow problems. All
he could rely upon now was his ability to gauge the audience
appeal of untried artists, which he had never had to do before.
Meanwhile he would try other kinds of acts. Always American.

Jayne Mansfield was the Pamela Anderson of her day. She had
begun in Hollywood as an instant film star, but by the sixties she
was divorced from her husband Mickey Hargitay, and was on the
cabaret circuit. My father met her through an American lawyer
called Marvin Mitchelson, who had got her Mexican divorce
made legal in California, so he decided to bring her over for a
tour of working men's clubs in the north of England. Because
she had this glamorous identity, he would take a whole floor of
a hotel. As this would then be locked off, everyone would leave

their bedroom doors open, and if my mum and I weren't going to see her perform at night, we'd have a good old mooch around her room trying things on. What fascinated me most were her bras. I had just started to be interested in such things. They were huge, something like 44DD, and that's not an exaggeration. So I'd be wandering around wearing them strapped round my chest and my feet stuffed into calf-length white leather boots with kitten heels that were then her big thing. As a tour, it was another disaster.

Then my father finally struck lucky. In 1964, on the northern leg of the Chuck Berry tour, he'd put in a support band called the Alan Price Combo who Peter Grant had recommended – he was now acting as a scout for my father. This time his obsession with all things American paid off when he persuaded them to make their first single an old New Orleans classic they'd played on the tour, and 'The House Of The Rising Sun' went straight to No. 1. The Animals – as they were renamed – became only the second English band after the Beatles to have a number-one hit in America.

The last person that my mother wanted to see in her smart new Mayfair surroundings was Dolly. Since we'd moved from Brixton we'd hardly seen her. I can't say I was sorry, because I still hated the way she stank and how she fawned over David and didn't notice me. One Saturday, my mum and I had planned to go out, when Dolly turned up. She'd managed to find her way to the seventh floor. I opened the door, and there she was: same old hairstyle, same old red bow, same old fag hanging out of her mouth, smeared with lipstick. She had somehow found her way to the apartment, and my mum was so pissed off that we just walked her back to Green Park, put her on a bus to Wandsworth Common and didn't even give her a cup of tea.

She never did it again. Perhaps my mother paid regular visits to Elsynge Road, but I doubt it. The next time I saw Dolly was quite a while later. It must have been the summer, because I remember the roses in her street were out. Her flat was at the far end, on the first floor in a big old mansion block. We got into the building without any trouble, but then we had to slam on the door for a good few minutes before this person who looked like a witch eventually let us in. She hadn't heard us knock, she said, because she was in bed. And it was obvious as soon as you got inside the door that she'd been there for weeks. The place stank of cat's piss and shit. There were cats everywhere, and we couldn't see a thing. This flat was always dark anyway, because it was so big and went back so far, but now it was pitch dark because the electricity had run out. While my mother started tidying Dolly up, I went to try and get some milk and tea and some change for the meter from a parade of shops on St John's Road. Eventually we left her with a pile of shillings, though as she would have to climb to reach the meter I didn't see how she would do it, given the state she was in. And then, just as we were walking over the bridge at Clapham Junction, I felt this itching, and I looked down at my legs and saw that I was covered in a creeping carpet of black fur. And then I realised what it was. Fleas! Eventually my mother found a taxi and I was screaming with horror over these things that were feeding on me, and she got me back to Hay Hill, she threw me in the bath, chucked in a whole bottle of Dettol and scrubbed me till all the fleas were dead. But she didn't seem that bothered about me or her mother, it was just, 'Don't you dare tell your father.'

Apart from Dolly, we knew nothing about my mother's family, but I now suspect that she was probably born illegitimate. People like your grandmother are always showing you their photographs and talking about your grandfather and the other relatives you're too young to have met but Dolly never did. All she had in the way of photographs were pictures of her with her troupe, the O'Shea whatever-it-was girls. They were famous for this thing she'd invented called the pony trot. Dolly was at the back with six girls in pairs in front of her, huge feathers on their heads and reins attached to their backs that she was holding, and they all wore thick flesh-coloured tights and little brown laced ankle boots.

But whenever we went down Acre Lane in Brixton, my mother would point to a huge Victorian house, far bigger than ours, and say that that was where she'd been brought up. That she'd lived there with her grandmother, and it had been her home. And the only photograph I ever saw of my mother as a child was when she must have been about six, standing with a severe-looking woman in the garden of this house in Acre Lane. And this woman, with her long dark skirt and white pinafore and stiff white collar and cuffs, was my great grandmother. I know nothing else about her. Not her name, not where she came from, nothing.

One day we were in Shepherd Market – the red-light district of Mayfair – and me, my brother and my mother were on our way to the sandwich shop next door to the off-licence. Suddenly my mother stops, goes into the off-licence, and of course we just follow her in. So then she starts introducing us to this man.

'Ira, this is Sharon.' Shake hands.

'And this is David.' Shake hands.

'Children, this is your uncle Ira.'

This Irishman with a Jewish name was my mother's brother! Until then we had no idea she had any family at all, apart from Dolly. Whether Ira was a full brother, or half a brother, she never said. It wasn't something she was going to talk about. But there certainly wasn't any great family reunion. After that we would see him occasionally. What I do know is that Dolly went to live with him for a while, but then when dementia set in, my mother got her into an old people's home in Elsynge Road, just down from where she'd lived for all those years. Eventually Dolly got pneumonia and died, and all those secrets died with her.

There was so much that I didn't know and didn't understand about my mother, particularly her mental health. She started to change about a year or so before we moved to Hay Hill. One Sunday we'd gone down to spend the day with the Kaye Sisters, just an outing, which was something we did quite often in the summer.

The Kaye Sisters were a singing act my father would use in his shows. In the fifties the sisters thing was big – the Beverley Sisters were another example. The Kaye Sisters' big hit was 'You Gotta Have Something In The Bank, Frank', advice my father would have done well to listen to.

Anyway, one of the sisters had married the manager and had done quite well for herself and they had this apartment on the front at Brighton, overlooking the sea. And we drove down to see them in our brand new car, a canary yellow Ford Consul. The sun shone and we went on the pier, played the slot machines and had fish and chips and generally had a great day. Then on the way back, it must have been somewhere around Croydon, without any warning this drunken driver comes straight towards us, clips the car on my mother's side, and there's a terrible crunching noise and we start veering across the road. None of us was hurt – apart from my mother, that is. With the force of the collision, the hook at the back of the passenger seat, the thing where you hang your jacket, got embedded in her temple.

She was in hospital for weeks and weeks – it was a month before we could even go and see her. As Richard had a job in a factory at the time, and Dixie wasn't there either, it meant our father had to look after us for the first time in his life. He had to get us dressed, he had to make us breakfast, he had to get us ready for school, and it was a big lesson for him to have two children to take care of on his own. When we finally got to visit her it was quite frightening. Her head was covered in bandages, and she was very quiet, hardly said a word to any of us. And we didn't say a word either as Don had warned us that if we made any fucking noise we'd get chucked out. As he didn't have a car, we'd have to go by bus and it took nearly the whole day.

My mother was never the same after that. I think it must have been some form of depression. She was always sleeping and always sick. When my father invited anybody over for dinner, it was always a fucking drama. And when he wanted to go out partying, she wouldn't go. Whether this depression was connected to the accident or the money problems, I don't know. But the accident must have been quite serious because she got a payout of £10,000, and you could buy a whole house for that in the sixties. Of course, my mother saw none of it. My father took the money and put it straight into the company.

Towards the end of 1964 Peter Grant suddenly disappeared from our lives. It was a real shock – we had known him for what seemed like for ever. It was like one day he was waiting for us outside the school gate, and the next it was taboo to mention his name. All I knew was that something had gone wrong business-wise. But from then on it was war. Whenever he and my father did happen to meet in the street, there would be scuffles and punches until somebody managed to pull them apart. And for the first time in my life I felt uneasy. Here was my father, who I thought was the most wonderful person in the world, beating the shit out of the nice man who used to buy us sweets and pick us up from school.

Much, much later I discovered that Peter Grant had been the tour manager who had taken the Animals to America for my father in 1964. And that when they were in New York, he had taken them to see Allen Klein (who later became the Beatles' business manager) and persuaded them to leave Don Arden and go with Klein. To say Don bore him a grudge is to misunderstand how my father operated. Even though it was Peter who brought the Animals to my father's attention in the first place, he never forgot and never forgave, because Peter Grant was tantamount to being family, and a betrayal in the family carried the death warrant. And this went on for years and years, because Peter went on to manage first the Yardbirds and then Led Zeppelin, and the music world is a small place.

It wasn't long before David and me were beating the shit out of each other at Conti's and Miss Conti said that one of us had to go. Naturally, as David was the blue-eyed boy who everyone adored, it had to be me.

So then I was sent to Ada Foster's, miles away in the other direction in Golders Green, and getting there every morning was a fucking nightmare, and from the moment I stepped through the door on the first day I hated everything about it. Unlike Conti's where you could wear anything you liked, here they had a uniform: pink pinafore dress, grey shirt and pink and grey striped tie. And when you went for auditions you had to wear this repulsive pink leotard and woollen knitted tights that were incredibly itchy. As for the people who ran the school – Mrs Foster, her daughter and her husband – they were horrible.

After two terms of misery there on my own, I begged Posy to leave Conti's and come and join me, and amazingly her parents let her. Having her there was the only thing that kept me sane. In fact, her journey up from the Elephant by tube was quicker than my bus from Park Lane, and we'd meet up at Golders Green bus station then catch another bus together for the last stage of the journey to hell.

To make the time pass more quickly when I was on my own, I'd get all the magazines and lose myself in their pages. From *Woman's Own* to *Honey* to *Nova* and even *Vogue*, when I could get the money, I drank them up. I longed to be glamorous and I'd read anything about Twiggy or Jean Shrimpton or Verushka, studying their make-up, and finding out everything there was to know about them, their lives, what they did, where they went, who they went out with, how they'd got where they had got. It was my dream world. I wasn't under any illusions that I could ever be a model myself, because I was too short and dumpy and they had legs like lamp-posts. I was an OK dancer, but I probably already knew I was never really going to make it. I was losing my drive and my commitment and as a dancer, without that commitment to do class for several hours every day, you're out.

When we went to auditions, other girls would be desperate to get picked, while I didn't care if I got in or not. For a lot of the kids it meant everything. I remember Olivia Hussey, who'd been with me at Conti's, getting down on her knees and praying before we went in. God obviously appreciated the effort because she went on to star in Zeffirelli's *Romeo and Juliet*. For me it was like, Oh good, a half-day off school.

I did get the occasional part. I did two seasons of panto at the London Palladium, once with Cliff Richard in *Cinderella*, once with Frank Ifield in *Babes in the Wood*, and I did a few ads like children's clothes for Marks & Spencer. For the first time in my life I was earning money, and it felt great.

In those days, 50 per cent of a child's performance fees had to be put into a savings account that you could only draw out bit by bit. One year, when I was about thirteen, my Post Office book didn't come back after it'd been sent off to have interest added, so they gave me a duplicate. A few weeks later the original one turned up, which meant I had two identical savings books, with identical amounts of money in them, and an idea occurred to me. What if I used both books? So I did, and spent it on clothes and records. A month or so later, there came a knock on the door early one Saturday morning and I heard my mother shout to my father, 'Don, the police are here. They want to talk to Sharon.'

I knew immediately what it must be about and pulled the sheets over my head as if that could make me disappear, and when my mother came to get me I was shaking with fear. I agreed that I had taken money out of both books, but told the police I didn't think I was doing anything wrong. My face must have told a different story. My father paid the money back, and I got some mild sort of ticking off, but in fact I think it made him laugh to see his daughter a chip off the old block. It was the end of my criminal activities for ever. That terror was just not worth it.

I was always auditioning. I must have auditioned ten times for *Fiddler on the Roof* and *The Sound of Music*. Each time there was a cast change, there I'd be. I'd go on stage, throw myself around for a few minutes while bashing out a few bars of 'Do, A Deer, A Female Deer', or for *Fiddler* it would be 'Kids! I don't know what's wrong with these kids today! They're noisy, crazy, sloppy, lazy'. I suspect I got a certain pleasure out of singing that because it could have been me. I'd get down to the last few and then get booted. And no wonder when I think how I behaved. I was really obnoxious to the people who were auditioning me.

'So, Sharon, perhaps you could tell us, what do you read in your spare time?'

'*Playboy*.'

I was a brat, an absolute brat, because I didn't give a shit. It was just, fuck it, I can get a bag of chips on the way home.

My parents didn't care what I did. My mother was always in bed and my father was either in shit or in clover. But as far as the world knew he was the Godfather of Rock in his smart office in Royalty House, Dean Street, centre of the music industry. He might have missed out with the Animals but over the next few years he would have the Nashville Teens, then the Small Faces, then Amen Corner, then The Move. Not a bad list: but then there were also the ones no one's ever heard of: Attack, Johnny Neal and the Starliners, Raymond Froggatt, Neil Christian. All belonged to Don Arden at one time or another.

I say Don Arden, but nothing was ever in his name. My father's number-one rule was never put yourself on the front line. His entire empire, all the companies, all the management contracts, all the mortgages, all the bank loans were signed not by him but by my mother. And then when one of these companies would go bankrupt (as they did regularly) it would be my mother who would have to go along to the bankruptcy hearings. Here today, gone tomorrow, like Top Ten hits, only to be replaced by another one, exactly the same, but with a different name. All it needed was new stationery. That was it. That was all.

But whenever my mother was involved in yet another of these bankruptcy proceedings, she would get really strung up and emotional and take to her bed for days at a time. She was a pawn, just as I had been when I'd been forced to open the front door to the bailiffs or process servers on Angell Road.

Eventually she said she just couldn't take it any more and that was it; she never worked with my father again. But luckily for him, there were other mugs in the family ready to pick up the pen. First off the conveyor belt came David, who joined the business in 1966 when he was fifteen.

Now my brother had left Conti's, I was allowed to move back there again. The bad news was that it was really too late to stop the rot: I had lost the dedication to dance. That real desire. And I would procrastinate: 'I'll go dance tomorrow.' Tomorrow, tomorrow. Always tomorrow.

Eighteen months later the tomorrows ran out and I said good-bye to what had passed for my education. I was fifteen and three months old, the earliest the law allowed you to leave school in those days. I had no qualifications, not a one. Not an O level, not a CSE, nothing to my name except a few useless dance cer-tificates. Nobody in their right mind would have employed me. And nobody did, although I did try. And then came the inevitable: 'After the summer, Sha, you'll come in and we'll teach you the business.'

By this time the office had moved. Dean Street had gone – rent defaulted on, too many bailiffs at the door, who knows – and we were now in Carnaby Street, the heart of Swinging London.

Although I was still too young to sign things – in those days you had to be twenty-one – I was learning the guiding princi-ples of how my father ran his business. I was the receptionist, the person who did the meet and greet at the door. I was also in charge of the switchboard, one of those old kind where you had plugs and wires that if you weren't careful would turn into a spaghetti junction. And finally all those years of accents and improvisation were about to bear fruit, when I put in my calls to the bank manager.

'Is this Mr So-and-so?' To be said with a Brooklyn/Bronx/Queens accent. 'This is New York . . . a person-to-person call. Please hold . . . I have a Mr Don Arden on the line . . . Putting you through . . .' In those days you couldn't dial direct.

Sometimes I'd have to go and see Mr So-and-so in person, my role changed to that of the loyal daughter, desperate to shield her blameless father from shame and ignominy. More improvisation, including the use of the word 'Daddy', which I rarely called my father. When I was younger he was Dad, but from the moment I started working for him, he was Don.

My speech, carefully rehearsed on the bus from Soho to the City, would go along the lines of: 'My daddy has bagfuls of money in New York, and he'll be back on Monday, and then he'll have all this cash, plenty to pay off everything we owe you, and more . . . Please just wait another few days . . .' This bank was the infamous London and County Securities and after it collapsed in 1973, the very same Mr So-and-so came to work for my father.

And, guess what, I turned out to be good at all this bullshit. Finally something I could do that my father approved of. And so I did it for him again and again, lied for him again and again, to bank managers, to artists, to anybody he asked me to.

In fact, I quite enjoyed being at the office, being part of the extended family, because that's what it was like. My father always socialised with the people who worked for him, which was why he'd felt so betrayed over Peter Grant. There was the usual array of heavies – although the one who had replaced Peter Grant, another ex-stunt man called Patrick Meehan, was different from the rest. He had been with my father since the early sixties, having also started as a driver for Gene Vincent. When Peter Grant and my father had fallen out in 1964, Patrick Meehan moved to working in the office and doing the day-to-day. He was very well put together, quite well educated and always conducted himself in a dignified business-type manner, though I never really liked him. He was always a bit superior, like he was a schoolmaster.

He had a son, another Patrick, a friend of David's, who was working at Thomas Cook and always hoping to break into the music industry as a producer. He used to have little practices when there was any spare studio time. Mrs Meehan was always really nice to me. She was Italian – they all spoke Italian when they were at home – and had tremendous style. I remember her once buying me the most beautiful leather bag from somewhere very expensive and glamorous in Bond Street. It was olive green and I loved the smell of it.

Another of the heavies was a man called Wilf Pine. This time it was my brother who brought him in. It was in 1968, just before I started working there, and Amen Corner looked as if they were going to go the way of the Small Faces, who had dispensed with Don Arden as manager in 1967. My father had never got on with singer and front man Andy Fairweather-Lowe. According to David, who had come across Wilf Pine when he was booking The Move into a dance hall in the Isle of Wight, Pine was 'handy' and 'talked their language' and he also knew another member of the band, so my father thought it worth bringing him in to deal with the situation. In fact, it proved only a stay of execution.

I hated Wilf Pine from the moment I met him. He was real low life, and was always talking about sorting this one out, knocking this one off. And you just knew that if you didn't do what he wanted, he'd beat the shit out of you. Perfect for the work my father had in mind, but I kept well out of his way.

It was through Wilf Pine that my father made his first real connections with big-time gangsters, both in London and in New York. He had met the Krays briefly, because they were often at the Astor Club in Mayfair, where we would sometimes go, but Wilf's connections went far deeper than that.

When the Carnaby Street office had to go (more process servers, more bailiffs), my father moved the office into the apartment in Hay Hill, and we all moved out to Margate, to the little house he had bought for weekends when we still lived in Brixton. It must have been seventy or eighty miles out of London and just getting in and out every day was another fucking *schlep*.

By this time Richard had left home, which led to an improvement in the atmosphere at the apartment. David and Richard had had to share a bedroom and it was a truly horrible relationship. David had picked up my father's attitude to his brother. He was very dismissive and violent towards him. One time he got him down on the floor and smashed a light bulb into his ear. So basically, after years of verbal and physical abuse, Richard just said, 'Fuck it, I'm off. I'm going.' And he married his girlfriend and opened a shop selling model soldiers in Kingston, which had always been his passion. Anyway, one afternoon I'm in the office and David makes a sign that he wants to talk to me.

'The old man's gone nuts this time,' he said. He and my father had been down to see Richard that afternoon, and they had driven back through Wimbledon and Don had pulled the Rolls up in front of a house that was brand new. Less a house, more of a mansion, David said, overlooking the common.

'And so he goes, "Love that." And now he says he's going to get it, whatever it costs. But I tell you what, Sis, that place is gonna cost a fucking fortune, and he's just not got it.'

---

20 April 2005, morning
Doheny Road, Beverly Hills

I want to wake up in the morning and not feel terrified of the knock on the door. I want to wake up with no debts, no commitments, no lawsuits, and then I want to fuck off and buy a little house in Italy and learn Italian. And if my children want to come and see us, they can. But I need some place of calm. I need my animals and I need to be settled. Most of all I want to wake up and not hear that voice screaming inside of me. Oh God, how do I get out of this, how do I get out of that. I want a funky little house I can put my bits of shit in that I love and wake up happy. And if I want to lie in bed, I can lie in bed. If I want to do the garden, I will do the garden. If I want to do anything, I can do it.

I can't live for other people any more.

3

Wimbledon

Somehow the devious old fox did it. Somehow he managed to persuade the builders or the developers or whoever it was to let him have this palace for £5,000 down and the rest in a year's time, and 45 Parkside was his. I couldn't believe it when we went to see it. A huge house in the most expensive road in one of the most expensive suburbs of south London. It looked straight out over the common, and the back garden stretched back as far as the road behind it.

Being brand new, it needed everything done. At the time, my father had a band out of Manchester called Sampson who weren't doing very much, so he got them in to do the decorating. But, of course, what with having to furnish it and carpet it and get all the curtains made, the money soon ran out. Before too long the gas was cut off. Then the electricity was cut off and the bailiffs were called in. For two weeks we lived with candles. My job was to arrange weekly payments. So I would have to go out and stand there in the porch, full of embarrassment. 'Please, can we work out a payment plan?'. . . 'I promise that by next week I'll have it' . . . or pleading with them not to take this, or not to take that.

The most important difference moving to Wimbledon made to me was that I got a cat. My mother had always had dogs when we were in Brixton but strangely I didn't like them then. I didn't actively dislike them, I just never had a connection. And then there were all David's animals, budgerigars, rabbits, guinea pigs, snakes, lizards. But they were things that no way could you get affection from, and that were kept out the back in hutches that Nigel Heathhorn had made.

I called my moggy Mrs Smedley, after the frozen peas, and I found her the first weekend we moved in. She was black and white and really fluffy and as soon as I saw her in the pet shop in Wimbledon High Street that was it: she was mine! Mrs Smedley was more like a dog than a cat and would follow me to work and sit on the wall until the bus came. In a way, she even came with me.

'Good morning. Can I help you?'

'Is Don there?'

'I'm afraid Mr Arden is in a closed meeting and can't be disturbed.'

'Oh, right. And – er – if I could have your name, Miss . . . ?'

'Smedley. Deanie Smedley.'

It made me laugh when they would later call up and ask for my puss.

The Deanie came from a Natalie Wood film that I had been to see with Posy called *Splendour in the Grass*. It was all about smouldering love and Deanie wanting to escape from the confines of her parents. Suffocating parents I knew about, but smouldering love had no parallels in my own life. Boys weren't interested in me. I had spots, I was short, I was fat. I was dieting, I was not dieting. Now that I wasn't dancing, I was putting on weight fast. And in a mistaken belief that it would make me look less dumpy, I'd cut my hair. Having it long had made it look reasonably straight. Now I had tight curls: fanny brown, fanny texture.

Although this was the sixties and everyone seemed to be sleeping around, sex for me was never a way out. Whenever my father talked about this girl or that girl, it was always 'that slag' or 'that whore' and after all I'd witnessed with Dixie, I knew that no one was good enough for him. Better to have no boyfriend at all – and being fat, I realised, made it easier for men not to be interested in me in that way. I'd be the mouthy one they could have a laugh with, not the sexy one they wanted to fuck. And so I ate. Not because I was hungry. Not because it was dinnertime, breakfast-time or lunchtime. I just ate. And the fatter I got, the more I ate.

It was about this time that I first met Charlie Kray. He was the twins' less famous older brother, and it was like Prince Philip was coming to tea. And for the impending royal visit, the house had to be cleaned from top to bottom. So my mother got in the flowers, got out the silver service. And I can see her now sitting at the kitchen table the night before, Silvo everywhere, Marigolds up to her elbows, polishing the lot. She even made finger sandwiches, crusts off, and bought in a box of iced dainties.

So the next day we're all there in the living room waiting for the ceremony of afternoon tea, my father, me, my brother and little Charlie Kray, and my mother comes in dressed in her Sunday best, dripping with diamonds, with this big silver salver and the silver teapot, silver creamer, silver sugar bowl and the best china. And as she goes to put the tray on the coffee table, I see that her skirt is all caught up at the back, leaving her arse hanging out. And I stuff my hand in my mouth, but I can't stop laughing. And then my father gets up, pretending to help her – 'Here, Paddles, let me give you a hand' – as he desperately tries to pull the dress out of her girdle without Charlie Kray getting an eyeful. But by this time I'm laughing so much, I'm wetting myself, so holding my crotch I run for the door, my hand already soaking.

I spent the rest of the afternoon on the phone to Posy.

The way my father lived, violence wasn't the last resort – it was the first resort. The idea of calling the police would never have occurred to him. Who needed the police when he had his gangster friends? You knew they were villains just from the way they talked, bragging away like drug addicts or alcoholics do when they're together:

'I used to shoot up five times a day.'

'Five times! I used to shoot up ten times!'

'I used to drink five bottles of scotch a day.'

'That all? You're just a beginner. I used to drink ten before breakfast!'

So it was like:

'I got out my gun and I fuckin' killed him, one bullet right between the fuckin' eyes.'

'One bullet! I used half a fuckin' bullet.'

It was a pissing contest.

As for all that shit about them being 'incredibly nice people' and their code of honour and how they looked after their own, it was pure crap. The Krays weren't an unknown commodity. We all knew what they did, all about concrete overcoats and people being cut up and fed to the pigs.

Don Arden loved the power and he loved the fear that it put into people. I swear, after he saw *The Godfather*, it sent him bonkers. He thought he was the godfather. And he lived his life like that. He was a street fighter: he was brought up on the street, he had to fight for everything and he'd had very little education.

All of that I get. But he was a bad businessman and he came from the mentality of 'You fuck me, I'll fuck you twice'. Instead of going to the lawyer or going to the police, he'd always deal with it himself in his own way.

I can remember one time, a year or so later, we had a huge party at the house. Everybody would always want to come to the Ardens' parties because they were great parties. I made sure they were. I loved throwing parties, and I still do.

Anyway, at this particular party, somebody was found in my parents' bedroom rifling through my mother's jewellery and my father and two thugs began beating the shit out of him, and then he was just taken away and dumped somewhere out on the common. He wasn't dead, but he could have been.

And at that same party, a gatecrasher jumped over the fence and got in, and my father had him down on the ground and was battering him, and I joined in and began kicking him myself, because that was what you did. And as I was kicking this man, all I could think was: my dad's going to think I'm really spot on for doing this. I was doing it to impress him. For years and years I looked on him as this pillar of strength. Always putting us first, even though the whole world was against him for some reason and he never got a break. Morally he was unimpeachable, the best family man in the world, and he had 'great ethics'. The first time I heard the word ethics was when my father was talking about himself.

One evening in February 1970, I went with my father to the Marquee in Wardour Street. There was a buzz in the industry about this unknown band out of Birmingham who had an album about to be released. They were managed by some small-fry local manager, so the sharks in London were all hoping to land a big catch.

I had never been to the Marquee before because I wasn't

involved in the talent-spotting side and, in any case, I'd only recently joined the business and I was still only sixteen. But it was one of the premier gigs for an up-and-coming artist to play at that time, and it struck me as very seedy for somewhere with that kind of reputation: outside just a hole in the wall, and inside the sort of place where your feet stick to the floor, and you can barely breathe for the fug and stink of cigarettes and crammed-together bodies, and where sweat was running down the walls. When we first went in, another band was on. And then the band we'd come to hear began to play, and suddenly I had goose pimples on my arms and felt the hairs stand up on the back of my neck, and it was like What. The. Fuck. Is. This.! I had never heard anything like it. I must have been to hundreds of gigs before, flashy American R&B artists, pop groups, even rock and roll, but nothing, nothing remotely like this. It might not have been my kind of music, but the atmosphere and the ambiance around them were incredible. And it was just a brilliant show. You didn't have to know anything about the genre – and none of us did, because it didn't really exist until Black Sabbath invented it.

They belonged in a category that at the time might have contained Led Zeppelin and Deep Purple. But the truth is that they were out on their own. They looked angry, austere, and the singer's voice was truly otherworldly. If you remember that during the same period Gary Glitter was asking the fans if they wanted to be in his gang, you can see just how different they really were. And whereas Led Zeppelin were musically brilliant, they also sold sex – Robert Plant wore vests and tight jeans, a complete look-at-my-lunchbox merchant – Sabbath were nothing like that at all. With them the sound and the atmosphere were the thing.

My father had already set up an appointment for the following day. And now, having heard them, he was determined to get

them signed. In those days if an artist was available there'd be a
handful of managers auditioning for the part, so he put on a
show: the Rolls, the Mayfair office, everything to demonstrate
that Don Arden was the most powerful manager in England,
which in fact he was.

Sabbath were staying at some run-down boarding house in
Shepherd's Bush, where they were sleeping four to a room. Wilf
Pine was despatched in the Rolls to fetch them and I still
remember the buzz of excitement in the office as we waited.
Sure there were other managers out there, but my father had
already done well by several other bands out of Birmingham, so
they would know his name. And these were all working-class
boys who didn't know honey from pigshit. All they wanted was
to be rich and famous, and if Don Arden had done it for the
Small Faces, Amen Corner and The Move, he could do it for
them.

And so they arrived, ushered in by Wilf, and I did the meet
and greet. And they were a strange-looking sight. You could
barely see their faces for all that hair. The bass player was very
trendy, high-end fashion, but the singer – the only one without
the droopy moustache – was the strangest of them all. Although
it was winter, he was wearing open sandals. For a shirt he had a
pyjama top, and on a string round his neck was a tap. I asked
them to take a seat, so they sat down. But not on chairs, on the
floor. I asked if they wanted a cup of tea; they mumbled something I took to be a no. And so they were all huddled on the
ground mumbling to each other. I retreated to my switchboard
and stayed well clear as if they were a firework that looked safe
but might at any moment go off.

Eventually my father buzzed me through. The overture was
over, the first act was about to begin.

'If you'd like to come this way,' I said. 'Mr Arden will see you
now.'

When they finally came out, my father got Patrick and Wilf to take the band back to the hotel, to buy them drinks and generally find out how the land lay.

'So how did it go then?' I asked him, once I'd heard the lift go clunking down.

My father took a satisfied puff on his cigar. 'You know what, Sha? I think we're in business.'

But we weren't. We heard nothing back from them at all. Not a word. However, a week or so later, Patrick Meehan and Wilf didn't turn up for work . . .

Not only had they taken them back to the hotel, they'd taken them on to the Speakeasy, then the hippest club in London, for a bit of a chat. And what Sabbath had told them was that they would really like to go with Don, but they were scared of him. And so these two had said, 'Well, how about us? We're the ones who do all the work, why don't you come with us?'

And that's what happened. Patrick Meehan bankrolled the whole thing, put in his son as executive producer. The two Meehans managed, and Wilf Pine ran the company.

From their very first record Sabbath were a hit, and they went from strength to strength, getting bigger and bigger and bigger, because in the musical world of the early seventies nobody had heard anything as dark as their music, with such riffs and lyrics. It was entirely new. And the Meehans built a huge corporation around them. It was Black Sabbath who bankrolled everything, Black Sabbath who gave them credibility in the industry. Eventually they bought out Brian Epstein's NEMS empire, his artists, his building, his everything. They got involved with film production, merging with David Hemmings' company Hemdale.

And it was hard to take. But that's how it was. Cut-throat. And there was nothing you could do. Every band was stolen from. Everybody stole from everybody. They were just like pirates.

They didn't plan it. How could you plan to have a gold mine fall into your lap? No, the opportunity was suddenly there in front of them, and they went for it. What is harder to forgive is how they subsequently raped and pillaged Sabbath. All Sabbath got was a weekly wage of about £200–£300. The Meehans took all the royalties, took all the publishing and sucked them dry. Millions went missing. But we didn't know that then.

But it broke my father's heart. Not only did he lose a great band that went on to make millions, but those people he had trusted had betrayed him. Patrick Meehan had been with my father for years, and everything he knew he'd learnt from him.

Don Arden was a pioneer in the industry. His skills were entirely his own. First you were an artist, and the next biggest thing was to be an agent, so he became an agent, then it was a manager, and then you owned your own record company, and that's what he did. He wrote the book. And they had stabbed him in the back. Like Peter Grant before him, only more so, Patrick Meehan was family.

The feud between my father and the Meehans went on for the next ten years.

With my father there was black and there was white. You were either with him or against him. And if you were against him you had to die. You had to be eliminated, wiped out, never to be seen or spoken about again. The *News of the World* called him the Al Capone of music. If you were in his clan, he would protect you. If someone said something against one of his artists, he'd go round to the office and punch his head off. But if you did anything outside his clan, he'd go down with one bullet left in his gun.

Of course, the young man in the sandals with the tap was Ozzy. He had just turned twenty-one. I can't even remember now if I registered his name. I certainly never considered any one of them as boyfriend material; the people I spent most of my time with were gay – I felt much more comfortable with them. They weren't a threat, I wasn't a threat, and we could just have a laugh.

A little over six months later, however, I became involved with someone who was very definitely not gay. Adrian Williams was in a band called Judas Jump that my father managed. It was a sort of supergroup made up of a couple of guys from Amen Corner, a guy from Peter Frampton's band, and Adrian was the singer. They had one semi-hit single, and lasted one album before they disbanded. We began going out when I was seventeen and he's stayed in my life ever since.

We were friends before we were anything else. He thought I was funny, I made him laugh. And I think he saw it as a bit of a challenge that I knew nothing about sex. Nothing. I remember him having to explain to me what a blow job was. And then I discovered I was pregnant.

What do you do when you're seventeen and that happens? You go to your mother.

'You've got to get rid of it.'

'But—'

'There is no way you can have a child, Sharon. It will destroy your life.'

'But—'

'You have to have an abortion.'

There was a bitterness in her voice that I realise now had nothing to do with me. My mother had been only nineteen when she had Dixie, and whether she was pregnant before she married Mr Shaw I don't know. But she was the eternal romantic. Her bedside table was always piled high with romances: Barbara Cartland, Georgette Heyer. She loved all that historical romance shit. I had read *The Diary of Anne Frank* when we were living in Mayfair, which just tore my heart out: *that* was real.

Even at that age I couldn't take all that fantasy. It only confirmed what I already knew: that we had nothing in common. Nothing.

Abortion had only recently been legalised in England, but it was still an under-the-counter business. Basically you had to claim that it would be dangerous to either the baby or the mother for the pregnancy to continue. Girls couldn't just turn up and say they'd rather not have it. So I went to one doctor who sent me to another doctor who sent me to a third. And it was dealt with: too young, couldn't cope, psychological damage, whatever. Adrian paid.

The abortion clinic was a house in Avenue Road between Regent's Park and Swiss Cottage, and I was absolutely terrified. It was arranged for a Saturday and I had to be there at seven in the morning, and Adrian dropped me off. And I remember going through the doors, carrying my overnight case and seeing all these young girls, all terrified, all not looking at each other, and not a word being said. And every hour somebody's name would be called out, and a nurse would lead them away. And then it was my name, and I remember feeling the terror, as if my legs were going to give way. Then nearly forgetting to pick up my bag, and walking up the stairs to where it all happened. And I can remember lying down on the bed and screaming and crying. And when I came round I was still screaming and crying and this nurse was telling me to shut up because I was disturbing everybody.

So I grabbed my clothes from where they'd been hung and got dressed. I was still dizzy from the anaesthetic but I knew I couldn't stay. So I staggered outside, found a phone box and called Adrian, and I was weeping and weeping for him to come and get me.

My eyes were so swollen with crying I could hardly see. They were like two puffballs, and I was bleeding, bleeding. The huge sanitary towel hanging between my legs, attached to an elastic belt, was sodden. And Adrian drove me back to Wimbledon, put me into bed and then left. And I lay there Saturday night, all day Sunday, and on the Monday he came back. I couldn't move. All I had managed to do was dump the sanitary towel and put an ordinary towel between my legs and just lay there and tried to sleep.

In all that time my mother never came in, never so much as put her head round the door or offered me a cup of tea. It was her way of saying, 'You got yourself into it, you get yourself out.' I do understand what she was trying to do. But on the other hand it was really hard. The only person I had to talk to was Mrs Smedley. Just like Minnie, years later, when I had cancer, she never left my side.

Soon after that Adrian started working for my father and then moved into the house with me in Wimbledon and we were together for the next five years. But he wasn't ready to settle down, and neither was I. We were both so young. I know he was fond of me, but he was always embarrassed about my weight and didn't want his friends to see me, so that wasn't great for my self-esteem. I wasn't fat but I was definitely tubby. Obviously it must have suited him at the beginning, otherwise he wouldn't have done it. My parents said they would prefer him to be there and at least know where I was. But with him being a huge, huge womaniser, it was always going to be a problem.

As is often the way, Adrian was also attractive to men, and there was one guy who I knew was trying to fuck my boyfriend. I first met him at the stall in Kensington Market where he used to sell trousers he'd made himself, and his name was Freddie Mercury. At the time he was bisexual and living with a girl called Mary Austin. Freddie and I just hit it off right from the start.

A couple of years later, it must have been just before

Christmas 1975 when Queen were already selling huge numbers of records, Freddie asked if he could speak to my father. They were unhappy with their manager, he said, and needed some advice about what to do. So Don talked to them and succeeded in getting them out of their management deal with whoever it was, and then it was like, 'Would you look after us?' With two hit albums behind them, this was an offer you could not refuse. But less than a month later, at one of our famous Christmas parties, I introduced Freddie to another of my gay friends, John Reid, who I'd got to know when he worked at EMI, and who was then managing Elton John.

When Freddie phoned the next day, it wasn't to say thank you for the lovely party.

'Darling, I hope you're not going to be MAD with me. But I want to change managers . . . you see, I ADORE John!'

I was heartbroken. We had managed them for little over a month and Queen were – and honestly still are – my favourite band ever. But you know when somebody makes up their mind in circumstances like that, there is nothing they or you can do. For once my father was very good about it. He knew it was something beyond anyone's control. It wasn't like they thought John Reid was a better manager, or he could do more for them, it was just a friendship. Not that it stopped my father offering Adrian £1,000 if he would 'fuck Freddie'. But I always remained friendly with Freddie and the rest of the guys, and would go and see their gigs whenever I could. I absolutely adored him.

One of the reasons my father could be so magnanimous with Queen was that since 1972 he'd had a gold mine of his own: the Electric Light Orchestra – better known as ELO.

20 April 2005, morning
Doheny Road: in my bath

'Sharon?'

A female voice from the landing. I reach over and run some more water from the hot tap.

'Well, if it isn't Mel-linda from Down Under,' I say in my Dame Edna voice. She's heard it before. In fact, several times a day. But what the fuck. Melinda is Awe-straye-lian and I am sure she gets terribly, terribly homesick for the old mother tongue. Melinda has been with us now for four years. She started as Kelly and Jackie Boy's nanny, which basically meant she had to get them up and get them to school. Now they've gone, she nannies me.

'Can I come in?'

'Course you can, Mel-Linda, luv. You've seen a didgeridoo before . . .'

Melinda Varga is my counterpoint to Michael. She rants, she raves, she cries. Most importantly, she laughs.

'My God, Sharon, it smells like a Turkish massage parlour in here. What the fuck happened?'

'I had a little accident with the bath oil . . .' says the naughty girl.

'Not the Jo Malone . . .'

You bet your bottom dollar the Jo Malone. The whole fucking bottle.

4

Leaving

In spite of my father saying that we were never, ever, on pain of death, to have anything to do with the Meehans, David and I were still in touch with Patrick Jnr. The music business was too small a world, at least for kids like us, to hold grudges like that. And in fact he had done nothing wrong whatsoever. Could you really blame him for handing in his notice at Thomas Cook when the chance came to manage Black Sabbath? And we'd grown up with him; he was like a childhood friend.

Whenever my father would see either of the Meehans or Wilf Pine, invariably there would be a fight, a scuffle on the pavement, a squaring up, a punch thrown, threats, whatever. Yet still there was always that relationship between the Meehans and the Ardens.

For example, after a couple of years running his model soldier shop in Kingston, my brother Richard went to Don to borrow some money to tide him over. Things weren't going well and he was in danger of losing the shop, he said. At the time – around 1973, I think – my father was going through a bad patch and so had nothing to lend. But instead of telling him no, he swallowed his pride and went to Patrick Meehan Snr (who had always had a soft spot for my half-brother) and got him to lend Richard the money, even though he was at daggers drawn.

Patrick Jnr would occasionally ask David and me over to a party at his house, and so we'd go and there'd be the Lamborghini or the Ferrari in the drive, and the swimming pool and this, that and the other. The Meehans were always good in business, in the way that my father never was. Even though Don went on to have huge success with ELO, he never had the infrastructure that the Meehans had. I don't think they had any more money than my father – it was still all smoke and mirrors – but they just seemed to manage it better.

Whereas all my father wanted was the wealth, the Meehans wanted the social position to go with it. So they had the house in the country, and it was, 'Oh darling, you must come to our yacht, and Lady Bumfuck is going to be there,' and 'Let's pop over to Argentina for a spot of polo.' It was by no means a lifestyle they were born into. They just adopted it. Yet still, because of the Wilf Pine connection, they were surrounded by heavies and two-bit hoods. They made sure they took care of Wilf – it would have been extremely misguided not to – but at the heart of the Meehan organisation it was father and son. The whole of that world was father and son orientated, no need to look further than Don and David. But if you were a girl, then you weren't really part of anything. It was just like, give-her-a-job-until-she-gets-married, keep-her-busy sort of thing.

Just before Christmas 1974, Black Sabbath had a big show in London at the Rainbow, and Patrick Jnr invited David and me along as his guests. I hadn't seen any of them since the day they came into the office nearly five years earlier. And now they were huge. After the gig we went back to the after party at Patrick's house, and I got horribly, horribly drunk.

I didn't really drink very much in those days. I hated the taste of alcohol and would have things like vodka and orange to try and disguise it. Ozzy wasn't at the after party, and I spent most of the evening talking to Tony Iommi, Sabbath's lead guitar player. My brother inevitably knew him better than I did, because he was always out on the road, but that evening I was enjoying the attention I was getting, which is perhaps how I ended up drinking too much. Anyway, I liked Tony. He was very unassuming, very low key, and although I never found him that good-looking, my girlfriends thought he was gorgeous. Having said that, if he had made a move, then who knows what might have happened. But he never did. His taste was for leggy blondes, not a short, fat, furry matzo ball. For me it was that thing of showing off to the girls: Tony Iommi is my friend and I can hang out with him any time. Which of course I did. But he was just a friend.

The party ended for me that night in Patrick's wife's wardrobe. Feeling suddenly very unwell, I opened the sliding mirror doors, fell in and threw up all over her shoes. And when my brother found me, he grabbed me, pulled me out, shoved me in the car and yelled at me all the way home.

I would still see Patrick from time to time, and one day I was telling him how pissed off I was with living out at Wimbledon, and how I really wanted my own place, but of course couldn't afford one. Although my father would pass out banknotes when he felt like it – Buy yourself this, Buy yourself that – no way was he ever going to buy me somewhere to live. He wanted me where he could see me. Then Patrick said he was moving out of his house in Adam and Eve Mews, so why didn't I rent that?

'Just take it for a while, and if and when you can afford to buy it, then we'll cut a deal.'

I could scarcely believe it. Adam and Eve Mews was just off Kensington High Street. Nowhere near Mayfair, nowhere near Wimbledon. It was a quiet little cul-de-sac, miniature houses where grooms used to live when everyone had horses, and the yard was still cobbled. And it seemed too good to be true. I had the cinema less than fifty yards away, restaurants I could walk to and Kensington Gardens just round the corner. But most importantly, for the first time I would have a home of my own, to do with exactly as I liked. So I said all right.

'I'll come into the office and we'll work it out.'

So the next day there I was sitting in these smart Mayfair offices, the former NEMS HQ, talking to Patrick Jnr, when suddenly someone came crashing through the door with a gun out in front of him. My father. And I was looking at him and he was looking at me, and neither of us said a word. But the expression on my father's face was stunned amazement. He had no idea that I still had anything to do with the Meehans. So after glaring at me, he goes over and puts the gun to Patrick's head.

'How dare you, you little piece of shit!' *Oh fuck, there goes my house . . .*

'Now hold on, Don. Let's not get excited.'

'Withdraw it, you cunt, or you'll be sorry.'

'Seriously, I don't know what you're talking about.'

'I'm warning you, you motherfucker . . .'

'And I'm warning you. If you don't leave now I'm calling the police.'

Whether Patrick Jnr knew what my father was talking about, I don't know. I certainly didn't. But it turned out the Meehans were in the process of suing my father for the money Patrick Snr had lent Richard to keep his model soldier business going, and that the first my father knew about it was a notice he'd seen in the paper that morning. And so of course he went fucking mad. In fact, I sometimes think that my father was genuinely mad, in the sense of not the full shilling, which is why I forgive him so much of what he did in his life. He would act in a way that went in the face of any rational behaviour. I mean, what did he think he would achieve by pointing a gun in Patrick Jnr's face in broad daylight in the heart of Mayfair with secretaries and other clients and who-knows-who-else around? Anyway, Patrick said that he would get the writ withdrawn, and my father left. Meanwhile all I thought about was the mews house that I had just waved good-bye to.

But this wasn't the end of the story. Patrick did, in fact, call the police and that night they turned up in Wimbledon. We were all at home. No prizes for guessing who got to answer the door.

'Ah, Miss Arden. Your father in, is he?'

'No,' I said. And he wasn't. As soon as he'd seen the squad car pull up, Don had done a runner, out the back door, through the garden, to a gate that took you to another road at the rear. The plainclothes policemen showed me the search warrant. I shrugged. 'You can look for whatever you want,' I said. They didn't find anything.

As for the writ, Patrick Jnr didn't turn up for the hearing, so the case was thrown out. Perhaps that was him keeping his word.

What made the business with the gun so insane was that my father could easily have paid back the loan. ELO had proved just the cash cow he needed. In addition to the management and promotion side, he now had his own record label, Jet Records, which naturally ELO were signed to. Hay Hill had gone, and we were working out of two large houses joined together in Gloucester Place, just north of Oxford Street, where we employed around fifty staff.

All this expansion meant huge overheads. And although we were awash with money, it was being spent like water: there'd be David asking for money for his racehorses, me buying paintings and antiques, and my mother simply hoarding it. 'What about getting yourself a nice car, eh, Sha?' he would say. Or a piece of jewellery. At least he knew I'd wear it. What better way to show the world just how wealthy he really was? He would buy stuff for my mother but she would keep it in the box.

For once ELO hadn't been filched from anybody else. There are only ever a finite number of talented musicians, and the cast of characters was always interchanging. ELO was a Don Arden home-grown product. By 1971 The Move had disbanded, but Roy Wood had stayed with my father. Roy is an amazing innovative character, and he had always had this dream of mixing classical music with rock. So, together with Bev Bevan, the original drummer from The Move, and a singer-songwriter called Jeff Lynne from a band called Idle Race, also from Birmingham, Roy came up with the Electric Light Orchestra. So Roy and Jeff worked on the idea, wrote one album and did a couple of gigs, but it just wasn't happening. A clash of egos, basically. Then Roy walked away: although ELO was his brainchild, he was probably the weaker and the nicer of the two. Roy started up Roy Wood's Wizzard and left ELO to Jeff.

I have always been especially fond of Roy. I have known him since the days of The Move. I must have been about fourteen, and he'd say to me, 'Here's fifty quid, go get yourself something nice to wear at the gig.' And he would mean *Top of the Pops*. So I'd go there with a couple of friends from school, and he'd introduce me to people like Marc Bolan of T-Rex. One time, I remember, he bought me a bottle of Diorama. He is just a very nice man, very kind and sort of like a teddy bear. And Roy Wood's Wizzard is still out there, and he brought his daughter – Holly Wood – to Ozzy's last show in England. But I never feel he's had the success that he deserves.

Nobody really thought the rock/classical mix would last. But Roy was right: the Beatles had opened the door with their use of orchestra and strings, and with them no longer around the field was clear. It wasn't long before ELO's 'art rock', as it was being called, was a phenomenon on both sides of the Atlantic. They had their first chart success in 1972 and were touring right through to the nineties.

Another signing to Jet Records was a singer-songwriter called Lynsey de Paul, who, of course, my father also managed. She'd had a big hit with the theme tune for a TV sit-com called *No – Honestly* and I was her day-to-day person in the office, basically because I was the only woman. She was very vampy, blonde and white-skinned, and she played the piano. A beautiful looking girl really, with thick blonde hair and beautiful eyes and everybody wanted to fuck her. The nearest I ever came to getting any of that rub off on me was when she sold me her bed.

When she decided she needed a holiday, I was the obvious person to go with her and, because it was winter, we went to the Seychelles. Once again, I was drinking. And once again I disgraced myself. Not vomiting this time, but pissing. And not in a wardrobe, but into Lynsey's conveniently positioned suitcase.

I was basically very, very unhappy. Although Adrian and I had been together over five years, I knew in my heart we were going nowhere. By this time he had moved out of my parents' house and bought a place of his own in Sutton, still in south London, but further out. It was a cute little house in a new terrace. I'd helped him decorate it; we'd chosen everything together, curtains, lamps, pots, pans, the dinner service, sheets, towels, the lot. But it wasn't mine. And I think I sensed this wasn't going to be a happy-ever-after story. But he was still working for my father, so I'd see him in the office every day, and it was sometimes very painful because of course I thought I was in love with him. I'd have to pretend I hadn't been wondering where he was when I'd called and he hadn't been in – all that shit. And so I'd have to be this good-time girl, always ready with the one-liners, having a wonderful time, always ready to party and show the boys how bloody boring their stick-thin girlfriends were.

He'd said he'd be waiting for me when I got back to Heathrow. He wasn't. So I got a taxi to his house. And let myself in. And my gut was telling me that this was all wrong. But I open the door and I go upstairs. And he's in bed with his hairdresser. And she jumps up and pulls on a kimono. My kimono. And then I go absolutely fucking ballistic. I start throwing everything through the window – lamps, pots, then her clothes and her shoes and calling her every kind of cunt under the sun, and him every wanker, every little piece of shit.

And Adrian is pleading with me: 'The neighbours, Sharon, please think about the neighbours.' Fuck the bloody neighbours. I wasn't going to have to live with them. I went downstairs and continued the mayhem, throwing stuff out of the kitchen window, and then I start on the living room and there's glass everywhere. And then I get a knife and go back upstairs.

'You can take that off, you hear me, you cow, you piece of shit!' And I grabbed it off her and then ripped it into shreds with the knife. Very dramatic. Very Shakespearean. I gave the most brilliant performance. But after ten minutes I was utterly exhausted.

Basically I had destroyed the house. There was just one problem: Adrian was still working for my father and due in the office at ten the next morning.

To be fair, he was in an impossible situation. He worked for my father, he was going out with me. How could he tell me it was over? I think that subconsciously he had worked out a way of my finding out for myself.

Of course, I was completely devastated, completely obsessed. I'd see him every day. He was there in my face. And I was mean to him, I was horrible, I was like a woman possessed. But I couldn't stop myself. And he had gone off with his fucking hairdresser from Vidal Sassoon's, and she was very beautiful, very talented, very artistic and very thin.

It broke my heart. And, to make matters worse, Mrs Smedley had disappeared while I was away. I went searching for her on the common, put up notices on lamp-posts, but it was useless. Wimbledon Common is a huge, wild stretch of land, the nearest thing you get to the country in London, and it must have seemed too enticing. But it's a haven for foxes, and she probably made one excursion too many. And I wept and wept and wept. For her, for Adrian, for me.

So when Lynsey de Paul said she was going out to Los Angeles to live with her boyfriend Bernie Taupin, I just said, I'm coming with you. With Mrs Smedley gone, I had nothing more to keep me in England.

And, oh, the relief. To the world it looked as if it was happening naturally. Sharon Arden going over to California to take care of her father's business. After four years of touring around America with ELO, my brother had had enough of being out of England. So I would take over. And there would be more, with David finding new artists and shipping them out. We already had an office in LA, so the transition wouldn't be difficult and I wouldn't be entirely on my own. My father had always wanted to live in Los Angeles, and now – thanks to ELO – he could have his dream. A house in Hollywood . . .

But in the meantime, I was obsessed. I would cry every night, I would wake up in the morning and for a few brief moments my mind would be blank, then there it would be again, pounding around my head. I would go to receptions, and he would be there with her and she was so beautiful and lovely and so gracious. She was never horrible to me. I was horrible to her, because I was a witch. OK, we'd gone out for five years, so what? He was a free agent. He'd finished with me. She didn't take him away from me. He just went.

Yet even when I moved to America my pain wouldn't go. I cried every night and I would call him and cry on the phone and he would come and visit me. He came twice to visit me in LA. Always completely chaste. He would come as my friend.

Then, about two years later, when I was back in England for some reason, I was driving down the King's Road in Chelsea heading towards Sloane Square, and there's a zebra crossing there, by Peter Jones, where there are always people, and I stopped the car. And I saw this couple walking across the zebra crossing laughing and kissing, and I looked at them and I saw that it was Adrian and his girlfriend Vivien.

And they were so much in love and so happy. And I sat there behind the steering wheel and watched them go across the zebra crossing, and I drove around Sloane Square and came back the way I'd come, and I watched them walk up the King's Road. And they never saw me. And I thought, what am I doing? I mean, look at them. Look how much they love each other. And it all fell away. It was as if everything lifted away from my body. All the jealousy, all the resentment, just went. And it was only then that I let it go. And Vivien became my friend, as Adrian had always been my friend. They were together a long time.

---

20 April 2005, morning
Doheny Road: my bathroom

'Now about tomorrow, Sharon . . .'
   It's Melinda being efficient.
   'Yuurrrrs.'
   'The flowers are being delivered to security at seven.'
   'Just as long as he doesn't see them.'
   'I'll get Sam to put them in the laundry room. Oh, and there's a

package come for him. I think it's from Elton. Shall I give it him now or wait till tomorrow?'

'Let me think about it.'

Tomorrow is a big, big day for my husband. Tomorrow he will have been sober for one whole year. No drink, no drugs, no bottles of painkillers thrown down his neck. Not a one. This is the longest Ozzy has been clean since I first met him. And he's just a totally different person. His life has changed. I would like to say changed for ever, but as they always warn you in AA, it's one day at a time. So I'm giving him 365 red roses, one for each difficult day, and throwing a surprise party: a barbecue in the garden, for fifty people, immediately after the AA meeting that's held at the house every Wednesday.

The celebration he thinks he's getting is a special dinner this evening with his sober sponsor Billy Morrison and Jen, his wife. Best glasses, best china, best cooking, best everything except wine. Cranberry juice or iced tea. FAAB-ulous. The balloons (fifty-two for the number of weeks) have already arrived, and David Withers our cook from England is working his butt off doing both the dinner and the barbecue at the same time: all Ozzy's favourite things for the dinner, and enough ribs and kebabs and chicken legs to keep the dogs happy for a year.

I smile. From downstairs I can hear 'Touch Me And I Bleed'. With the new songs Ozzy and his co-writer Mark Hudson have written in the last few days, Ozzy's rock opera about Rasputin is finally coming together, and it's fucking brilliant. And I feel as if my heart could break as Ozzy's voice and Aimee's soar upwards in a duet.

'Sharon?' Here's my husband now, standing at the bathroom door. 'Did you hear that?'

I wipe my eyes. 'Mmmm.' I'm out of the bath and I'm doing my teeth.

'You know something, Shaz: Aimee has a real gift. She has such perfect fucking pitch it's scary. I mean, she hits every note full on. I don't know why she won't use it.'

'Because it's just not her time, Dadda.'

'I remember when she was about fourteen and she would wander round the house singing opera stuff. She needs to have happen to her what you did to me. D'you remember, Mama?'

'Mmmmm.'

'And what was that, Ozzy?' Melinda picks up the ball. Bonza girl, Mel-Linda.

'When I was in Black Sabbath I'd sing from the wings. And it was Sharon who said, "Here's the mike, fucking use the stage," and she showed me how to do it.'

There's a pause as he walks through to my dressing room and I know he's staring at a pile of clothes taking up half the floor.

'Sharon . . .'

'Yeseeee.'

'Are you having a jumble sale, or something?'

'No, I'm packing.'

'What for?'

'For Thailand. We're going to see Jack do his match, don't you remember?'

'When are we going?'

'Next Monday, after we've been to see Kel in New York.'

'Sharon . . .'

'Yes, Dadda?'

'When are we going to stop following the children around?'

5

Los Angeles

Lynsey de Paul and I flew into Los Angeles in April 1976, when I was twenty-two. It was eight years since I had first fallen under its spell when my father had taken us there for a family holiday in 1968. I had been back several times since, but I never forgot that first time; hippies would sit in the middle of the street and give you flowers. The first hotel we stayed in was the Hyatt House on Sunset, known as the Riot House because of all the bands who stayed there and wrecked it. And when you stood on the balcony you could see right over the city from the Hollywood Hills to the coast. Then we moved to the Beverly Wilshire where in those days they had a huge soda fountain, part of the drug store that was in the lobby, and I remember seeing Simon and Garfunkel in the elevator.

The person who showed us around was Marvin Mitchelson, the man who'd introduced my father to Jayne Mansfield. He was one of the top celebrity divorce lawyers and became famous as the man who invented palimony, the California special where you didn't even need to be married to get your share of the money. He and his wife took us to all the hippest places, like the Whisky à Go Go, the elite club at the time, where we heard Smokey Robinson, and then the Rainbow and the Factory, where you took a lift right into the ground and Red Buttons was with us.

With someone like Marvin Mitchelson oiling the wheels, nothing could go wrong. Or that's what we thought.

'Who farted?' my father asked as we went down in the lift to the Factory. It wasn't farting, it was me belching. And my belching smelled of shit, the first symptom, as it turned out, of Hong Kong flu, an epidemic that was sweeping the world and had just reached America. So while the rest of the Arden family were going out and about and enjoying themselves, I was lying in a darkened room with a temperature of 104 degrees and all my mother could do was sponge me down with alcohol rub. The good thing was that when I got back to England, I found I had lost a shitload of weight.

Eight years later when Lynsey and I arrived at LAX, Los Angeles' less-than-wonderful airport, immigration asked her what she did, and she said, 'Singer-songwriter.'

'And your friend?'

'She's my bodyguard.'

Once we got through, I grabbed hold of her arm, twisting it hard.

'Don't you ever refer to me as your bodyguard again, you little cunt.'

There was no love lost between us at this juncture. We checked into the Beverly Hills Hotel. Lynsey to see how it went with her boyfriend before she moved in with him, me until I found a rental. Within days she'd checked out.

The Beverly Hills Hotel was where my father always stayed when he came to LA, and so the staff all made a great fuss of me.

Ever since that time, that pink palace has been my security blanket: I never like to stray too far from it.

Not everyone was nice to me. There was a guy named Greg who had been running the LA side of things for my father out of a small office on Sunset. Basically he didn't want me to be there at all, as I was queering his pitch. There were obviously certain things I needed to know, but he was fucked if he was going to teach them to me. He treated me as some 22-year-old kid, and he was a big bastard, which didn't make life any easier.

I found us new offices in a brand new development in Century City on the fourth floor of 2049 Century Park East, one of two triangular towers, where everybody else was doctors, dentists, lawyers and accountants. In 1968 it had been green fields with a railroad for freight trains running down the middle of the street to the coast; now it was all marble and glass skyscrapers built on land that had been sold off by MGM.

The rental house I found belonged to Sidney Sheldon. He had been a playwright, a Hollywood screenwriter – he wrote *Easter Parade* which starred Judy Garland and Fred Astaire – and even won an Oscar, but went on to become the most translated novelist in the world, with every single one of his novels a number-one bestseller. Whenever he writes a book, he goes to the place he is writing about, and in 1976 that was Italy. His house was 214 St Pierre Road, Bel Air, a semi-gated estate of large properties between Beverly Hills and Westwood built around a golf course. His was the first house you arrived at once you came in through Gate 15 and it came with everything, including a Filipino housekeeper, so all I had to do was buy new sheets and towels. It even had a guest cottage attached, which meant people could come and stay without you having to deal with them in your jammies.

Being Don Arden's daughter made it very easy for me to meet people. And in that first year I got some really good girlfriends who became a big part of my life. I was lucky, I was working. If you come to a new country and you're not working, it's much harder to make friends and become part of the community. Looking back now, I realise I must have been lonely. For so many years I'd lived in this hive of activity, where your house was also your business, where all the talk was of business. But I soon learnt that if you've got enough to do, you can just push your loneliness to one side and fill it up with work. And that's what I did.

I went out with a few men, but it was always me paying the bill, or me getting tickets for this and for that. Gay men were my salvation. I became very good friends with Michel who ran the Dôme restaurant on Sunset and he introduced me to just about everyone. Then I had my circle of gay friends from London who would call whenever they were in LA. One of these was John Reid, Elton's then manager, who I'd introduced to Freddie Mercury and who in turn introduced me to Elton. Elton's career was well under way, and it was like a phenomenon, watching as it exploded until it seemed you couldn't turn on the radio anywhere in the world without hearing that familiar voice.

Life in California was better than I could have imagined. Paulita, the housekeeper, would wake me up in the morning and feed me huge breakfasts. She would come to the office and feed me huge lunches. She would do everything for me. Like so many people in Los Angeles, she was working her butt off to send money back to her family in the Philippines.

Then just after New Year, when I had been at the house about six months, she arrives with the breakfast tray as usual, but then tells me about how she needs $10,000 to bring her children over and get them educated. And of course I listen and nod, as you do. But I'm thinking, *ten thousand dollars*? It's a lot of money now, but thirty years ago it was five times, ten times as much.

'I don't feel good about this, Don,' I said when I next spoke to my father on the phone. And as we talked, he told me that after he'd been over at Christmas he'd noticed two shirts had gone missing. And David had mentioned he couldn't find some jewellery he'd had. And when I put the phone down, it was like: there's something funny going on here. There was that ring that hadn't turned up, and a necklace I hadn't seen in a while. At the time I'd thought I'd mislaid them: wrong drawer, under something. But what about all those towels I'd bought when I moved in? When I'd got the guesthouse ready one time, we seemed to be very low. Towels? In the end I narrowed it down to Paulita or another lady who would come in to help when there were guests to stay. And when my father flew over a few days later, I had to tell him that I was convinced it was her.

'Leave it to me,' he said. He didn't want me involved. He told me later what happened.

First he calls her into the office in Century City and says, 'Paulita, you've been stealing, haven't you?' And she says she doesn't know what he's talking about. So then he ties her to the chair, tilts it back on its legs, takes off the thick gold Cartier chain he always wore round his neck, wraps it round his hand and starts punching her in the face.

'So that's how I get it out of her,' he told me. '"Yes, I've been stealing." So then I says to her, "Paulita, now I want you to take me to your house."'

And together with a heavy he'd taken with him, they went to her place, and my father said he'd never seen anything like it. Up in her attic were rails and rails of stuff. It was total chaos: boxes, bags, piled high. Not only things she'd stolen from me, but things she'd stolen from Sidney Sheldon and another one of the people she worked for, Gert Silverstein, an interior designer in Beverly Hills. And stuff from department stores, still with the price tags on. At this stage my father called the police. He didn't tell them anything about the punching and the rest of it; just faced them with the evidence. The police called the Sheldons and Gert Silverstein. The Sheldons were still in Italy, but Gert Silverstein came and he couldn't believe it. And Paulita at this stage was still there, and suddenly she picked up a paperweight and went to hit one of the police officers. She was arrested and charged. And I had to go to the prison where she was being held to make a deposition and when she thought no one would see she was pointing her finger at me and mouthing: *I kill you, I kill you, I kill you.* She went to jail for about five years.

MIDEM is held in Cannes every January. Everyone who is in the business goes to buy and sell publishing, buy and sell artists, and artists go there to perform, and every record company has parties. It's like the film festival for the music industry.

And in January 1977 I flew from Los Angeles to Nice, via Paris, with my mum and my dad. And Patrick Meehan was there, and Patrick Meehan's father was there and Patrick Meehan's Italian mobsters were there, thanks to the Wilf Pine connection that had by this time gone international. And the Meehans had chartered a yacht, and theirs was the main party boat that year, and everybody was talking about the drugs and the hookers. And the Meehans were in their element: zey speek French, dey spika Italian, they're the bee's fucking knees.

So one evening we were in the casino at the Carlton, the smartest hotel on La Croisette, and it was all chandeliers and waiters in tailcoats – there's nothing dark and dim about gambling in France as there is in Las Vegas – and everybody was there. Including me: I'd been invited to dinner with a guy called Don King who ran K-tel, a compilation label. He was very nice, and actually it was a date.

My mother and father were somewhere around but where, or what they were doing, I had no idea and didn't care: I was enjoying being flirted with. Then suddenly I heard screaming and there were people running as if the place was on fire. So obviously I got up along with everyone else to go see what was happening. And what did I see but my father, in his silk dinner jacket and his smart hand-made Jermyn Street lace-up shoes, and he'd got Patrick Meehan Jnr on the ground and was kicking the shit out of him. Suddenly one of the Meehan bodyguards picked up this glass coffee table – a huge thing, all chrome edges and legs – and was holding it over his head, about to smash it down on my father.

So I didn't even think about it. I made a dash at this guy and threw myself at him. As he lost his balance, he lurched sideways, the weight of the coffee table pulling him down. And then we started really fighting. He went over, and while I was trying to hold him down, he continued to punch me, so I curled up into a ball. I had brothers: I knew how to protect myself. I also knew by now that my Italian mobster had a gun strapped to his calf. Everyone was crowding around, and a lawyer called Gerry Rubenstein was trying to break it up, but other people had got involved in the actual fight, and it had gone from two, to four, to six, to eight. When casino security arrived, we were separated into teams as if there was a line drawn down the middle. By the time the police turned up, everyone was silent, and in shock.

My father was quite badly beaten. No bones broken but he had a black eye. I was bruised and my arm was bleeding from where the glass table had cracked, but nothing that needed stitches.

We all got interviewed by the police, but nobody said a word. Not the Meehans, not my father. There were no charges; we just had for pay for the damage. The Meehans and my father went fifty-fifty.

Obviously my evening of romance was at an end. There was I, my first date in a year, sitting with this guy buying me steak and frites, and I'm thinking this isn't bad. And within seconds I'm getting punched by some shit-arsed Italian meatball.

It was really ugly and horrible but it could have been much worse. That table could have killed my father. It could have sliced his head off. And it was insane, crazy behaviour, everything I hated, and here I was being drawn back into it again. I'd gone to America only to be pulled back into this whirlpool of shit.

When I had arrived in LA, I couldn't get over how clean everything was: the sun and the blue sky and the cool breeze and no mess in the streets. It was manicured perfection, and then there were the people. I was amazed at how everyone could be so good-looking. Of course, I didn't realise then that they were as manicured as the lawns. Even people who have everyday jobs are manicured: a waitress still goes and has a facial, still goes and gets her nails done.

Everything in LA is about the way you look. The first thing people say is, 'God, you're lookin' great!' Not how are you, how's the family. Then the next thing is, 'You've lost weight!' People were always saying to me how I was losing weight. And why? Because they thought I was fat, so that would be a nice thing to say, they thought, which shows how shallow people can be.

When the penny begins to drop, you want to go Fuck Off. But I just came back with: 'Wrong, actually – I've put it on.'

'Oh, well, you don't look like it!'

'Yes, I do!'

'But you look like you've lost weight.'

'Actually, I know I haven't.' And it was true. I could be twenty pounds heavier since the last time I'd seen them and they'd say the same thing. I was angry because I was being made a fool of. And people would shrug, but I knew what they were thinking about me.

My father was always immaculately
dressed and rarely went without a tie.

My father was ten years younger than my
mother, though it didn't show till later.

I was a happy baby.

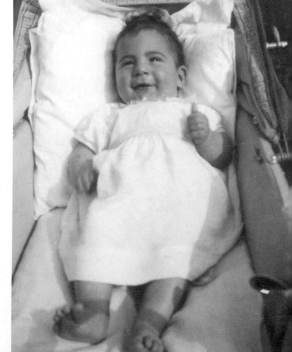

In order of size, my half-brother Richard, David and me at Margate, our usual holiday destination.

Angell Road, Brixton. My half-sister Dixie must be about eighteen in this picture, and was more like a mother to David and me.

Taken in the Black Forest during one of my father's tours of the army bases.

My sister Dixie made this outfit for me for one of my dance displays.

At one of Biddy Pinchard's ballet classes on Brixton Hill.

With Cindy in the Hay Hill apartment in Mayfair.

Dressed up in best sixties gear in Kent. The Small Faces were coming over for a meeting with my dad.

From left to right: Sally, my grandmother; my mother; my father; Michel, who managed the Dôme restaurant; and me. We're at the Howard Hughes house, celebrating my birthday.

This was taken in Las Vegas. I was spending the weekend with my father.

Black Sabbath – the one without the moustache is Ozzy. (Michael Ochs Archives/Redferns)

With Ozzy and Randy. This
was the very last picture of
us together. It was taken the
night before the accident.

My beloved Rachel in the
courtyard of the Howard
Hughes house, in front of
my cottage window.

Ozz 'n' Shazz.

Our wedding photo.
Maui, 1982.

I might have been a nobody, but my father was one of the most powerful men in the music industry. I was so naive that I didn't realise this might make a difference. It took a couple of years for the glitter to lose its sparkle.

'Can I borrow this? I'll bring it back.' It never comes back.

'Can I borrow your car? Mine's in the shop.'

'Can I borrow a couple of grand? You know, right now I'm short.'

'Could you get me sorted with clothes?' A young guy asked me this one time, as he'd just got his first job with an agency. He didn't mean could I give him advice. He meant buy him suits and trousers, because I could. And what's more, I did.

That whole business of Paulita had made me very uneasy about renting, and when the lease of the Sidney Sheldon house came to an end, my father said this time we should buy; no more problems with staff we hadn't chosen ourselves. I saw a couple of places, but there was always something that put me off and I had by now decided I wanted a view.

Then a real estate woman called Thelma Orloff called. She was hugely wealthy, and famous for having gone out with Cary Grant when she was younger. Not that she mentioned that when we passed his house on the way to view the place she had in mind. All she did was nod at a big pair of gates at a hairpin bend and say Cary Grant lived there.

Benedict Canyon runs up into the hills from Sunset, just past my hub, the Beverly Hills Hotel. The road had begun to climb when we turned a sharp right. Up, up we went, skidding on the remains of a mudslide. Then took another side road, to the left this time, then stopped by a large pair of wooden gates. Once inside she parked the car in front of a long line of garages. Behind them I could see the wire of a tennis court. Then through another smaller pair of gates into another smaller court-yard, this time with the house framing it on three sides, the fourth side, to the right, opening out onto Benedict Canyon. I walked across and looked over the edge. At that time of year it was green and lush.

'Great view,' I said.

'Just wait,' she said, already turning the key in the front door. 'As Al Jolson once said, "You ain't seen nothing yet!"'

The house was built in a traditional Spanish style but with a thirties filmstar take, single storey, with pale adobe-covered walls, terracotta tiles and terracotta roof. I followed her in. From the outside it had looked inconsequential but as soon as you opened the doors you were in a huge series of spaces open up to the rafters, cathedral roof as they call it in California, and on the left of the front door the whole ceiling slid back, separating in the middle. Arches went off this way and that way. To the right a view across the canyon again, and still she marched on across the vast high-ceilinged room that was flooded with light coming from a wall made up entirely of folding glass doors, opening onto a terrace where I could see nothing but the dazzle of sunshine. And then I walked outside, and stopped in my tracks. There it was: Los Angeles, spread out like a vision of Xanadu, and nothing but garden and cactus and desert plants in-between. You could have been on a little promontory in Mexico.

'Lovely, don't you think?' she said.

I couldn't speak. It was spectacular: the view, the house, everything about this place was spectacular. I had fallen madly in love. And then she was off again, down the series of terraces to show me the swimming pool, the pool house, the this, the that. But all I wanted was to say to her: yes, yes, I want it, where do I sign?

And then it was back into the house again, up the one small staircase that took you to the tower room – the room that eventually I turned into a library and dressing room for my father. On the side near the canyon was a smaller room that I made into

David's area. Then into the kitchen and staff quarters that backed onto the inner courtyard. And lastly to the guesthouse, which was the other side of the small courtyard that was covered with a purple-flowered creeper. And as soon as I walked into it, I knew that this would be mine. The rooms were small, it didn't have the view, except over the canyon, but here I could be free: I had my own little kitchen, my own bedroom, my own sitting room. My parents and David, I knew, would love the view during the short periods when they were in LA, but I could have it all the time. My mother didn't like Los Angeles and so my father only came out when he had business. A week, perhaps, every month.

'I've found a house,' I told him when I called. It was three in the morning in Los Angeles, but I couldn't sleep.

'How much is it?'

'One point seven million.'

'How much?'

'But, Don, once you see it—'

'How many bedrooms?'

'Well – three in the main house, but—'

'Three! That's over half a million a room. You're nuts.'

I bought it the next day. And how come I didn't need my father's signature? Because he never put his signature on anything. My father would arrange the financing, but the house would be in my sole name, like nearly everything else in his world: companies, loans, mortgages. I was only twenty-three, yet I already had two years of signing for my father under my belt. I was used to it.

And Thelma Orloff didn't even blink.

It had been built by Howard Hughes, who gave it to Jean Peters after their divorce. Although it looked like a thirties house, it was probably more recent; nothing in Hollywood lasts long and houses are pulled down as soon as somebody dies. Egos are too big to want anybody's dreams but their own.

Jean Peters was a starlet Howard Hughes had helped push up the career ladder in 1946 when he was working at 20th Century Fox. Over the next ten years she worked with Humphrey Bogart, Spencer Tracy, Burt Lancaster and Marlon Brando. They had married secretly in 1957 but they'd been involved for over ten years. They were divorced in 1971 and he'd given her this as a parting gift. It was on a huge plot of land, about three acres. There were three other houses on it. One was a teardown, but the others could be refurbished.

And then I began to fill it with beautiful things. I chose every single piece of furniture, every lamp, every painting, every piece of sculpture, every sheet, every towel. I put my heart and soul into that house. I kept everything simple, everything in character – you would really have ruined it had you tried to do anything different. No paint on the walls, just the natural plaster. The woodwork – beams, doors – was left natural, not so much brown as grey from weathering. I had the pool done out in dark blue mosaic – it was just rough blue concrete before but I like to feel smoothness under my feet – and had stars put in on the bottom.

One of the first things I bought for the house was a big old-fashioned telescope, which I kept in the living-room area. And the first thing I did every night when I came home was to go to the spyglass and look out across the city to the Mormon Temple on Santa Monica Boulevard. On top is a golden angel blowing a horn that glints at sunset. It was my ritual, a way of anchoring myself. And at night, with the city lit up, it was breathtaking. And I built a hot tub on the top terrace where you could sit and look out at it all glittering beneath you. To show I was here to stay I bought a Great Dane called Jet, named after our record label. In America they usually clip their ears so that they stand up, but I could never do anything cruel so his ears always flopped over.

Before I moved in, I had another cottage built, a replica of mine but on the other side of the courtyard, directly behind the staff quarters. Because – in spite of the size of the house – there were no other guest rooms. I built a guardhouse by the front gate. I did up the pool house and had two changing rooms made with showers.

I had hoped I might find something left of Howard Hughes and Jean Peters, intertwined initials perhaps. But there was nothing except an ancient projector and a projection room that eventually I turned into a library bar and filled with books and black and white photographs.

Everywhere I look in my life, everything is to extreme measure. It's the same with my housekeepers; I have either had monsters or angels. Paulita had made me terrified to take on anybody else, but then Rachel came into my life.

Rachel was born in Texas, and since the age of thirteen she had been in service. She told me how her first employer would send her to collect packages from Neiman Marcus in Dallas and how she'd had to go round the back, because if you were black you weren't allowed in the store. Later she came to California where, although there was still discrimination, it was nothing like it was in the South. Her money either went back to her family, or she would give it to the church.

Rachel had no children, and she had never married. I was twenty-three and she was fifty-something, and so I think I became the daughter she never had. She insisted on calling me Miss Sharon. She was a very special woman. She would cook for me and take care of me, and I absolutely adored her. I can remember one time when she wasn't well, I went to Santa Monica to see her and she couldn't believe that I had come to her house.

Of course, one way of her loving me was to feed me. In fact,

I had met her first at the Sidney Sheldon house where she had done the catering for a party. So I would eat, eat, eat.

---

20 April 2005, morning
Doheny Road, Beverly Hills

I'm having lunch with Gloria Butler at the Ivy and by the time I get out of the house I've already changed three times. Although it's only April, it's so hot out there. I flick through the rail at the end of the bedroom and pull out a pair of cut-off linen trousers and a Nehru-necked embroidered top in lime green cotton voile. Oh the joy of not having to wear black all the time. But then Melinda tells me she can see my bra. And that will never do for the Ivy since there are always photographers waiting outside. I solve the problem by wearing a white tank underneath.

No make-up. In the old days I used to trowel it on, but since I lost all my weight, I only use it when I absolutely have to. But today not even moisturiser, as my first stop is the skin doctor. I haven't had spots since I was a teenager. But I have one now. A mother-fucker of a volcano about to erupt on my chin. I think it's the toxins coming out after the colonic. Ozzy thinks it's leprosy.

My husband has always been a hypochondriac; when he has a headache, it's a brain tumour. But if it wasn't for him insisting I have a yearly check-up, my colon cancer would have killed me.

I haven't had breakfast. Saba pushes a piece of toast into my hand and I grab a couple of chocolate truffles from the bowl in the hall. It's something I have in all the houses. I always have to have mints or chocolates to grab on the way out to keep up the blood sugar levels. Perkins, one of our security guys, has already opened the door of my Bentley, my lovely Bentley. Minnie thinks she's coming but she's not. Not today. Not to the doctor's, not to the Ivy. And I know that until

I get back she will sulk. I put on my dark glasses. Who am I kidding? The volcano is nowhere near my eyes. The security cameras show some girls standing in front of the house, probably waiting for Jack. Little do they know he's several million miles away in a third world country learning to fight with his feet. Hah! The front gates glide open and – a manic wave to the fans – I'm off, nearly running over a dog walker. Everyone has a dog walker in LA. They should be called dog followers, because that's what they do.

The skin doctor is at the junction of Roxbury and Wilshire in Beverly Hills, the bit they call the Golden Triangle. I take Sunset, then swing left down Rodeo Drive, with its phoney art deco monstrosities and mock-Tudor bungalows, then across Santa Monica into the stretch everybody's heard of: Ralph Lauren, Chanel, Armani, Gucci, Prada, with its trees like bouquets, and so clean you could lick your ice cream from the sidewalk. Then right onto Wilshire, past Barneys, my FAV-ourite department store, then right again into Roxbury. I hand my keys to the parking attendant and take the elevator up. For once I'm on time.

'Mrs Osbourne?' The receptionist looks flustered. 'We weren't expecting you so soon.'

'I'm sorry – I had my appointment down for twelve.'

'Yes, that's right. But the doctor thought you might be late, I mean – er – held up, so he took an early lunch.'

Years of bad behaviour return to haunt me. I can see her neck turning a bright crimson.

'Look, I can call him on his cell . . . I'm sure he won't mind. He should only be about twenty minutes.'

'Don't worry.' I smile. 'I've got things to read. I can wait.'

6

On the Road

When I arrived in America in 1976, my father got me a green card by paying a senator a shitload of money. My father didn't know this particular senator, but he knew someone who did. Artie Mogul was then the head of United Artists Records and knew a lot of people in high places. A work visa wasn't enough for what my father had in mind for me. He needed me to be permanently resident, complete with social security number, because without that I couldn't sign tax returns or do the other money manipulations he needed me to do. I would fly to New York and I'd be ushered into a room and there'd be tax advisers from Washington. And my father would be there, and he'd tell me that I'd be going to Singapore in a week, or Switzerland. And there'd be this tax shelter, this company to be set up. And this went on year after year: 'Sign this here . . . Sign that there.'

And was I thinking, Hey, wait a moment, how come he doesn't do this himself, what's wrong with his own signature?

No. I'm thinking, how important am I! Isn't this amazing that my father trusts me this much! That he needs me this much to do this for him! It was like an honour. I mean, he loved me this much.

These attorneys with their expense accounts, their silk suits, their degrees from Harvard and their fine houses and their children in private schools, they all knew I didn't have my own lawyer, that I wasn't represented. I was an uneducated kid who left school at fifteen without a piece of paper to her name. But, what the fuck, they got me to sign anyway. Who cared that I didn't understand what I was doing? My father was making money hand over fist, which was why he needed to give less of it to the tax man.

Even when things were going well, my father couldn't resist a scam. He got off on it, just like he got off on going around with Mafia hoods in New York, walking into some greasy spaghetti dump in Little Italy with 'the boys'. I went with him a couple of times and it was like watching a fucking B movie. They were badly dressed in shiny grey suits, and ugly with bad teeth and smelling of garlic and guns in their boots. Not an Al Pacino or Robert de Niro among them. It was pure fantasy.

An example of a Don Arden scam. In the early seventies when ELO were new and hot, three labels in America were desperate to sign them: United Artists, Warner Brothers and EMI. So how did he choose which one to go with? He didn't. He simply delivered ELO's tapes to all three and pocketed a huge advance from each of them. Fraud? No, no, no. This was just 'playing the game' or 'business'. In the end there was some sort of compromise: ELO ended up with UA in America, EMI in England and Warner Bros in Fuck-all-land.

Artie Mogul, then head of UA, was involved in a long-running scam with my father, in which I played the messenger boy.

The idea was simple. My father would tell Artie Mogul that he had tapes of some new band he had 'discovered' – let's call them the Two-headed Twat. UA would agree an advance to the Two-headed Twat. I would deliver the tapes and I would sign the contract. 'Here you are,' I would say, 'you now own the rights to the tapes of the Two-headed Twat.' A cheque for, say, $100,000 or $200,000 would be given to me with a smile. I would bank the cheque and I would give each of the four people involved a payout. Split the sum four ways, and write four equal cheques to Artie Mogul and two other co-scammers. Oh, and my father. There was no such band. It didn't exist. As for what was on the tape? Nothing. Farting, nothing. Yet each month another artist with a ridiculous name would miraculously appear, and there'd be another delivery from Don Arden's daughter. They didn't pay millions – nothing to excite anybody's attention, just a couple of hundred thousand dollars a time – fifty grand apiece – nothing too greedy, but it was on a regular basis. And I never thought twice about it. Everyone used to laugh and I laughed with them. In those days I looked at it this way: it's a huge corporation, nobody knows, it's nobody's money anyway, who gives a shit? It wasn't hurting anyone.

And what was in it for me? Why, the pleasure of knowing that I had been such a help to my father. I might go to Tiffany or Van Cleef and buy a piece of jewellery and put it on my Diners account. But I didn't own it. It wasn't mine. On the company payroll I was paid between $200 and $500 a week. Obviously this was worth a lot more than it is today, but I wasn't well paid by the standards of the industry at that time; several people in the organisation got more than me. I was never considered an exec-utive, because my father would never have given anybody the position of an executive. We were all worker bees and he was the queen. The Diners card – and later, when they came in, all the credit cards – had to be in my name as my father couldn't be seen to be an entity; he simply had a second card on 'my' accounts. I didn't even see the bills. They'd be sent to the company and the company accountant would pay.

When I wasn't signing for my father, I was busy at the rock face, managing our LA-based artists. I had Britt Ekland who was trying to launch a singing career but, as she had just split up from Rod Stewart, it was hard going. For the first time in my life I witnessed someone with a broken heart. I saw that beautiful woman turn into an anorexic wreck, get heavily into drugs and lose her hair. I'm not blaming Rod, because I don't know what went on, but he did break her heart.

Then there was Glenn Hughes, a singer/bass player who'd been with Deep Purple, who I put together with a guitar player called Gary Moore. At his peak, Glenn had been a gorgeous good-looking guy, but now he'd done a Jim Morrison: he was grossly overweight and unhealthy looking. To make it worse he'd always had beautiful long hair, and he'd cut it off. So it was an uphill job. In those days to have any chance of success you had to have thin legs and wear tight trousers. You were in competition with rock gods like Robert Plant and Mick Jagger.

But Glenn was addicted to anything he could put in his mouth, and he'd come to the house and be eating chocolate and drinking, and whining about his weight and saying 'Oh God, I can't finish my record', and one day I was so fed up with this constant self-pitying drone that I just spat in his face and gobbed in his beer to stop him drinking it. He was dumbfounded. All musicians did drugs or drank, but this was the first time I was having to deal with the result, because if he didn't do something about it, I was wasting my time. Thirty years later, Glenn Hughes is clean and sober, looks amazing and is doing fantastic – he's an AA miracle.

*

I have no idea how my father and Tony Curtis became friends, perhaps through Marvin Mitchelson. Tony was a genuine fan of ELO to the extent that Don got him to introduce them at stadium concerts on more than one occasion. In 1977 a friend of my father's was getting married and wanted something quiet and simple, so Tony Curtis suggested they use his house. So there was this guy, his bride, Tony Curtis, my father and mother and me.

Tony was living in Bel Air at the time, and his house had this room with a wonderful window with a great view of the hills. And it was sunset and it was all lovely, and it gets to the part where the rabbi starts to sing. And the moment he started, another sound came up, like a group of backing singers. It was Tony's three dogs, who'd been banned from the ceremony itself but had been standing the other side of the picture window, their noses pressed up against the glass. Once the singing started, the dogs collectively put their heads up and began to howl at the sky. They were wailing up a storm but everyone ignored them except me.

I started to giggle. My father gave me a look, but I couldn't stop. And then it was the old problem. I started to piss. You could hear it. I did everything I could do to stop it, crossed my legs, pulled at my muscles, but none of it did any good. Soon the black suede boots I was wearing were like black patent leather. The ivory-coloured carpet had been Scotchguarded so instead of it soaking in, there was one big pool. I did what I could to help it soak in, making these weird movements with my feet. Thank God, only my father and mother noticed. After the ceremony, Tony said how he had never in his life got attached to houses or possessions. 'It's too dangerous, because you will always be heartbroken.' I wonder if he thought that when he saw what I'd done to his carpet.

*

I was still in touch with Tony Iommi. Whenever he came to LA he'd call me; I was like the little sister, and I had all the connections. So he might ask me where he could find a sweat suit, or if I could get him a massage. He liked to go places and meet people, so I'd take him. Or if my father was away he might come up to the house. If it seemed a little clandestine, it was only because if Don ever found out Tony had been there, he'd go utterly insane. Tony was the reminder of the Meehans' betrayal.

One time he asked me to a Sabbath gig when they were playing Long Beach, just down the coast. This was around November 1976, and I hadn't been in LA that long. I'd seen Sabbath a few times over the years, and occasionally I'd bump into Ozzy in a hotel somewhere wandering around, though I'd never really talked to him.

So I was in the dressing room backstage, and it was one of those things where Ozzy and I happened to be sitting opposite each other, around a coffee table. And we must have talked for about half an hour, and he just made me laugh and laugh. And I remember thinking, God, this is such a sweet funny guy. And he has such a lovely face and such a lovely smile. What I couldn't understand was how the others were always making fun of him. 'Oh, it's only Ozzy.' Ozzy was 'the goofball', 'the idiot'. If anything went wrong, it was always Ozzy's fault. Even then, it seemed odd, because the public absolutely adored him, and when people thought about Black Sabbath, they thought about Ozzy, yet whenever the band spoke about him, he was like the band joke.

Then, a month or two later, around the time of the MIDEM fight, I had a call from Tony saying how if I was going to be in Europe we should try to hook up. They were doing a gig in Amsterdam that worked for us both. 'Just don't tell anybody else you're coming,' he added.

Tony was always very private with his personal life, and never liked the other guys knowing his business. So I fly over, get to the hotel, and we meet up, have dinner and then he goes off to the gig. He didn't want me going to the gig, he said, in case any of the band saw me, but he'd see me later. So, it's oh, all right. And I went to my room, watched some TV and waited for him to ring. Nothing. I waited and waited. What a waste of time. I was being made to feel like a little tart, even though our relationship wasn't about that anyway. And around two in the morning, it was suddenly: Fuck this. What the hell am I doing here? So I booked the first flight out at seven that morning. I was just leaving, the hotel as quiet as a morgue, when who do I see but Ozzy, doing his usual can't-sleep wandering thing.

'Sharon?'

'Hi, Ozzy.'

'What are you doing here?'

'Don't even ask,' I said. But suddenly things didn't seem so bad, and there we were laughing in the hallway and chatting as if it was the most natural thing in the world, even though it must have been four in the morning. We could have been talking for only five minutes at most, because I suddenly realised where I was, and what I was doing.

'Look, I've got to go, I've got a flight . . .'

'Oh, OK.'

'So, see you, Ozzy.'

'OK.'

Then sitting in the taxi on my way to the airport, the noise of the windscreen wipers thumping across the windscreen, it was like, Oh my God, he is just so cute and so funny.

Ozzy says that for him that five minutes in Amsterdam was the moment he knew that he fancied me. He says that I reminded him of a cherub. But I knew he was married; not only married, but married with two children. But it was like my ears pricked up at a high-pitched sound that only dogs can hear.

By the time my father next came out to LA, his anger at the MIDEM fight was displaced by hand-rubbing self-satisfaction. He was about to buy out United Artist Records from Transamerica who owned the company at the time. It was a joint thing with his friend Artie Mogul, he said. He was going to be president, Artie was going to be the chairman. David was going to be doing this, I was going to be doing that.

'It's gonna be amazing, Sha. Just you wait.'

Then one morning the telephone rings, and I pick it up.

'Sharon? Hi. It's Artie. Don there?'

I'm in my bungalow, so I pass it through to my dad, and I know it has to be about the deal, as it was about the time it was going to come down. So I put on my dressing gown and go over to the house to hear what's happening.

Even before I open the door I know something has gone very wrong. I can hear my father screaming down the phone, effing and blinding: you lying sons of bitches, motherfucker this, cock-sucker that. And Artie Mogul has called to tell him that the deal was sunk. But that it didn't include him. They had signed it the night before, and my father was out.

The veins on his neck were standing out like ropes, you could see them pulsating, and I thought they were going to burst. I was furious too. I hadn't been a party to everything that had gone on, but to a good half of the conversations I had. And, of course, it was then obvious to me that Artie Mogul never had any intention of including my father in the deal. But at that time ELO were UA's most profitable artists and they needed them on board before the deal could be closed, and if my father had had any idea of what they were up to, he'd have taken ELO elsewhere.

My father then went to the lawyers and served them with every sort of paper to try to get the band away from them. Over the next few weeks Artie Mogul tried to reach Don on the phone, but by then he had gone back to England, so he had to deal with me.

'Sharon, hey, listen. Let's you and me try to sort this thing out, there's nothing that can't be fixed.'

'No, Artie, you listen to me. You're a piece of shit, and if I ever see you I'll fucking kill you. Because you're a liar, a bare-faced fucking liar.'

But he was just one among many. The business was full of lying, cheating mobsters. There was barely a decent person among them. Everywhere I turned there was another liar, another bull-shitter, another fake.

Eventually my father settled, which gave him the right to take ELO someplace else, and he took them to CBS, run by Walter Yetnikoff, which later turned into Sony. But it was too late: the back catalogue was slowly being destroyed.

How? Very simply. Artie Mogul gave the ELO masters – the tapes, the artwork for the album covers – to a man called Morris Levy, the biggest bootlegger in North America, who was involved with the mob in New Jersey.

And so the market was flooded. And when it became obvious what was happening, Artie Mogul held up his hands and said, 'Not me! We're not pressing them!' No, quite right they weren't; it was Morris Levy pressing out millions and millions and selling them worldwide and making a fortune for himself and for Artie Mogul and his henchmen. As these were all bootlegs, they weren't being accounted for in terms of publishing or record royalties, so the band didn't get a penny.

As soon as he was free of UA, my father got ELO into the studio and got them to tour, and Jeff wrote great songs and they had one hit after another. The main damage to the band was done by Morris Levy who bootlegged their double album *Out of the Blue*, a brilliant piece of work, and milked it and milked it and nobody got a penny from it but Artie Mogul and Morris Levy.

In 1977 it was my job to take ELO out on the road. I'd toured with my father and with David, but this was my first time solo. I was the novice and ELO the veterans. I had very little to do – just charter the planes and make sure everybody got on, pay the hotels and deal with any problems. Because they were such veterans there were no problems, except those caused by me. The money from each show would go straight to the agent who had set up the tour, so I had nothing to do with that side. I was soon extremely bored: a flight every morning, snatched food, sound check, gig and another hotel room, and we did something like forty cities in fifty days.

David had tour-managed ELO's four previous US tours, and Jeff and he had got on well, and Jeff didn't hide the fact that he was irritated at having me along. I felt like I belonged to a completely different generation. I mean, I was twenty-three, while they were in their thirties, and married. They were all tour-hardened professionals, had been doing it for years, and were basically sensible and normal. If there had been some young boy in the band I wouldn't have minded, but there wasn't even anyone in the crew. As a result I was very badly behaved and would get drunk every single night because I was so fucking bored. Rachel came with me. She acted as our dresser, she washed and ironed and mended and did her best to keep me under control, but mainly she laughed.

'Oh, Miss Sharon, now you come to bed! Come to your bed!'

I remember one time at the Peachtree Plaza Hotel in Atlanta, Andy Gibb – the Bee Gee who had a solo career and died young – invited Jeff and Bev Bevan and me up to his room, and I threw up over his record collection. I don't know if it was the same night – how could I possibly remember, given the state I was in – but in this same hotel there were these enormous fountains, and I was so pissed that I was just flopping around, in and out of the water, until Jeff dragged me out.

In Washington there was great excitement because no less than the President of the United States – Jimmy Carter it was then – had invited us all to the White House. So the night before, I'd had everyone back at my suite – which I often did, the idea being that I'd end up paying for the drinks. I was already out of my skull when I noticed there was a place where the wallpaper was coming unstuck. It was that time in the seventies when flock wallpaper was all the rage. So, just to see what would happen, I began to pull at a corner, and it came away as easily as an old plaster, and suddenly a whole strip had peeled off.

'What say we just wreck the room?' I said to the guys. And so that's what we did. Not just more wallpaper, but the TV, the oven, the hot plate, all went out through the window. We utterly destroyed it. The next day the hotel called the police. And the others go: 'We had nothing to do with it. She did it all by herself!'

As for the White House, nothing was going to stop that. They went; I stayed behind dealing with the police and paying for the room.

Flock wallpaper was a particular source of destructive pleasure to me in the seventies, and I attacked it at least one other time. It was at a CBS convention when Walter Yetnikoff was in charge, those things where they fly everyone in from around the world and do their bullshit. That year it was held at the Century Plaza Hotel in Century City. Yetnikoff was one of the most unpleasant people I have ever come across in all my years in the music business. At that time I was only a girl, but he was always incredibly rude whenever I would see him. To me, he was the kind of man for whom the term 'chauvinist pig' was invented, who

thought that all I was good for was lying on my back or scrub-
bing floors. So my girlfriend and I – she had also suffered from
his unpleasantness – decided to show him what we thought of
him. In those days there was a shop on the ground floor of the
Century Plaza selling tacky clothes, so we went in and bought
really repulsive dresses and put them on his account. We didn't
wear them, it was just like a Fuck You. And we ate in the restaurant all week, and signed everything to his room, because
nobody checked anything.

So the last night of the convention we go up to his penthouse
suite, and he's sitting there on the floor smoking dope with a
promoter from San Francisco called Bill Graham, both of them
much older than I was, and here am I, the new breed. And they
have the shrimps, the oysters, the champagne, and they were
going in and out of the bathroom. Yetnikoff was a big cocaine
user.

So while these two were otherwise engaged in the bathroom,
I took all this seafood that came presented in huge South Sea
island type shells the size of babies' baths, and threw it off the
balcony. And nobody even noticed. Everybody in those days was
stoned. Then, because I was so drunk and so bored, I started to
wreck the room, starting naturally with the flock wallpaper, in
my small way showing my total lack of respect for him. He
wasn't a musician, he couldn't read or write music, he had never
sung, he didn't have a musical note up his arse.

In those days, almost everybody in the industry knew about
music, and there he was, nothing but a two-bit lawyer, running
the biggest record company in the world. He was the beginning
of the end. From then on the lawyers took over. And you would
go into his office and there were pictures of him arm-in-arm
with the artists. Arm-in-arm with Barbra Streisand, arm-in-arm
with Bruce Springsteen, arm-in-arm with Michael Jackson. But
when asked at a charity event a few years later if he wanted a

picture taken arm-in-arm with Ozzy, he said no. And if I could have cut his heart out, I would have done. But his callous behaviour motivated me: I'm going to be bigger and better than you and when you are fired and at home in front of the TV I will still be doing this. And that was like an oath I gave myself. I will see you out of this business, and I have done. Arsehole.

Through Tony Iommi, I kept in touch with what was happening with Sabbath, and by 1978 the news was not good. Things were beginning to seriously unravel with the Meehans. It might have taken them eight years for the penny to drop, but Sabbath now knew they'd been stitched up like kippers.

By the time Sabbath played the Marquee that February night in 1970, the groundwork for their future success had already been laid. They had already toured; they already had a huge fan base. It was organic and from the street, and when the Meehans picked up their management, it was simply the right time and the right place. The truth is that Sabbath would have made it whoever they had gone with.

All the people around them were self-serving, so it was one shark fighting another shark, all biting each other's tails. Sabbath were complete innocents and had no idea they were being ripped off. They had no concept of how much they were worth. They were paid a weekly wage, but in the early seventies credit cards were not in everyday use so everything would be sent direct to the office, their phone bills, clothes bills, everything. That's the way it was in those days.

'You want a car? Sure you can have a car. What car do you want? You want a Rolls-Royce? OK, here's the Rolls-Royce.' So the car would be delivered. But it wasn't their name on the registration document.

Or they wanted to go on holiday. These were working-class boys from Birmingham – they didn't know they could have got a private plane to fly them to the Caribbean and charter a yacht. They'd take their kids for two weeks to Lanzarote and think they were doing well.

They'd say we've seen a house we want to buy, and these boys' experience was so limited it wasn't like they saw it advertised in *Country Life*. They would never imagine they could have ever afforded palatial or extravagant. And so the house would be bought. But it was never their names on the deeds. Ozzy had 'bought' his parents a house, but when Sabbath left the Meehans, his parents got thrown out. Like all the other Sabbath houses, it turned out they were owned by one of the Meehans' companies.

Worst of all the sharks circling round them were the music publishers. Their music publishing had been signed away 'in perpetuity'. Ozzy now says he didn't even know what the word meant. 'We were four guys in a fucking barrel. I thought "perpetuity" was a fucking disease.'

It was the most obscene thing in the world to take four young guys who were so untarnished and bleed them dry. But that's exactly what the Meehans did, by lying to them, using their money as their own. They had absolutely no respect for them, as people, as musicians, as anything. And that's really what started the rot, because it set the tone for Sabbath's entire professional careers. They felt worthless, they didn't trust anyone. And neither should they have. Everyone around them had lied and cheated, till Sabbath felt they had nothing left to give. At the end of the day the Meehans took away their will to play, which is a terrible thing to do to an artist. Because what were they working for? They never got any real money, any encouragement or any self-worth.

Then one day Tony Iommi called me from England. Sabbath were in a bad way, he said. They had left the Meehans, but now it was all turning into a nightmare. Did I think that Don would consider taking over their management?

20 April 2005, midday
Mickey Fine's Drugstore, Beverly Hills

'Well hi, Sharon! God, you're looking great!'

'I'm doing great!'

'Hey! Saw you guys on Jay Leno last week. Didn't Ozzy look great? You both looked great!'

'Why thank you!'

'And what can I get for you today?'

'Could you fix this for me, please?' I hand over my prescription. Nothing to get over-excited about. Just some antiseptic spot-disguising medication. My volcano isn't leprosy. My self-diagnosis, that it might be something to do with the colonic, is probably right, the doctor says. He also gave me a Botox injection in my forehead for good luck, so once again I am ready to face the world.

I'm in the drugstore at the base of the doctor's building. I don't know this woman, but she knows all about me. Ever since *The Osbournes*, it's been like that. Everywhere. When we were in Australia at the beginning of March it was the same, on a bloody South Sea island people were staring, taking pictures with their mobile phones, asking if they could take a picture of me with their boyfriend or girlfriend or mother or sister or brother or their fucking kangaroo. Because they think they know me. So I put my hand round a shoulder, smile to the camera. I tell Ozzy that the day people stop asking for your autograph is the day you have to worry because your career is over. It doesn't harm anyone to be nice. But I'm the sort of person, you treat me nice, I'm nice to you. You treat me mean and I'm even meaner to you. I am extremes. But sometimes all you want is to be left alone, just to buy an ice cream and wander along the harbour and sit in a café like anybody else without the whole world staring at you as if your tits were hanging out.

Mickey Fine's is an old-fashioned American drugstore, like the one I first went to in the Beverly Wilshire all those years ago, a time when there seemed to be one on every corner. You'd have a soda, buy a magazine and wait for your medication to be dispensed, like Schwab's on Sunset, which was famous as the place where all the directors and producers used to hang out in the thirties and forties and discover movie stars. Now it's a Virgin Megastore.

In fact, I am probably left alone here more than anywhere else. It's being medical that does it. You have the right to be invisible. Nobody asks you what you're doing, in case you tell them that your fanny is itching or your scrotum is playing up.

7

—

Split

I knew from previous conversations that Black Sabbath were all very bruised and very demoralised. Everyone had taken advantage of them: music publishers, managers, lawyers. Because they were just Birmingham boys who knew nothing. Prime targets to be abused. And they were abused. Basically the industry nearly destroyed them, ate them up and shat them out.

Tony had always been Sabbath's spokesperson, and it was because of him that they had stayed so long with the Meehans. He'd always been close to Patrick Jnr and they'd be out together, each with the red Ferrari, each with the model on his arm. And by now the Meehans had lost all their big companies, all their big entities. They'd spent lavishly, on Ferraris, on Lamborghinis, on houses, on drugs. Because they thought it was never going to end. They owned the Black Sabbath record catalogue for the world except North America, and they continued doing so into the late eighties. They kept pressing and pressing, doing compilations and greatest hits, and milked and milked and milked that back catalogue, and Sabbath never got anything. And they never paid a penny in royalties to Sabbath. Never a penny.

So I called my father who at that time was in England, and asked if he would see Tony and the band and help them out and, of course, he said he would. So they had this meeting and it was all 'We love you, Don, we made a mistake', and my father agreed to try to extricate them from the terrible mess they were now in. Just one example: they were chased for the tax, although they never got the original money.

Would it have been any different if they'd gone with my father in the first place? In my view these people were all shysters, they were all dishonest and all in it for their own good. My father would have stolen from them, absolutely he would. But they would have been left with something. Now they were in this whirlpool, faced with years of endless court battles, with fortunes being spent in legal fees. If their money didn't go to Patrick Meehan it went to lawyers. It was a saga that didn't end for another twenty years, in the mid-nineties.

It was 1979 by the time we got Sabbath's management, and my job was to get them re-motivated, writing and recording, to get them back on the road again, because that was the only means by which they could begin to scratch their way out.

So we brought them over to California and I rented a house in Bel Air and had a studio built in the garage there. I sorted them out with a housekeeper and cars, because that's what management did in those days. I looked after them, literally looked after them, as if I was their mummy.

As for the creative side, it was hard work because they were at each other's throats. When you have four egos in a band, every one of them thinks: 'This band is good because of me.' What none of them seemed to understand was that it was a collective force. Nobody could do Ozzy's melody lines, just as nobody could do Tony's guitar riffs, nobody could do Geezer's lyrics and nobody could do Bill's drum fills. But the main focus for all their anger and discontent was Ozzy, as it always had been.

It started bad when Ozzy was late getting to the house. He'd had a drugs bust in 1970 so every time he came to America he had to reapply for an entry visa, which took for ever. So by the time he did finally turn up, the others had already settled in. Even the day he landed it had taken him five hours to get out of the airport. I can still remember sitting round that kitchen table in Bel Air as Ozzy re-enacted how immigration had strip-searched him and gone looking for drugs up his bum, and how I completely cracked up.

The rest of the guys had already seen where I lived. But when I took Ozzy up to see the Howard Hughes house, he was taken aback by its beauty. He just couldn't believe it. He had never seen anything like it, never even imagined such a place could exist and be lived in by ordinary people. From then on, while the others would still be asleep, he'd get a cab to bring him up every morning, and by seven he'd be in the kitchen with Rachel cooking him breakfast, and then he'd go down to the pool or sit on the terrace. By this time our office had moved to one of the other houses on the property that I had done up, and he'd wander up there. And each day I would spend more time with him, at the house and at the office. And though Tony Iommi and Bill Ward would come up too, they never overlapped because they were night people. Geezer Butler was the only one who rarely appeared, but that was largely because he was already dating Gloria.

All this while Ozzy assumed I was involved with Tony. First there was our dawn meeting in Amsterdam – what other con-clusion could he come to? Then he was constantly seeing me coming out of Tony's bedroom at the Bel Air house. It would always be the middle of the night when they'd need me to listen to something, so I'd go over in my jammies and a dressing gown, and then later Tony would want to talk to me alone. He was going through a divorce, and so I would go to his room and sit on the floor for hours listening to him as if I was his agony aunt, so people automatically thought there must be something going on between us. My father certainly thought so.

I was doing my best to encourage and motivate the band, but it was like pulling teeth: 'That's a good track, save that track,' I'd say brightly. Or, 'Let's work on this, guys.' It was ridiculous really, because I knew that they only had to be in a room together and it would be magic. And if a song needed work, then as long as the bones were there, we could fix it. But they wouldn't. Although to the outsider it might have looked as if they were working together, they weren't. They were like a family who, although they sit down and have breakfast, won't even pass one another the cereal.

One day Tony just appeared at the house and said he wanted to talk. About Ozzy. I was used to it. It was evening, and the sun was going down over the Santa Monica hills, and I poured us both a drink.

'OK, Tony, so what is it now?'

'We want him out.'

I couldn't believe what I'd heard. I knew they'd tried it two years before and it hadn't worked.

'You've got to be insane. You can't get rid of Ozzy! Without Ozzy Black Sabbath isn't Black Sabbath, you know that.' And this went on month after month. They just couldn't work with Ozzy, they said. He was doing too much dope and coke. But they were all doing dope and coke. The difference was that the others could maintain a semblance of control; they wouldn't be staggering around crying or in a heap on the floor like Ozzy. He might as well have had a neon sign on his head with red flashing lights saying 'Stoned'.

I found them a producer called Sandy Pearlman, and they began to work in the studio and to write, putting down backing tracks, but whatever vocal line Ozzy put on, they hated.

Ozzy was equally unhappy. The atmosphere in the house was terrible, he said. He and Tony had gone to the same school, and he told me how Tony had been one of the school bullies and how the other bully at their school, Albert Chapman, had been brought in as their tour manager. He'd always be yanking on Ozzy's chain, knowing that he would take it.

It was a ridiculous situation and all of us, my father, my brother and me, were telling all four of them: 'You're crazy, you've got to make this work, you've got to make this work.' We were desperate. We had invested all that time and effort and we knew that all they had to do was come up with a good record, and they could do it blindfold.

People think that being a manager is a great job: it's not. It's the worst job in the industry. There'd be a ring at the door and Bill would be there with a tape in his hand saying, 'Listen to this, it's shit.' It could be three in the morning. In the record business there is no ten to six. Managers are like parents; artists want praise, unconditional praise, and they want you to do everything from working out contracts to making hair appointments. If things go right, they could have done it without you. If things go wrong, it's your fault.

However I tried to cool the situation, it did no good. Tony and Bill and Geezer were adamant that Ozzy had to go, and then one day they just fired him. So I got in my car, picked him up and put him into an apartment hotel called Le Parc in West Hollywood, about the same distance from the Howard Hughes house as Bel Air but in the opposite direction. I thought it would blow over. I thought that once they'd had time to calm down and reconsider, we'd sort it out.

And then Tony called me and asked about a singer I'd mentioned to him a couple of years back.

'Ronnie Dio,' I said.

Could I find him for them? Sure I could find him; he lived in LA. He had a band called Elf, which was a good description of him. From the outside he was a little Munchkin but his ego more than made up for it. And did they really think that this little man could take over from Ozzy Osbourne? Perhaps this was the way to make them see sense.

So Sabbath and Ronnie Dio got together and when somebody new comes in like that, you know how it is, you fall in love with them, and everything they do is amazing and fantastic and everyone is overly nice and overly complimentary. And so Ronnie Dio was Amazing, Humble and Sweet and Nice, and his wife was Gorgeous and he probably shit Gold.

Meanwhile Ozzy was on his own at the Le Parc getting more and more depressed, drinking and doing coke. However dreadful the last few months with Sabbath had been, they were his security blanket and now he had nothing. I put one of ELO's roadies with him, so he would drive him around, but he couldn't be there twenty-four hours a day. I did what I could to reassure him.

'Look, Ozzy, believe me, this new guy won't work. I know him, they don't, and in no way can he fit in your shoes. Just give it a bit more time and it'll fall apart.'

At the same time I was still dealing with Sabbath, and it turned out that Ronnie liked the producer, the producer liked him, so Sabbath liked Ronnie even more. And everything that I thought would fall apart didn't. What they couldn't understand was why Ozzy was still in LA.

'Because we're still managing him, of course,' I told Tony.

'What do you mean?' he said. 'You can't do that. You can't manage both of us; it's got to be one or the other.'

It had never occurred to me that this would be a problem. 'But why?' I said. 'You've both got careers, you've both got futures.'

The band refused to give way. 'You have to choose. You cannot keep both.'

I said I would discuss it with my father and David.

It was obvious now that they were never going to take Ozzy back, yet he had great song ideas and a huge following. So while we were working out what to do to keep everybody happy, Sandy Pearlman, the producer I put in, asked for a meeting. He had been looking to get into management, he said, so why didn't he take Sabbath on? My father and David and I talked about it, and in the end we said, 'Fine.' David had loads of English artists that he'd signed, so it was just like OK, go. Nobody was crying. And at least the headache was gone.

The next thing was to put together a band for Ozzy. I knew that this was exactly what he'd wanted to do for a couple of years. He even had a name for his first record, which he'd had printed on a T-shirt that he'd worn with Sabbath: *The Blizzard of Ozz*. So half of him must have known in his soul that it was over with them. But the other half wasn't brave enough to think he could do it on his own. It was like a tired marriage. You get used to it and it's like, Oh it'll get better, we'll work it out, but in your heart you know it's over. That was the stage he was at with Sabbath.

'OK, Ozzy,' I said. 'Let's put a band together, you can do it.' And the more he lived with the idea, and the longer he was away from them, the more his confidence came back. He didn't have anyone telling him he was no good, he didn't have people saying, 'You're a joke and an idiot, stand at the side of the stage.' And there was no more bullying. No more practical jokes being played on him. They were all big practical joke pullers, and they used to do really mean things to each other for fun, like the time they set Bill's beard on fire and Tony shat in the guacamole dip and let them eat it. Things that they thought were unbelievably funny. But you look back and you think: you're sick. And Ozzy always came out the worst because he wasn't much of a fighter. Not then, not now.

Ozzy doesn't like confrontation. He will always back away. And when you have three people and your crew against you, it gets too much. And after having been away from that for a while, Ozzy was so relieved to wake up and not be thinking, Oh God, what's going to happen today.

After a month or two he started getting himself together, writing and putting down melodies. And then we started to audition musicians for a band, which is always a nightmare. The best way to get people is word of mouth, so we went to a place called Mates, a rehearsal room in LA, and put a notice on the board saying that Ozzy was looking for musicians and giving the office number.

Although Ozzy had new ideas in terms of where he wanted his music to go, we asked them to play Black Sabbath as a starting point. We would hear absolutely anyone. It was an open call so they'd line up and it would be first come, first served. We paid other guys to stand in, so on the day we were auditioning for a bass player we had session musicians doing lead guitar and drums.

These guys are really good at what they do, but with a rock band you have to have the complete package. It's no use being sixty years old, however technically brilliant. It's very easy to tell if they've got it, especially with a drummer. He's the metronome of the band and if he's out of time or has the wrong drum fills, it shows. Ozzy and I would pull up a couple of chairs and sit there and listen, but there was nobody, and this went on for months.

Then Ozzy hooked up with a bass player called Dana Strum. Although he wasn't right for the band, he was very nice and befriended Ozzy and he kept talking about a fantastic guitar player he knew by the name of Randy Rhoads, who played in a local band called Quiet Riot. So Dana arranged for him to come down and audition.

Randy completely blew Ozzy away. He was like a gift from God. He was nice and funny and a brilliant musician, and he had drive. He was great looking with a tiny body, like Prince, but with a mane of golden hair. And Ozzy and him connected so well. Everything about him was perfect.

We still couldn't find a drummer, still couldn't find a bass player, but the main thing was the guitar player, so Ozzy decided he'd had enough. He'd been away from his family for months, and he was pining to go home and see his children, and now that he had the nucleus of his band there was nothing to stop him. So that's what happened. They both went back to England and Randy stayed at Ozzy's house in Stafford with his family, and they began to write, while my brother took over the search for a drummer and bass player. And gradually it started to bear fruit. Randy played guitar, Ozzy sang his melody lines and they would work on their riffs together, and it was just perfect.

But for me, still in Los Angeles, it was strange suddenly not having Ozzy in town, popping in for breakfast, hanging around the pool. And putting my energies into Glenn Hughes and Gary Moore hardly made me want to jump out of bed every morning. I'd put them with a drummer called Cozy Powell, who I'd hoped to put with Ozzy, but he was way too expensive. It was the same with Gary: he thought he was too good to be messing with somebody like Ozzy Osbourne. And thank God, because otherwise we'd never have found Randy.

My father had begun to spend much more time in California,

but I would come and go and do my own thing, and it wasn't like we'd have breakfast, lunch and dinner together. But then I hardly saw him in the office either. And it's not until something happens that you begin to put two and two together.

One night I got back to the house. It was late, well after midnight. Colin Newman, our accountant from England, was in town and we'd been out to dinner. He was more my age than my father's and so we were mates. As Colin had only just flown in, we went straight out onto the terrace to look at the lights twinkling below, and it was then I noticed my father's briefcase on the floor. I went to pick it up, to tidy it away and take it back to his room or whatever I had been planning to do, but it flopped open, so I looked inside. And what did I see but a tiny pair of see-through thongs. Briefs in a briefcase. And a little note: 'Something to remind you of me.'

A couple of days before I'd gone up to see my father in the office in the tower above his bedroom – somewhere I didn't often go – and there was this great big stone monkey there, like a gorilla made out of concrete with hideous glass eyes. New, not antique, like something you might pick up at a truck stop, the sort of place that sells signs saying 'You don't have to be mad to work here, but it helps' or 'My other car's a Porsche'.

'So where did you get that, Don?'

'Oh, somebody gave it to me. Isn't it fabulous?'

So I'm looking at this thing going, yeeeesss, *quite* fabulous.

And it was horrible. Horrible. The only thing in the entire house that I had not bought. And now another thing that I didn't buy: a pair of see-through pink knickers. The note was signed Meredith. So I went in his phonebook, also in the briefcase, and there was a number for a Meredith. And I called the number, and my father answered.

'I think you ought to come home,' I said. I didn't think twice. Because suddenly all those things people had said began to hammer in my head, how Don had this suite at the Beverly Hills Hotel for his prostitutes, and then there was a note I'd found under the windscreen wipers on the Rolls saying, 'I miss you, why haven't you called?' And this was the man I thought was so squeaky clean.

So I went upstairs to the tower room, picked up this stone gorilla and lugged it down to the front door. It was about two feet high and made of concrete. On the head of the monkey I arranged the pink knickers. And then I lifted up my skirt, and I squatted down and shat on it. So there was this fucking gorilla, vaguely Buddha-like, pink knickers on its head, topped by a turd.

And by this time Colin saw what I was doing and was jumping around going, 'No, no. Sharon, stop it!' Because of course he'd known about my father and his mistress all the time. Everybody knew except me. And Rachel had heard the commotion, but she was laughing her head off, saying, 'Oh my God!' Even she had known. She'd tried to warn me. When I was away on tour she'd say things like, 'Miss Sharon, please, please come home. The house needs you, Miss Sharon.' And later she told me how Meredith would be there when I was away, ordering the staff around and going into my bedroom and going through my things.

I didn't think my father would come. I didn't think he would have the nerve, but I decided to keep Colin up just in case, because I was scared.

'You're bloody staying.'

'Look, Sharon, I'm dead on my feet, I'm jet-lagged . . .'

'You're bloody staying here.' And so he was pacing round the house with his hands in his pockets like a father-to-be outside a labour ward.

And then my father came in. He was fuming, and his shirt was undone at the neck – something that rarely happened; he was always dressed perfectly. He came storming in, and of course he had to pass the monkey to get in the door. And he looked at it and went pale.

'How dare you get the dog to shit on my monkey,' he spat. He thought I had got Jet to shit on the fucking thing. Colin put him right.

'It wasn't the dog,' he said. 'It was your daughter.'

And then my father started screaming at me: 'How dare you go through my private things. Whatever I do is none of your business.' He was absolutely right. He could have fucked who he wanted, he could have fucked the Supremes, he could have fucked the Four Tops, it was none of my business. But I was stunned because my father was so moral, so opinionated about everybody else who was having affairs on their wives. My world had shattered.

Over the next few days I was in a terrible state. The doctor prescribed me some Valium, and one night I took an overdose. It wasn't on purpose; it was simply that every time I woke up I thought they weren't working, so I'd take another one or two. It was Colin who found me. And it was so terrifying to see how easy it was to take too many when you're woozy and you don't know what you're doing. And now, when I read about people committing suicide by taking too many pills, I wonder if it really was that, because it's so bloody easy to do it accidentally.

And then I started drinking. The whole structure to my life had imploded. Everything I thought was good and right, and everything I'd fought for and fought other people for, was all bullshit. Everything that people had said about my father was true. I felt conned. I felt utterly conned. Two days later I spoke to my brother, although we were hardly in constant touch. He knew: it had been going on for about a year, he said. A whole year.

I didn't tell my mother. Firstly, it was none of my business and secondly my father would have fucking killed me. Yes, I would stand up to him. I had the courage to say no, I'm not doing that, or you're wrong. But only up to a point. I never really thought he would physically attack me. But he didn't have to. The tone in his voice when he was angry was so frightening it would really rattle your insides. Like with my mother: he only went for her verbally, but when my father went verbally, you would rather that he hit you. It was much easier to take. But I was scared he would lose his temper so bad that he couldn't pull himself back, and he'd lash out and I'd end up getting hit by default.

My mother found out when she next came to California. She didn't come often, she didn't like LA, and, in 1979, she was sixty-three years old. It happened when she was going through some of his papers and found a prenuptial agreement between Don and Meredith. Yes, my father had asked Meredith to marry him. And the prenuptial was things like: when we get married, you don't get this, this and this. And when my mother told me, I just said, 'I know.'

A month or so later, when I was back in England, she talked to me about it. Her husband had never been faithful to her, she said. One time she'd sent a suit to the cleaners so had gone through the pockets, as you do, and found a key to the Cunard Hotel in Hammersmith.

'I've always known that he cheated on me', she said, 'but it's something that I turn a blind eye to. I lost one husband through cheating and I'm not going to lose another.' And that was it.

But the day she found the prenuptial she confronted him. In the Howard Hughes house that very evening. I wasn't there, I wasn't party to it. So they did whatever they did about it. Then she went back to England.

From then on whenever they were together it was always very strained. And my mother would call me, crying on the phone, like when she found an insurance claim filed by Meredith for pearls that had been stolen from the Dorchester in London when my father was supposed to be living in Wimbledon. And she only had me to talk to, and then I would have to have a go at my father. I was the go-between. I was the voice that she didn't have. I was the raging bull that she wished she was. She had always been passive. She should have beaten the shit out of him and thrown him out. It turned out my father hadn't slept with my mother for years and years. On the one hand I felt terribly sorry for her, but I should never have allowed myself to be her mouthpiece. As I said, he could have fucked the Rolling Stones, the Beatles and the Supremes and it had nothing to do with me.

---

20 April 2005, midday
Mickey Fine's Drugstore, Beverly Hills

I pick up my medication and look at my watch. Do I have time to stop at Barneys? I need some new bras. I went to get one this morning and there was only one in the drawer. Saba says Kelly has taken them all.

My cellphone goes. It's Michael in my office: an ongoing problem with the stage set for Black Sabbath. I tell him I'll call him back when I'm in the car. Since my husband had his accident, he and Sabbath do Ozzfest together. And now the band that come on before are trying to dictate what our stage set can be, because they need this and that and the other. And if it means they can't use some of their set because of our set, it being a construction problem, then our priority is Sabbath. They come first.

'Listen, Michael. My job is to take care of the band, and the band has to be treated like superstars. No other band, I don't care who they are, takes precedence. I will not let them use their stage set if it means Sabbath cannot use theirs. They can shove it up their arse. I cannot send Ozzy out there naked. It makes my husband feel like a second-class citizen. They can have balloons, whistles, fucking fire-engines. They can set themselves alight for all I care, I don't give a shit, as long as the stage is cleared within fifteen minutes ready for Sabbath. So find me a professional stage-set designer. I don't want some half-baked roadie sitting at home doing a drawing on the back of an envelope. I need a fucking professional. OK, so what else, Mikey?'

'Insurance. Non-appearance.'

'I told you, Michael, I do not want non-appearance. I will get up and sing if Ozzy can't sing. Zakk will play if Bill Ward is sick.'

'But it's a tour cost—'

'Of course it's a tour cost, but I need to put that money on the stage to make my band look the best they can. If Ozzy can't sing, I will fucking go on. I am not spending money on insurance. They never pay up. They will always find a loophole so as not to pay when you make a claim. Forget it.'

8

Ozzy

Whenever he was in LA, Jeff Lynne would stay at the house. In early summer 1980 he was in the guest cottage with his girlfriend. He had his own entrance and I wouldn't see him from one day to the next. The tour was long over and ELO were in LA recording their next album. That's how it works. You write the album, you record the album, then you do the tour of the album, which is when the money comes rolling in.

And it was about three o'clock in the morning, one of those late-night piss jobs, and he'd come over to the main house and I'd just poured him a beer. And then he came out with his bombshell.

'Sharon,' he began. 'Your father's been stealing from me.'

I looked at him. 'What do you mean, stealing?'

'I mean, your father is a fucking thief.'

'Jeff, do you know what you're saying?'

'Your father owes me four million dollars.'

'You can't mean this—'

'Your father has stolen from me and I want my fucking money.'

His voice was low. There was no shouting or anything. It was just quiet and matter-of-fact.

I knew that my father was having problems with ELO, particularly with Jeff. Jeff was great in the studio, a great songwriter, a great producer, but he was horrible live and he didn't enjoy it: in fact he hated it. But the drummer, Bev Bevan, loved to play live. And these two, Jeff and Bev, were the nucleus of ELO.

ELO was our cash cow but, thanks to Morris Levy's bootlegging, there was no money coming in from the back catalogue and so my father was desperate to get them out on the road again, because tours generate much more than record sales. And basically Jeff was refusing to play ball.

I knew things weren't doing good in the business because I'd come home and find things gone. Like my car. I'd bought a classic sixties Mercedes and had it redone to perfection, cherry red, ivory leather seating, beautiful mahogany wood dash, the interior completely refurbished, and it was an absolute jewel. And one day I came back to the house and the car had disappeared. I knew then that my father was up to his old tricks. He'd decided he needed some money, so, boom, the car went. He had other cars, but no, it had to be mine. 'We'll get rid of that one.' But that was my car, wasn't it? Not according to Don. Nothing was mine. It was his.

And then he'd start on my jewellery. I'd go back to my bungalow and think we'd had a theft. I had a cabinet where I kept all my jewellery, a wooden apothecary's cabinet with all the little drawers, the porcelain handles and gold lettering with the names of the drugs that originally had been kept in it. It was about three feet high and I had it in my dressing room. And he would just go in, take what he wanted and hock it, take the cash and that would be it. Not a note, nothing. And I could say nothing, because nothing was mine. I could use it, but that was all. My father was the biggest Indian giver who ever existed. He would say, Sha? I want to buy you a painting. So he would buy me a painting, for my birthday or whatever, but then I'd come back one day and it would be gone.

'It's not yours. I bought it.'

As long as you were there in his house, under his roof, that was fine. You could use these things. But if you left, you left with nothing. You owned nothing.

So, feeling suddenly as cold as ice, I tried to think what to do as Jeff looked at me, and I said, 'Look, if Don owes you the money, I know he'll give it you.'

He said he didn't want to put pressure on me, but he just thought I should know that his lawyers were now on to it, and they said that Don owed ELO $4 million in royalties.

The next day I called my father in New York. I told him what Jeff had said, and he went ape shit.

'How dare he say that,' he screeched down the phone. 'That motherfucker, I'll kill him.' Later, when he calmed down, he said he was working on the situation, that he was getting the cash together from all different sources and he'd pay him and make it right.

I stayed out of it. Accountants had to be given access to the books, and appointments had to be made, but I had nothing to do with any of it. As for trying to sort it out with ELO, it had gone beyond anything my brother or I could do in the way of salvaging something.

'The situation is fixable,' my father had said. But the situation was not fixable, the damage was done. In time, he got them the money, but there was no changing their minds. They wanted out. They wanted nothing more to do with him. Losing ELO was a huge blow to my father, and later on he told everyone that I was the reason they'd left. That I had spent the money he had owed to Jeff. I became his excuse for everything.

*

There are times in your life when you know that things will never be the same again. And for me this was the turning point.

I was trapped. I had gone to America to get away from exactly this, but it had followed me, and now I was clawing to get out. Half of me wanted to be loyal to my father and to take care of him as I always had done. The other half just wanted to go away, to get a life. I knew there was another way of living, and I wanted to find it. But I just couldn't get out.

My brother went along with everything my father said. And I always felt he resented me. In the past I'd coped with unhappiness by eating, but for some reason this was different and I started to lose weight. I was at my wits' end. My father's affair, the company going bad. It was like a train wreck.

I had lost contact with Ozzy and I was simply trying to hold myself together and think what I wanted to do, where I wanted to go. Get out of the music business.

I don't want to be seen as a victim, someone who was taken advantage of. When I was younger, it was true that I didn't know what was happening. But by this time, I knew that much of what my father did was wrong. But I chose to turn a blind eye and say nothing. I would do what he wanted me to do, albeit under duress. I could have left before, but I chose to stay because I liked the lifestyle and didn't want to give up the luxury. But now I had made my decision. I had to go.

And that's what I told my father. And he was still saying, 'You can't do this to me', and then, 'I need you to sign one more paper.' It was always one more paper. Just one more. And then one day I had complete and utter meltdown.

It was about two weeks after Jeff Lynne's bombshell. My father already knew I wanted out, but I wasn't following through. That evening, something broke and I started screaming at him, and punching, and thumping his chest, and he was trying to calm me down, holding my arms.

'I just can't take this any more, I just can't! I can't!'

And then I started throwing anything I could pick up, smashing everything. I began on the living room in the main house, then went over to my bungalow and continued to destroy. Swiping everything off the tables, wiping them clean with one sweep of my hand, picking up antique lamps, throwing them, throwing everything. I even destroyed a Ming vase. It's terrible destroying something of beauty, but there are some times where you just can't control yourself, and there are some times when you are so frustrated, you are so beyond the point of reason, that there's nothing you can do. It's when you know you are powerless and you just can't take any more.

And at the end of all the destruction, I got down on my knees in a state of total exhaustion and I must have cried for days. I had nothing left. And I took to my bed and I didn't move. My father was probably concerned, but he didn't come near me, he knew to stay away. But then, after a couple of months it started again: 'Could you just sign this for the last time?' 'Could you just make that phone call for me for the last time?' And everything was for the last fucking time.

It was now about six months since Ozzy and Randy had left LA. They'd been staying at Ozzy's house in Stafford with his wife and family, with Randy going off every weekend, being driven by his roadie to Scotland, Cornwall, Wales. He never stopped wanting to learn, wanting to find out.

My brother had failed to turn up either a bass player or drummer and this was now an urgent problem as they would soon be ready to record the album. So David put in a bass player we all knew called Bob Daisley. He was an Australian living in London who'd been in a couple of bands my father had managed – Widowmaker was one. Technically he was good, but I'd come across him a few times when the band he was with at the time was supporting ELO on their American tour, and he wasn't one of my favourite people.

But he wasn't coming in as one of the band, we just put him on a wage, what's called pay and play. Randy was in an entirely different category, and because my father basically couldn't give a fuck about anything else except his new woman, he also didn't get Randy's talent, so he was signed to me for management, publishing, everything.

That still left a drummer.

In my book, a good drummer is crucially important to a band. He needs to stand out as an individual, as a special personality, and in the history of rock there's been just a handful of classic drummers: John Bonham from Led Zeppelin, Keith Moon of the Who, who died in 1978, and Cozy Powell, who had been in lots of different bands but who is the only drummer to have had an individual hit record: 'Dance With The Devil'. Needless to say, no one like this was either available or interested.

I talked to Ozzy on the phone from time to time, and he seemed up and happy and I was pleased for him. The studio was booked, the engineer was booked, but there was still no drummer. Then Bob Daisley recommended a friend of his to David.

'Who did you say?' I asked Ozzy when he told me his name. It meant nothing to me.

'Lee Kerslake. David says he was with Uriah Heep.'

So I went over to London and met with Lee Kerslake. I didn't really like him, but we had run out of time.

Anyway, they went in and recorded *The Blizzard of Ozz* in about six or seven weeks at Ridge Farm Studios, near Dorking, in Surrey. I came over again when it was finished. And it was brilliant. One of those things that was just on. The right time, the right place and everything was perfect. But the instant I saw the band together, I could see the dynamics didn't work, but we were too far down the line and there was nothing I could do. I said what I had to say, and then went back to LA.

But something at least had changed. I knew now I had to get away from my father. I couldn't take his affairs and I couldn't take working for him. I'd heard all these stories from my mother, and I now realised he was a liar and a thief and a hypocrite. OK, so that might be his business. But also as a human being, as a father, as a husband, I saw that he was a creep. And it was then that I started to question everything. And the full realisation of what I'd been doing for him over these last few years suddenly became clear. I had signed my life away for him: every bank loan, every mortgage, it was my name at the bottom of the paper.

And so what happened to all these bank loans? My father defaulted. And in America, if a company goes out of business, there are companies who buy up the debts. Then, if and when they manage to collect on them, they keep whatever they get.

The First LA Bank was one of the places we banked in California, and I'd made friends with the bank manager there. She was very kind to me, and was a nice woman. My father wanted me to get a loan off her. And so I did. In my name, with him as guarantor. It was just to get us through the next month, he said: the usual cash-flow problem. So I borrowed the money, paid it into the company and that was that.

He never paid her back.

Over the years I forgot about it. Not forgot entirely: I always lived in dread that one day it would come back to haunt me. And it did. In 2004, nearly twenty-five years later, the company that had bought this debt found me. How? Through the publicity generated by *The Osbournes*. The fact that it was not my debt, that I had never seen a penny of the money, was neither here nor there. It was my signature on the loan. I was responsible for its repayment, which, when interest was added, amounted to $300,000.

It was Wimbledon all over again. Everything was closing in. I'd come back to the house and find the entrance was barred with red tape saying Caution. I knew what it meant. In America when you don't pay your tax, they come and repossess your house. So I would call my father. He said he would 'deal with it'. I don't know what that meant: talking to his lawyers, or his tax advisers, saying it's 'in the post' or borrowing from Peter to pay Paul. This happened several times, but my father always managed to pull back from the edge.

So I would just turn the car round and go back down the hill to the Beverly Hills Hotel, as I knew that, no matter what, we could always go back there. You wouldn't be allowed in the house for any reason, not to get a change of clothes or a toothbrush or any damn thing. It was no big deal. I'd just go and buy more, like when you lose a piece of luggage. I got used to it.

It was the same when the police came. My father had had a visit from one of his Mafia hoods from New York and the next day the FBI arrived at the house. First there was a call from the guardhouse, where we always had a guard with a big fucking gun at the front gates.

'Miss Arden, we need to ask you a few questions.'

So OK.

'Yesterday we recorded you had a visitor, a Joe Pagano. We'd like to know what your relationship is with this man.'

'Hey, listen. I don't know him, and I don't want to know him. Speak to my father. You'll find him at his office.'

I wasn't interested. I didn't want to know.

I had to get out. But I had to move as diplomatically as I could, because I had no lawyer and no money. There were only his people. If I went to a lawyer, who would pay for it? I couldn't. And if the bill was sent to the company, my father would find out and all hell would break loose. I knew I had to tread very carefully.

*

Then in August 1980 my brother's wife had a baby, three months premature, and they didn't think the baby was going to live. Although my father controlled everything, David was the front man in London, just as I was in LA. My father called and asked if I'd go back to London to keep the office going. The business was going downhill, he said, and he gave me carte blanche to do whatever it took to prevent a further slide. And so I went and discovered that it was a mess, far worse than I had realised: the company was virtually bankrupt.

The Blizzard of Ozz, Ozzy's first solo album, was about to be released. The tour was about to start, first England then Europe, and it was going to cost. And then we had all these other artists signed with the record label that wanted advances and paying, and we had huge overheads and a huge staff. Even the secretaries had secretaries. I went in, cut half the staff, put the buildings up for sale and got rid of half the artists – which wasn't that simple because they were all under contract, they all had deals. When they complained, I told them there was no money, so what were they going to do?

'Listen,' I said. 'You can try suing, but we haven't got anything, mate, so either join the queue, or you can take ten grand and fuck off. And if you're good you'll make it, so good luck.'

It was clear that if we wanted to stay in the industry, we had to trim down and consolidate, and this was the only way to do it. But then my father made my brother come in and take the buildings off the market, and the next I heard a band I'd just got rid of were back in the studio with a 200-piece orchestra behind them.

'Who's going to pay the bill?' I demanded.

But my priority now was with Ozzy. He was booked to do the Reading Festival. Everyone would be there, other bands, the press, not to mention the fans. So I went down to see him in rehearsal, and I panicked. The band was nowhere near ready to perform at a festival, let alone a big deal like Reading. They had never stood on a stage together, let alone performed, and it was obvious they needed to go out and do warm-up gigs. Reading was only two weeks away and Ozzy was meant to be debuting, and I just couldn't risk it, so I decided to cancel and find a replacement. Fortunately for everybody we got Slade. It was great for them; it resurrected them and they were fabulous.

Next I had to get Ozzy out there performing some unannounced shows to break the band in. And so we did four little gigs, Blackpool being the first. I was so nervous. After all I'd been through with them, I felt like they really were my baby. And so we went to Shepperton Film Studios in west London to do a big full-scale rehearsal, trying to pull the show together before they went out. The album was being pressed and was about to be released any day. I knew it was important to make Ozzy's band completely different from Sabbath. Ozzy's approach was totally different, and the image of the band was totally different, though it was still Ozzy's genre. As for the music, it was a lot more melodic and a lot more accessible for radio than Black Sabbath had ever been. Everything was hanging on it. Ozzy's future was hanging on it. But I was so happy to be doing it for him, and I threw myself into it like I hadn't thrown myself into anything before. My only focus was Ozzy.

Bob Daisley and Lee Kerslake were beginning to drive me mad, always wanting this or that changed, and I wasn't prepared to tolerate it. 'Listen, you are stand-ins. And if you don't like the routing of the tour, or you don't like anything else, then go.' They were, 'We're in the band', and I was, 'No, this isn't a band, it's Ozzy. And I manage Ozzy and Randy, I do not manage you and you are totally non-important to me.'

So there was a lot of turmoil. At least Ozzy, Randy and I knew by then that they weren't staying: we had their replacements already lined up. For years Ozzy had a dream drummer he had always wanted to work with called Tommy Aldridge. He played with an American band called Pat Travers, who were quite famous at the time, and they had played the same gigs when Ozzy was with Sabbath. And I'd met Tommy one day at Ozzy's agent, Rod McSween, and I'd sounded him out. He said he would love to work with Ozzy, but that he had one more tour commitment with Pat Travers and then he was out.

The same thing had happened with the bass player. Randy had found us the bass player from his former band Quiet Riot. His name was Rudy Sarzo and he was on board. Just a question of finishing his commitments. And the four of them were so great together, and we had a blast. Eventually.

Ozzy's first show was Blackpool, a tiny venue where they would play to an audience of between two and three hundred. It was too far to drive, I decided, so I went up by train. It stopped at Birmingham, and who should get on but Ozzy's wife, Thelma. I recognised her because we had met once before when she and Ozzy had come to our annual Christmas party in Wimbledon.

We sat opposite each other, which was appropriate, as there wasn't much to connect us. She was a mum, I wasn't. In fact, she was on her second marriage and had a child by her first husband. I was very loud, very confident, she wasn't. She was one of those women who would go with the kids and stand with a placard at Greenham Common, and I was, 'Where the fuck's Greenham Common?' She was a tree-hugger. She went to Oxfam, I went into debt. She knew nothing about the music business. We instantly sussed each other out and knew there was no common ground.

She didn't like what I represented, and I had no idea what she represented. She was just somebody's wife. We'd been thrown together because she was going to support her husband and I was going to work.

*

The place was even smaller than I thought. Backstage was just some little room with no space to turn round, disgustingly grimy and with graffiti covering the walls. And we were all so nervous. And then the doors opened, and I smiled at Ozzy, gave him a hug and went out front. Roy Wood, my old friend from The Move, was there to give moral support. There was a real buzz of excitement because although this was a surprise gig it had been leaked. And when Ozzy came out, he gave the peace sign that he always does, and the kids in the audience do it too. And I was standing next to Thelma, so as my right arm went up, I was grabbing Thelma's arm to hold it up, but she pulled it away. And while I was all 'Isn't this amazing!', she looked at me as if I was out of my mind. And then it began, and I was screaming and clapping to egg the audience on. But I didn't need to, because it was brilliant, and at the end of the show I can remember crying because it was Magic. And the crowd just adored Ozzy, and Randy was phenomenal, and it was one of those nights that you will never forget. One of those nights where everything was perfect and the adrenalin was high, and all the journey that Ozzy had been through, and all the torments and the cheating and the demoralisation were over, and it was like, Oh My God. He's Done It.

So we all went back to the B&B, somewhere in the backstreets of Blackpool, and the crew and the band and Roy, we were all celebrating. As for me, I felt like a butterfly who'd just emerged out of a hairy caterpillar. Since the trauma with my father I had gone down from a size 18 to an 8. And, although the place was a dump, I couldn't have cared less. We had a great night celebrating, and we were all pissed, except Thelma, and on the registration book I proceeded to write Fuck You, and changed everybody's name to some foul name. And we made a noise all night long. I behaved really badly. Why? Because I could, because I was very happy, because it was like, Oh God! We've shown them!

20 April 2005, Lunch
The Ivy, Beverly Hills

The valet takes the Bentley, and I can see Gloria's blonde mane from the sidewalk. She is already sitting on the terrace. And I know I'm going to have fun. Gloria and I have known each other since 1979 when she was dating Geezer Butler, whose real name is Terry, and we've always had fun. Over the years, when Sabbath and Ozzy weren't talking, then we weren't supposed to talk either. But we always did. It's like Sabbath themselves. We always say there's this invisible thread that holds them all together. From time to time they disliked each other, yet they were bonded together, and whether they were with each other or they weren't, they remained a huge part of each other's lives. It's like a sibling thing, Gloria says. You can go for years without speaking but then pick up immediately as if it was only yesterday. Like the Sabbath lunch we had last year at the Peninsula Hotel in Chicago. All the wives and children came. It was like the second generation of Sabbath.

Our lives have been so intertwined over so many years that all the things we have said and argued and disagreed on, hurtful things we have said about each other and to each other, have only brought us closer. And there we all were with our families together as one.

And the band themselves, they've got to the point where they're old enough to accept each other for what they are, and they know themselves so well they don't even need to talk. They can just walk onto a stage without even looking at each other. They know instinctively what they're doing.

'Is it true what Ozzy said on *The Dr. Phil Show*?'

'What did he say?'

'That you're thinking of selling Doheny?'

'I've been thinking of selling Doheny since I first bought it,' I said. 'But Ozzy doesn't want to move.'

'Men never want to move.'

'Kelly says I can't walk down the street without looking for houses. Jack says it feeds my spending habit. But I like decorating.' And it's true. If I had another life, that's what I'd do. I'd become a decorator and get paid for it.

'It's just that I heard there's a house for sale just down the hill from us.'

'You're kidding me!'

'No. It's completely tucked away, the main house is smaller than Doheny, but there's a separate guesthouse with its own swimming pool.'

'What say we go see it?'

9

On the Road Again

Another reason for my bad behaviour that night at Blackpool was entirely subconscious: I was in love with a married man, and I knew he liked the wild streak in me. That whole night in Blackpool I was hugging him and not wanting to let him go.

Forget those tattoos on his knuckles,* Ozzy needed a tattoo on his forehead: Don't Even Think About It. Not only did we work together – a no-no in terms of a relationship – but he was married, had three young children – two of his own and one stepson – he drank to excess and he did drugs to excess. Plus he always had someone in tow, even if he did nothing with them, simply because he hated being alone. During the last few days at Shepperton he'd had this ridiculous Japanese girl (he was going through his John Lennon phase) who didn't speak one bloody

*O.Z.Z.Y. – self-tattooed at the age of seventeen.

word of English. Her face looked like a grinning frying pan, and she'd sit cross-legged on the floor and just stare at him. She was a pain in the arse and I nicknamed her Panface. Her English was limited. All I could imagine her saying was 'suck me', 'fuck me' and 'yes'. But what the fuck did I care, I was feeling so up; the rehearsal had been really buzzy and tight and I felt that we were ready to conquer the world.

We had finished around two in the morning. The band and I were staying at a motel near the studios but by the time we got back there the bar had obviously closed, so my old boyfriend Adrian Williams and Ronnie Fowler, another guy from the office, came back to my room with some booze they'd brought with them, and Ozzy came too. And then Adrian left, and it was just the three of us. And by this time I'm well away and Ozzy is getting very fruity and tickly and touchy, and I'm like, Oh shit, here we go.

'Don't you think it's time you were going home?' Ozzy kept telling Ronnie.

'No, mate. I'm staying. I don't like what's going on here.'

This happened a couple of times until it was gloves off and Ozzy said, 'Ronnie, I'm telling you – fuck off home.'

And that was it.

I thought it was a one-night stand. He was married; I'd met his kids . . . I was just another in a long line. It was only the drink talking, and in the morning we'd forget it had ever happened.

But God, did we have a great night. We had such a larky time, so much fun. We laughed, we made love, we had a big bubble bath together and then we went back to bed again, and had another bath, and then I left for the office. I'd had no sleep at all. And all the way into London I was just giggling, with the occasional Oh My God! And then I called Randy.

'Oh my God, Randy, you'll never guess what I've done!'

'Oh my God, Sharon, I've already heard!'

And so then we went to Blackpool, and Thelma was there . . .

But even though I told myself that the whole thing was ridiculous and I had to forget about it, I was still getting those looks from Ozzy, and there was that undercurrent, and that vibe, and it's oh no, no, no, no, no . . .

It was all a complete surprise. For the past year and more I had been living like a nun, directing all my emotional energy into finding a way to leave my father and get a new life. Yet, in spite of everything, I was no nearer leaving him than I had ever been. In fact, I seemed to have been pulled deeper and deeper into the vortex. Randy might have been signed to me, but Ozzy was still under contract to Don, and although I had washed my hands of sorting out the London office, I was in charge of our thing on the road, but only under my father's auspices.

We did three more warm-up shows and they were all sell-outs and the reception was tremendous. Thelma never showed her face again; she had done her support-your-husband bit, and that was it.

On 12 September 1980 we opened the first night of the tour at the Apollo Theatre, Glasgow, and we were all really, really nervous. In the days of variety, Glaswegians were said to be the most difficult of any audience in Britain, especially on a Friday night, which this was, when they got paid and got pissed. Ozzy was really nervous, on and off the toilet and shaking with stage fright – everything was resting on him. And the guys did the rehearsal, then the sound check, and it was all fine, and to get his mind off things, Ozzy and Randy and I went for a walk round the city, staring into shop windows. And when we got back to the theatre there were two boys from Newcastle at the stage door waiting for Ozzy to get his autograph, and they told us the show was sold out, though we could barely understand as their accent was so strong. But it was true: before the doors opened they were lining up round the block, and we were all in shock.

The show was unbelievable. At the end, Ozzy knelt down and kissed the stage. 'Thank you, thank you, I love you, love you,' he said, his voice breaking with emotion. And we all cried, the three of us: Ozzy, Randy and me, sobbing with tears of joy, and we could still hear voices from the auditorium calling for more . . . He had done it.

Glasgow was closed, so we went back to the hotel to celebrate. This was in the days when you could ask the night porter to get you something after hours, so about twenty of us were there, friends from the press, a couple of people from the office, and we're tipping the porter and buying drink after drink, until even the porter was legless.

And finally it wound down, and then of course, bedtime came . . . And Ozzy and I ended up together again, and it was like:

'Oh shit . . . '

'Oh what . . .'

'Oh why . . .'

'Oh God . . .'

It was really weird. It was only the second time we'd been together in any sense other than a business sense, yet we knew each other so well.

In fact, it could have started nearly eighteen months earlier, when Ozzy was staying at Le Parc, when we were trying to put the band together in LA. I was going to San Francisco for the weekend with Gary Moore and his girlfriend so, Ozzy being on his own, I said why don't you come with us, get out of the hotel? And we had a lovely time, just doing touristy things, going out, going shopping, going to Fisherman's Wharf. On the Saturday night we went to a restaurant and Ozzy behaved exceptionally badly, getting drunk, falling into plant pots and the rest of it, so I packed him off in a taxi to the hotel. But when I got back to my room, I remember thinking about him alone, and wondering if perhaps I should call him. Because although he'd been horribly drunk, he had been very funny. And he told me later how he'd been lying there wondering if I'd got back and whether he should give me a call. Neither of us did. Because in those days he was always ringing home, always talking about his wife, so it never crossed my mind that he might be interested in me.

And he was so sweet and nice and funny, even when he was drunk, and I just enjoyed his company and I really wanted to keep that safe and continue being part of what I was part of. And it was like, Oh God, what's going to happen . . .

I remember those next few weeks as some of the most carefree of my life. No pressure from my father, no calls from my mother. I was on the road and I was in love, not that I admitted it to myself or him. I had a Range Rover and Ozzy had a Mercedes and sometimes we'd go in his car, sometimes in mine, and one of the band would drive the other. And it was the same with the rooms: I would always book two, but we would always end up together. And I kept on thinking that it would have to end, but we were having so much fun, and then it would be the next gig and the next gig. And every show was sold out, and the shows themselves were everything a rock show could be and more, and *The Blizzard of Ozz* went straight into the charts and soon it was in the Top Ten, and he was getting unbelievable reviews, and we were adding more and more shows as the momentum kept building. In the end we added sixteen extra dates.

But when we played Birmingham, of course, Ozzy's wife would come with his children and it was so horribly hard. On the one hand I felt guilty, and yet I was twisted and tortured with jealousy. That first time in Birmingham Ozzy wanted an after-show party for all his family and the press and I literally couldn't go near him, so of course then it was as if I'd been stabbed.

Because I liked him so much. More than liked him. And as for Ozzy, it was a really weird situation. Although in the seven years he'd been married he had never been faithful, there had never been a permanent other one, just groupies. So whenever Thelma was around, I'd be around Randy, so that she would think that we were together. Randy had a girlfriend in California, called Jodie, and we all knew each other and got on great, so it was the perfect arrangement. Or as near perfect as anything could be in that situation.

My little bubble of happiness was punctured when we reached London and my father and brother decided to show up. Don kept telling me how this wasn't right and that wasn't right, that Randy overplayed and what was I going to do about it. He had always hated Randy and had never rated him as a guitar player, whereas Bob and Lee were 'top notch'. And then, of course, he was lording it over Ozzy, bragging how he'd turned him round and how all his success was due to him. But that's the way it always was. I didn't care; I wasn't looking for any awards.

The tour carried on right through till Christmas. Our last show was at Canterbury. And there was something so cosy about it, the cold weather that made us huddle into each other as we walked the streets, the ancient coaching inn where we stayed, the great cathedral that we walked around, all done out in Christmas candles. And I decided to have an end-of-tour party, so I booked the function room in the hotel and we asked those same two boys who'd wanted Ozzy's autograph back in Glasgow, and who'd been at every gig since, to come and join us. And the

food was like something from the war, curling fishpaste sandwiches, sweating cheese and crisps, but those kids were having
the time of their life.

As this was our last night together, there was nothing else to
do but be crazy. And, of course, Ozzy and me and the two fans
were the last ones to leave. We were just on our way along the
corridor back to the main staircase when Ozzy suddenly stopped.
Somebody had left their shoes outside their room to be cleaned.
They were big brown lace-ups. Without saying anything, and
quite as if it was the most natural thing in the world, Ozzy low-
ered his trousers to his ankles, squatted down, put his bum in the
air, put the shoe to his bottom and shat. While the two boys
were in total shock, I was cracking up on the floor. And at this
point, while Ozzy was still in mid-shit, the night porter came by.

'Can I help you, sir?' he said.

Ozzy waved his key in the air and said, 'It's OK, I'm staying
here.' We walked on, leaving his shit sticking out of the shoe like
ice cream in a cone.

We knew we wouldn't be seeing each other for a while, and
I couldn't bear to lose one minute of the time we had left
together. I didn't know what to do, where to go. Should I go to
America, or go back to Wimbledon for Christmas? I was just so,
so lost. We stayed awake all night, talking, holding onto each
other like monkeys in a tree. I just didn't want the morning to
come.

But it did, and we gave each other our Christmas gifts. Ozzy
had bought me a plate we'd chosen together from a china shop,
and I got him a silk shirt and some cologne. He was used to
wearing functional, practical things, chosen because they'd give
him a good five winters' wear, and to see his face when he put
on this shirt made me want to weep. He'd been a rock star for
ten years, yet had no experience of really beautiful clothes, things
that felt as lovely as they looked.

Ozzy should have left straight after breakfast as he was expected back by Thelma for Sunday lunch, but neither of us could bear it. So we said we'd have one last Christmas drink. It was like, anything to delay the moment. And the two fans were with us in the bar, and we all had one last drink together, and another last drink and another last drink and a friend who was giving him a lift was saying, 'Come on, Ozzy, we've got to go. We've got to go now.' But neither of us wanted to go and we just sat nestled into each other, clutching hands, while the two kids from Newcastle told us how they slept in telephone boxes or bus shelters throughout the tour and we hadn't realised it before. We asked how they were going to get back home.

'Hitchhike,' they said. Then Ozzy told them he would give them a lift to Birmingham, which would take them halfway there. And they were so excited, they couldn't wait to get going, but not me.

This would be the first time we'd been apart for months and I felt devastated, and I cried, clinging on to Ozzy for dear life, as if he was going off to a war zone rather than back to his family, though I think he feared it might be the same thing.

We said a final goodbye at the station. Ozzy took my bags and put me on the train and waited on the platform till it left. My face was so wet with tears that I could hardly see. I stood in the corridor and we just stared at each other as the train pulled out. We didn't even wave and when finally he was no more than a dot on the platform, I was too embarrassed to go and find a seat, because I was just sobbing. I was numb. Even though we'd planned that Ozzy was going to tell his wife and leave, part of me didn't quite believe it, because I knew what he felt for his children.

What went on over those few days in Stafford I can only surmise. I was a mass of nerves, and if I had any intuition that things weren't going right, they were drowned out by the tension involved in a family Christmas in Wimbledon.

And then my father had a phone call. Ozzy and Thelma wanted to come down and talk to him, he said. Ozzy and *Thelma* . . . ?

Instead of him telling Thelma he wanted to leave, Ozzy had simply admitted he was having an affair with me. But it was over, he said, and he told my father that I had to go and that David had to come back in.

And that was it. Nothing I could do. Ozzy was still signed to my father.

Our affair had been an open secret. I had never discussed it with my father, but the crew knew, all the guys in the office knew, so it was inevitable that my father knew. And my brother lashed out as if he was Mother Teresa and the Pope rolled into one.

'You're nothing but a home-wrecker,' he ranted. 'And him with children, how fucking dare you.'

'And you're nothing but a fucking hypocrite. You, who were fucking married and engaged to someone else at the same time, you pillock.'

And it was true. It wasn't only his 'fiancée' who never knew David was married; he hadn't even told our parents. He didn't tell anyone for more than two years. In fact, I was angrier with David than I was with my father, who was in an awkward situation because he didn't want to lose an artist, so what could he do except agree to everything?

But when Randy was told that David was back in charge, he went insane. Randy was signed to me. Since the tour had started, Randy had been the overnight sensation. 'It can't work without her. She's got to come back,' he said. I told Randy to just give it time. I'd been the one keeping it all together right from the beginning. It would all fall apart, I told him. My father had had nothing to do with the tour, and my brother was long since out of the loop. That was the reality.

And within ten days it was chaos in the camp. Nobody should have been surprised, including Ozzy. He knew that everybody else was unhappy that I'd gone, and he also knew in his heart that it would fall apart. The tour was finished, but it was like, what do we do now? What's the plan of action? And I wouldn't tell David what I'd planned, what I'd done, what I hadn't done. I wasn't telling anybody anything. So Ozzy phoned me up, and asked me to come back. Our relationship was over, he said, but he wanted me to come back. And I agreed. Both of us knew it wasn't over. I knew he was talking shit.

And did I feel angry with Ozzy? Not at all. Just dead. I understood the position he was in. I knew he loved me. I knew he wanted to be with me. But I also knew he loved and adored his children and wanted to be with them.

So I was just, 'Move on. I've got a responsibility to Randy, and I'm going to finish this.' But when the working day was over, I walked away. No jokes, no drinks. But it tore my heart out, seeing his beautiful smile when he didn't think I was there. Finding something he'd left in my car, stupid things that made my throat seize up. All I had to comfort me was an old T-shirt of his I'd found stuffed in my suitcase that I kept under my pillow and buried my face in before I went to sleep at night, filling my lungs with the smell of him.

We had four months to go before Tommy Aldridge, the drummer and Rudy Sarzo the bass player were available, and four months before *The Blizzard of Ozz* was released in North America. Meanwhile Ozzy and Randy had been busy writing the second album while they were on the road: they would get the structure of the song and then Lee and Bob would come in and put in their bass and drums. But I found them a pain in the arse to deal with. They were such a lot of work. You knew that whenever they called it was going to take five phone calls to sort out. 'I don't like this photo you're using . . . I didn't get the Branston Pickle . . . the wine's not cold . . . my suitcase is dented.'

I just had to bite my tongue. So it was, Right, guys, let's get in the studio, record the album so we have that under our belts and then we can just keep touring.

And that's what we did. I booked them into Ridge Farm Studios where they had done the first album. Same engineer, and co-producer Max Norman. And for the rehearsals and demo, we went to a studio in Monmouth on the border of England and Wales, an old fishing lodge by a trout stream in the heart of the countryside. Ozzy had been there with Sabbath and he felt comfortable there, which I was learning was always a big thing with him, and it was only an hour away by car from his family in Stafford.

The whole point of these places is that there are no diversions. Writing and recording an album is an intense, emotional experience and these emotions can't be allowed to dissipate by letting in too much of the outside world. We were several miles out of the little town and the only relaxation was a pool table, drinking and staring at the river. The studio itself was housed in a high barn attached to the house. It had been soundproofed but basically looked just as it must have done three hundred years before. The house itself was very old, a jumble of small rooms with staircases all over the place. The perfect setting for a farce. Which proved very appropriate, because as soon as we got down there, Ozzy's and my relationship got going again.

With Thelma living not far away, she would regularly turn up without warning, and I would have to hide in another room, going out one door as she'd be coming in another, going down one staircase as she'd be going up another. It might sound funny now, but in reality it was horrible and sometimes it got really,

really close. I wasn't there all the time and I'd be going up and down from London. But the more she would see me, of course, the more determined she was to make life difficult. It was hard on everyone. It was hard on Ozzy, hard on his wife, hard on me, and hard on Randy, who was still having to pretend that he and I were involved.

I don't know if Thelma loved Ozzy. But he was her husband and the father of their two children, and there was also her son from her first marriage whom he'd adopted. In a strange way it was not unlike my mother's situation with my father: a second marriage and not wanting to let that one go the same way as the first, hanging on to it even though it was completely dead and they had nothing in common. Thelma's trump card was the children, and she knew how to play it, turning up with them in tow.

Ozzy, I knew, was going through hell because of Louis and Jessica. He was leading two lives. But both of us had missed each other so much. And as much as I would pine for him, he would pine for me. It was something that neither of us had planned. It was just one of those things that happened so naturally you knew it was right. And both of us felt better with each other than without each other.

I had never enjoyed sex before I met Ozzy. But from our very first night together it was like, Oh my God, so this is what people mean. And now I knew how good it could be, and how loving it could be. And it was like, Yes, I finally get it and finally understand, and everything that had gone before was nothing. And he was so loving and gentle and cuddly, and for the first time I felt able to be myself, to be completely myself without needing to pretend. This man, this funny, crazy, clever man accepted me for who I was. He didn't care if I was fat or thin; the body might sometimes be useful, but it's not relevant. And I had never understood it before, all those songs, those films, those books – this was what they meant. And it was like a miracle that he seemed to feel the same way about me. And as much as I used to get butterflies and couldn't wait to see him, it was the same for him. Sometimes when we weren't together we would talk for four hours on the phone. And we just kept getting closer and closer. Yet already the passion was very volatile and unpredictable. The atmosphere at the farm didn't help, with everyone, apart from Randy, getting horribly drunk. And when Ozzy was pissed he would end up calling me Tharon, which was not calculated to put me in a good mood. I remember the glass smashing everywhere when I threw balls through the poolroom window.

By the middle of March the demo was finished, and we went back to Ridge Farm to record the album *Diary of a Madman*. When that was done, we finally said goodbye to Bob and Lee, and Ozzy, Randy and I flew to America where we picked up Rudy and Tommy. And the sound was immediately a whole lot better, and the stage performance was incomparably better. They were all so connected. Ozzy had always wanted to play with Tommy Aldridge. He had his ultimate guitar player and Rudy Sarzo was a very easy-going guy and never complained about anything and they were all personalities, they all contributed. For the first time it was a band, a real band. So they rehearsed, then boom: it was America, here we come!

20 April 2005, 3.00 p.m.
In the Bentley, heading west down Sunset

'Hello there, M'linda from Melb'n. It's Minnie's Mummy here. Listen, luv, Gloria's gonna be calling with the name of a realtor. See if you can get me a viewing for the house on Benedict she was talking about. Tomorrow morning, after Ozzy goes into the studio. I'm on my way to Malibu. I think Thailand is going to be very hot and very sweaty, so I'm going to pull some things out from the beach house. I'll be back at Doheny by the time Ozzy is through in the studio. Oh, and can you see if Kay can do my colour tomorrow, late morning, and Fariba can do my nails? If you need me, just call my cell. Bye.'

Sunset takes you right through to the coast at Pacific Palisades, and then it's only a few miles up the Pacific Coast Highway to Malibu. The PCH is a horror road that can't be any wider than it is because there's ocean one side and mountains the other. Our beach house is built on the few yards of land between the road and the shore. If it wasn't for the crashing of the surf right by the deck, the noise of the traffic would drive you mad.

The first time I came to Malibu was when Patrick Meehan brought me to dinner with some friends who lived here – it must have been 1974 or '75 – and I fell in love with it then. Later, after the children were born, we'd rent a house every summer to use as a base while Ozzy was touring. And it's a whole little community; everybody knows everybody else but nobody cares who you are. Peter Asher has a house here. I met him first with Rod Stewart back in 1977 when we were managing Britt Ekland; he's now with Kelly's record company. Ryan O'Neal lives one side of us and Leonard Bernstein's daughter the other. Charlize Theron is right on our stretch of beach, and so is Orlando Bloom. Leonardo DiCaprio has a house here as well. We only found out when Lola our English bulldog went exploring and Ozzy had to go over to fetch her back.

All our English friends love the Malibu house, and I could live here all the time, but Ozzy doesn't like having PCH up his arse. Everyone around here knows people who've been killed on the road, and Ozzy is frightened for the dogs. But when we're here just the two of us, it's as if we're incubated from the outside world.

10

Sailing

The history of singers who leave their bands to go solo is not great. In more recent years George Michael and Robbie Williams have done it, but back in 1980 CBS were as excited about signing Ozzy Osbourne as a 65-year-old fart. They took the deal because it was cheap – my father had sold Ozzy to them for a pathetic $65,000 – and when we arrived back in Los Angeles it was like, Oh yeah, the singer who left Black Sabbath.

The British tour had been a sell-out, and *The Blizzard of Ozz* was a huge hit all across Europe. But they couldn't have cared less: most Americans think you go past Canada and the world ends. And especially then, twenty years before 9/11, it didn't mean diddly shit. They couldn't spell Europe, let alone know where it was. As CBS was based in Century City, right by where I had found our offices five years before, we decided Ozzy should do a meet and greet, introduce himself to everyone from promotion to publicity to the sales force.

So the night before, we're up at the house thinking about

what to do. There had to be something to remember him by. And so we decided that we should get hold of a couple of doves, and once he was inside Ozzy would let them go as a symbol of peace and freedom and beauty. Not a publicity stunt, nobody from the press would be there to see it, just an offering.

So the next morning, we buy two doves from a pet shop in Beverly Hills, and by the time we get out of the car Ozzy has one in each pocket, because when birds are in the dark they go to sleep.

He is basically an incredibly shy person, particularly when he has to meet people he doesn't know, and so by the time we get in he's already tanked up, swigging away at a bottle of Cointreau. To make matters worse, it turns out he's not the only artist they're seeing; we're just one in a queue. So while we're waiting in reception for our turn, Ozzy is getting more and more nervous and incensed and I know that he's really on edge. I tell him to calm down, and next minute we're ushered in.

And it's the obligatory: 'Hello, how are you, lovely, lovely, lovely.' And Ozzy feels instantly that they haven't a clue who he is. And the marketing people are at the centre of this thing, so Ozzy sits down on one of the publicity girls' laps, and while she wasn't exactly hostile she was very, very cold – and this was the person who was supposed to be promoting him. Later he said that he just thought: Right, OK . . .

So he pulls out one bird, puts its head in his mouth and rips it off, spits it out on the girl's knee and says, 'Fuck you.' At the same time he's pulled the other one out and released it, so you've got this live bird flying dementedly round the room, while the headless one is still flapping on the boardroom table where Ozzy had thrown the body.

There's a split second of silence before this girl starts scream-ing, shortly followed by the sound of communal vomiting.

Within seconds security have arrived and everybody is backing away. I cannot believe what he has done.

And then I start laughing, and I just can't stop, weeping with uncontrollable laughter – shock, embarrassment, whatever. And as the security guy is escorting us out I am literally doubled up, helplessly clutching my crotch – no chance of asking if he could direct me to the ladies' rest room – so I pissed on the sidewalk in Century City. I was laughing and farting and pissing. And you could see the puddle as the piss was running down my legs onto the concrete, and I'd pissed in my shoes, and by the time we got back to the house my legs were all sore at the top where they'd been chafed raw with the piss.

Ozzy's behaviour was always unpredictable. Nobody told him to go in and do it. It was totally done on impulse, because that's just how he is. And when people say, 'How could he do such a thing?' – if you have worked in a slaughterhouse, like Ozzy had, and killed five hundred cows or five hundred sheep a day when you're fifteen, what is it to pull a bird's head off? In fact, when we got back, while I was trying to sort it all out with CBS on the phone from the office behind the house, Ozzy took an airgun belonging to my father and started shooting pigeons. Having wounded one – Jet brought it back to him – he then ripped *its* head off and left it in our receptionist's handbag. He was on a roll.

By this time CBS's legal department were already on the case. Not only were they threatening not to release *The Blizzard of Ozz*, due out the following week, but as he was still under contract, they said they would destroy him. They had never seen behaviour like it in their lives, and could not be associated with anyone who could be so foul and violent as to do something like that.

But although the album hadn't yet been put out, a first track

had already gone to radio – like a sample track, a standard procedure to get interest up. And as the week went on the story
grew: it wasn't a dove, it was a parrot, no, it was a fucking peli-
can. And by the end of that week 'Crazy Train' was No. 1 on
every rock station across America. So then, of course, CBS soon
forget about the bloody dove. Within six working days, CBS had
gone from: 'We will destroy you, and we never want you in this
building again' to: 'That track? – I tell ya, we fucking knew it
was a hit!' And then it just went bigger and bigger, it snowballed
and the tour dates went on sale and sold out instantly.

The dove incident was pure Ozzy. The show, however, was
me. However much I disliked my father's working methods, his
success as a showman was undeniable, and I was not about to
throw the baby out with the bathwater. Everything he knew
about putting on a show he had learnt in variety, and I look on
everything I do, even today, as variety. Variety, vaudeville, whatever you want to call it. You still have to go on and you still have
to put on a show. Just because the music's louder, it's still vaudeville, people still want to go and see a whole package, and if you
forget that as a promoter, you're dead. So I would give them a
show.

The support band was Motörhead, and although they were
big in Europe this was their first US outing. I made Ozzy's
white-fringed outfits more elaborate. Everything was more
theatrical, with make-up and colour. Eventually I dressed Ozzy
in red chain mail, and put Tommy up behind them, like on an
altar, backlit as if God had spoken and his drums were the apoca-
lyptic wake-up call.

I hadn't been on the road in America since ELO, and things
were very different for me this time round. ELO had flown
everywhere, but Ozzy liked to travel by bus. After the gig it was
get out, get in and hit the road. We had two buses: one for the
band, and one for the crew. And it was just how a band on

the road should be. Crazy and fun, and we really were like one big happy family.

American tour buses are much bigger than their European equivalents. In Europe there are problems with bridges that US buses don't face, and the bus we'd used in England was little better than a standard coach. But in the US, even thirty years ago, tour buses were custom-built palaces in comparison. In ours we had eight bunks, and the back lounge area was where Ozzy and I slept on a fold-down double bed and could be completely private. There was a little kitchen with a big fridge and cooking rings, and a bathroom with a shower and toilet. And this was our first home.

It was such freedom not to have to worry about whether Thelma was about to turn up or telephone, or even my father or my brother. There were no mobiles in those days. When we were in there, we felt completely safe, it was like we were sailing.

Most of the travelling was done at night, and the only real arguments were about music. In tour buses now each bunk has a flip-down TV linked to a satellite dish on the roof, where you can watch DVDs or listen to your own music with headphones, but in those days it was just cassettes that were played over the loudspeaker system.

Ozzy and Randy were obsessed with Phil Collins and they played *Face Value*, his first solo album, over and over and over again. And, as soon as 'In The Air Tonight'– their favourite track – announced itself, Rudy and Tommy would be going, 'Oh *no*, not this again . . .' And with Ozzy's ears already fucked by all those years with Sabbath, the volume was always as high as it could go. And after a month, the other guys got the tape and threw it out of a window.

'Has anyone seen my Phil Collins cassette?'

'Nooooooo.'

The next one to meet the same fate was Gerry Rafferty's *City to City*. Ozzy adored him too and this time is was 'Baker Street' thudding into our heads.

'Has anyone—?'

'Nooooooo.'

Then there was the Frank Sinatra and Dean Martin period. Ozzy would never listen to hard rock or metal. Never in a million years. When it comes to the genre of music that he's in, Ozzy prefers not to listen to it in his own time. When you've been working all day in a chocolate factory, you don't want to come home and eat a Mars bar. The music he was doing now was much more melodic, and in Randy he had found a soulmate.

Randy's mother ran a music school, and whenever he was back in LA, he'd teach the kids guitar. He told Ozzy how the only song they ever seemed to want to play was the old Sabbath classic 'Iron Man', and how it used to drive him mad. And every time we had a break — after a three-day run we'd always have one day off — he'd get the local Yellow Pages and find a classical teacher to give him a lesson. As if that wasn't enough, he was developing a system of notation that would revolutionise the way we write music, he said.

Randy was a true musician. When Ozzy had been with Black Sabbath, he'd basically had to sing in whatever key suited them, but now Randy would tailor his playing to suit Ozzy's range rather than the other way round. So I'd overhear him saying things like: 'If we do it in this key, you can get to the top note easier.'

And he basically gave Ozzy so much confidence. Now they were equal partners in the writing process, and the more Randy took up Ozzy's ideas, the more the ideas flowed. Yet until Randy came into Ozzy's life, he thought he was worthless because he didn't play an instrument.

*

Ever since I had given up trying to slim down the London office, I had been off the company payroll, so we were having to live off Ozzy's weekly retainer. Everything money-wise from the tour itself was going straight to my father, even though we were selling out.

He still hadn't paid Ozzy and Randy their advance on *Diary of a Madman*. I kept asking and asking for the money and in the end had to tell my father that they were refusing to perform unless they got paid, which was a lie. So finally he said to meet him in New York on one of our days off, so we must have been playing somewhere reasonably close.

While the only hotels we could afford were shitholes, Don Arden was staying at the Helmsley Palace in Manhattan. As soon as the door to his suite had closed behind us, he tossed two cheques onto the floor. There had been no 'Hello, how are you, how's it going?' No nothing. The only thing he said was: 'Don't make a noise when you go out, because I have a reputation to uphold.'

The cheques only related to the advance due on the second album, which had been recorded nearly a year before. Money for the shows was quite another matter. Every cheque from every performance was sent to my father direct, while we barely survived on the road.

The way it worked was this: the venue would pay half the fee upfront to the agent who had put together the tour; this was known as the guarantee. The agent would then send this, minus his commission, to Don. The remaining 50 per cent was payable on the night. If you sold out, then you went into percentage, the actual figure based on the power of the artist. And it's still like that today; everybody goes in with a different deal, just as everybody gets a different fee. And Ozzy's fee was going up because word had spread that he was selling out.

I actually liked the agent who did our bookings, but he was

under Don Arden's control, and I was already lining someone up that my father couldn't control, to whom he couldn't say, 'Send me the money.' Sometimes the local promoter could be persuaded to hand the settlement over to us instead of sending it to the agent. I tried to accumulate as much cash as I could like this, keeping it stashed away in a carpet bag I always carried, a Cartier tote made of suede, soft and squashy, because we were staying in motels with no safes. And it was this money I was having to use to cover our expenses. I was desperate for any cash I could legitimately get hold of.

The music business in those days was a boys' club, fuelled by cocaine and sexual favours. These were the days of payola and Mafia involvement, and the standard currency, if you were a woman, was a blow job, but men soon learnt that Sharon Arden was more likely to kick them in the balls than suck their dick.

The show was a sell-out wherever we went. At one small venue a promoter had the nerve to charge me for six weeks' advertising at a thousand dollars a week. This was a complete and utter lie, and his 'receipts' were false.

'You're not taking six grand off me when I know this gig has been sold out since the first day it went on sale,' I said.

'Well, I'd like to see what the fuck you are going to do about it.'

So I showed him. I head-butted him, and whacked him round the head and kicked him in the balls. The next thing I knew he was back with a uniformed cop in tow.

'I want you to arrest that woman,' the arsehole said. 'She assaulted me.'

The cop just laughed.

Apart from my father, I had no role model, so to a certain extent I had to make up the rules as I went along, but I didn't react well to being told what to do.

*

It is nearly impossible now for me to break down the following months. Even the names of the towns mean nothing. Two different albums, two separate tours, yet all the hotels meld into one. Every town was the same, every venue was the same. We weren't there on an educational trip; we didn't go to the art gallery or museum. We went to the radio station, the TV station, the gig and then out. The food was the pits. We lived on garbage. And the delicate butterfly that started out in England a year before had turned back into the familiar caterpillar munching its way through pizza at three in the morning. We'd stop at a truck stop, and I'd say, 'Oh, just get me a plate of fries.' Just shit. And the more stress I was under, the more I ate.

Ozzy's and my relationship was never conventional. Discussions rapidly descended into arguments settled either by fighting or by going to bed or more usually both. We were completely and utterly nuts. We beat each other to such a point and then we loved each other to such a point. Half the time we would start to laugh halfway through.

I smashed his precious gold discs, including the first gold for *The Blizzard of Ozz*. I hit him with the record, smashed it into pieces and threw it down a lift shaft, and it was sacred: all the work it took to get there. That was in Buffalo. We've been on trains where I've ripped up blueprints of stage sets and itineraries. I've thrown stuff out of the windows onto the highway. I've ripped up his clothes. I've torn up his passport. I was just childish and destructive for the sake of it. When I got like that, Ozzy called me psycho woman. And, not surprisingly, he would take his revenge. We were both drinking heavily, though I hated the stuff and was only doing it to keep up with him.

Some incidents stand out, but only because they had repercussions. Like the time I threw a full bottle of scotch and it hit him on the back of his head. He had been on his way out of the room. He then turned, came charging back and hammered me against the wall, so violently that my two front teeth broke off. Not only were the caps gone, but the original teeth under them had snapped, so the next morning I was on a plane back to Los Angeles to get them fixed.

The general pattern was that Ozzy would hit, and I would throw anything that I could pick up, from lamps to tables to telephones. One time in New York I threw a family-size bottle of mouthwash at him, but it hit Pete Mertons instead. I had known Pete since 1970. In one of those coincidences that shadowed our lives, he and Ozzy had been at school together, then he'd been a roadie for one of the Birmingham bands my father managed, and later David had put him with ELO. Now he worked with us.

Another of my father's old team we had along was a heavy called Harry Mohan, who had been a successful amateur boxer when he was younger. And one day Harry was there when Ozzy hit me, and so, to stop him, he punched Ozzy in the nose and said, 'Don't you ever touch her again.' Ozzy fired him on the spot. This was Ozzy's show, and no matter what the circumstances, or who was involved, nobody messed with him.

And one day, I just woke up and realised it had to stop. One of us, at least, had to stay sober. As it wasn't going to be Ozzy, it had to be me. My wake-up call was when I looked in the mirror that morning and hadn't recognised the person who looked back. One eye was completely closed and that side of my face was navy blue tinged with green. But worst of all, I had no memory whatsoever of it happening. This was insane behaviour. I didn't enjoy drinking, and now here I was blacking out with it. From then on, unless it was a glass of champagne to toast somebody, I drank no alcohol for the best part of twenty years.

*

The business of who we had as agent was an important one. It wasn't just a question of getting our hands on the money, it was a question of how good a deal was negotiated, and the level of venues we played. Even before we left Los Angeles, I'd had a phone call from someone who said he wanted to represent Ozzy.

'He's got an agent,' I said.

'I'm sure he has. But he needs me.'

Bill Elson was from ICM and he was the head of the music division, and ICM is global and Big Time. My father had put Ozzy with this small agency called Magna Artists, based out of LA. I could have said I don't want to play St Louis, I want to play Kansas City, and they would say, 'Well, I'm very sorry. That's where you're going because that's where your father wants you to go.' It wasn't their fault; they weren't part of any intrigue, but my father was Mr Big and that was that. Why would they listen to me? This was 1981, and I was a twenty-seven-year-old girl. I was just fucking the singer.

But instinctively I wasn't happy with Magna from the start. They had no other artists in Ozzy's genre; they mainly did country – people like Kris Kristofferson. And although in many ways I was still very naive, I was learning to go with my gut, and my gut would tell me when things weren't right.

So when Bill Elson called, I said, 'OK, come and see us on the road.' He did, and he courted us. He would fly out to different cities and talk to Ozzy and talk to the band, and we warmed to him. And in the end we really liked him.

He was older than us, around forty and a real family man, and totally straight – he always wore a suit and tie. He would come out to bloody Nevada in a suit and tie. Most important to me, he desperately wanted to represent Ozzy, even though he knew the situation with my father and knew his reputation.

So finally I told Don that this man from ICM wanted to handle Ozzy's agency, and that I wanted to have a meeting with him. My father said he would send 'one of the boys'. And so this Italian arrives, Johnny J, K or L. And the first thing he does is show me the gun down his boot, just in case I haven't under-stood his role, which is to intimidate me and relay everything back to my father. So he sits there through this meeting and never says a word, because these people never do. And Bill gives me the sales pitch and it was a good sales pitch: 'My contacts are bigger and I can get Ozzy more money. I can get Ozzy wherever you want Ozzy, and I will work for you.' Of course, I liked what he said, and it made sense. So then I called my father and said we wanted to change agents, and I wanted him to meet with Bill Elson.

'I don't think your father was too impressed with me,' Bill said when he called to tell me how it had gone. But Bill could have been the head of the CIA and it wouldn't have impressed my father, because he knew he couldn't control him. And to show his contempt, he conducted the whole meeting at the Helmsley Palace lying on his bed in a white towelling dressing gown, with Bill perching on the dressing-table stool.

'He's a cunt. An idiot, a *schmuck*. We're fine as we are.'

'But Ozzy likes him, Don. I like him. And we have to do the work on the road. I have to talk to these people.'

'He's a cunt.'

But in the end we did go with Bill, because Ozzy and the band insisted they needed better representation and Bill told Don he would keep him in the loop. But I knew that wasn't going to happen; Bill knew that wasn't going to happen, and so did Don.

After the dove incident, the story grew. And over the months kids started throwing things on the stage for Ozzy: anything from dead bullfrogs to snakes and rats would be thrown from the auditorium. In Rio there was a time somebody threw a live chicken on stage. In Japan they're more polite, and once we had chicken in a foil-wrapped takeaway bag that we all ate afterwards in his dressing room. But that was later.

The bat incident, the story that has become part of the Ozzy Osbourne myth, happened on the second leg of the tour. We were in Des Moines, Iowa, the heart of the American mid-west where nothing ever happens. And somebody threw this thing on the stage. Ozzy thought it was rubber, put it in his mouth and ripped its head off. But not only was it real, it was alive.

Once I realised that he'd had bat's blood in his mouth, I was horrified, and straight after the show went with him to the local hospital for an anti-rabies injection. Not just a little pinprick in your arm but a syringe the size of a cigar was injected directly into his stomach.

Anyway, the next afternoon we are in this shitty hotel room in the heart of corn country, and we turn on the television for the news. And suddenly there it is. God knows what was happening in the rest of the world, but the headline in Iowa was Ozzy Osbourne Bites Head Off Bat. And we laughed and laughed and laughed. Big bands have whole departments churning out publicity and are lucky if they get a mention on page 97. We hadn't even lifted up a phone – I'd been far too worried about Ozzy getting his shot – but the story was soon front-page news around the world. The publicity was not wholly good. We were banned from Boston to Baton Rouge. We were even banned from playing Las Vegas, which has to be the most decadent city in the entire world. It's unbelievable how rumours can turn people into morons. People of responsibility, mayors, governors, would take up this fight to ban us. It was like Chinese whispers. The most ridiculous idea was that we sacrificed dogs. At that time we travelled with Mr Pook, my Yorkshire terrier, and a dog called Bonehead, who, in fact, we had given to Randy. Jet was too big to tour.

*

At the end of July 1981 we were playing Fort Lauderdale on the coast of Florida, and at some time during the day Rachel had been down in the coffee shop of the hotel and had left our key on a table by mistake. She didn't think to mention it to me, but just got another one from the desk. And late that night, after the show, I went up to the room to pack; we had an early flight the next day, to New York and then straight on to Concorde for England. I was feeling very tense – we were playing a big festival at Port Vale, just down the road from where Ozzy lived in Staffordshire and Thelma and the children would be there. The English press would be there, so I had other things on my mind when I put my key in the door than the three guys with clipboards who appeared to be checking the sprinkler system.

It wasn't until we were on the plane that I realised we'd been robbed. Ozzy was dozing, so to find out how the time was going, I opened my jewellery case, flicking the little gold clasps to lift up the top. They had been very clever, leaving enough things inside – fashion jewellery, bangles, beads and shit – so that I wouldn't notice the change in weight, but everything of value had gone.

Rachel would always hide it so carefully, just like Ozzy's jewellery, which she would fold into his socks. Not that he had that much in those days, just his gold cross. The Cartier travelling case had been hidden in the back of the wardrobe under a quilt. So I sat there in this plane rigid with panic. I couldn't tell Ozzy, just couldn't. But once he woke up, he knew something was wrong and was getting increasingly desperate, saying, 'What have I done? Tell me what the fuck have I done?' But I couldn't tell him what had happened until I'd sorted out the insurance.

As soon as we got into New York I called Batyu Patel, the accountant in LA. He laughed.

'Sorry, Sharon. But you see I never made the cover.' My father had stopped it, he said. But for me to file a police complaint I would have had to go back to Fort Lauderdale. The Port Vale gig was too important. I only told Ozzy once we were on Concorde and headed for London because I didn't want him to be faced with having to make that decision, and he just put his head in his hands.

I had lost everything. Because the business was basically in the shit, I knew if I left stuff at home my father would just take it, either to pawn it for cash or to give a piece to his girlfriend. So this time I'd thought, fuck it. I'll take it with me. And I had a huge watch collection. I had three different Rolexes and five different Cartiers. And then there were my diamond earrings, and my ring collection. They had stolen probably about $500,000-worth of jewellery, including Ozzy's things that we didn't find out about till later, because Rachel had taken some of his stuff back with her to LA.

---

20 April 2005, 4.00 p.m.
In the Bentley, heading for Malibu

The in-car phone goes.

It's Dana Kiper, my LA accountant, who has been with me for ten years.

'Dana, just believe me, the woman is insane. I mean she has gorgeous stuff but she is un-fucking-believable. Never once did she mention insurance. Never once was it discussed. If she had told us, then I would have made arrangements.'

Dana loves a good drama, and now she thinks she has one, but she hasn't. The aptly named Goldie Ringstrom is a jeweller. She doesn't have a store, doesn't have a catalogue, she just has clients who are referred to by first names only. Halle or Barbra or Elizabeth. It was in the hope that a Sharon would join the list that she lent me a shitload of diamonds for the Oscars this year: and not only the ones that I wore but the ones I didn't wear, because – as every woman knows – you always need a choice.

At Oscar time, everyone is desperate to lend you jewellery. Why? Because it gets talked about: on TV, in magazines, framed by plunging necklines and beaming smiles. The Oscars is the jewellery equivalent of a trade fair. And they're all hoping that it'll be their stuff that you slip into your ears before the cameras begin to roll, that their diamonds will be the ones causing the cameramen to fit Polaroid filters to cut the glare. And so they troop in, the girl with the blonde hair and long legs, the two clean-cut guys, and the hand-tooled leather boxes lined in silk.

And so three days before the Oscars they're all there doing the same thing, the dress designers, the shoe designers, the stylists. Everybody is carrying this bag and that. And then Goldie (whom I have never met in my life) leaps up from the mass of plastic bags and shoe boxes and comes to greet me with the 'Hi, Sharon, you look so great!' Though it's Minnie who gets the biggest welcome. Since my chat show, Minnie is herself a celebrity. It's like a Tupperware party with these women pulling at things in plastic bags and scrabbling around on the floor for diamonds that have fallen out. Mattie is the long-legged girl she has helping her keep track. Meanwhile Goldie herself never draws breath.

'Look, if something isn't what you want then I can change it. I can lengthen it. So tell me what you're looking for. Do you want funky or diamondy? So what are you guys wearing? Debra has this in yellow diamonds. I like the pink. See, this becomes a choker and it's so chic. Oh you're so right. This is chicer. Quite expensive but it's quite funky. So try the pink diamonds. These all become necklaces too. Do you like the black ones? I love the black ones. You know what, they're pretty without the circle of white diamonds, but the centre I like. Bring me some of those without the circle, Mattie. Oh and this is a beautiful piece, I think I'm going to give it to Elizabeth on Sunday. It's her seventy-fifth, you know. But she'll probably end up telling me what she wants. Find her the turquoise snake. Show her the diamond bangles.'

And so I took the diamond bangles, and a choker and two pairs of earrings, and two bracelets, and another necklace, and two brooches, because it wasn't just the Oscars. Four days later I had the MTV Awards in Sydney with eight costume changes, and so I needed jewellery to go with that. And I like wearing jewellery, and not only on camera. I'll wear something like the bangles for a few weeks without taking them off, and then send them back.

And I did wear the choker and the earrings, then they got returned the next day, together with a 12-carat diamond ring – the band was so thin I thought it would break. And the things for Australia got returned when I got back to LA.

And now Dana says that Goldie is billing us for the insurance.

'Don't waste any more time on this, Dana. Because she's got everything back. I know she's got everything back. And when Tiffany lends me jewellery or Van Cleef lends me jewellery, they always cover the insurance. So just forget it, Dana. The woman's a lunatic and you can tell her to go fuck herself.'

11

Leesburg

One night in March 1982 we were in Florida again, driving through the night on our way from Knoxville, Tennessee, to Orlando, where we had a festival date with Foreigner the following day. Later we found out that there was some problem with the air-conditioning, so the driver had told our tour manager that he could get it sorted out at the hub, the bus company's headquarters, and that we were going to be passing anyway, so they might as well stop. I knew nothing about it. When we had got on the bus in Knoxville, I was out for the count in our little back lounge, though Ozzy stayed up later. What I also didn't know was that the driver had his wife on board, sitting up front with him in what's called the shotgun seat. If I'd been asked, I wouldn't have allowed it. When you're so long on the road, the bus becomes your home, and the last thing you want is another person pissing in the toilet. No interlopers, ever.

Ozzy says that he didn't get to bed till about six. But I remember him telling me how Randy had been saying how he wanted to give up rock and roll and go back to college. And Ozzy had said, 'Wait a few more albums and you can buy your own college.'

The next thing I remember is a terrible noise, and then being thrown onto the floor. Crash was the word that filled my head. There was a roar of noise, and the first thing I do is look out of the window, and all that I see is a green field, and then the screaming starts. Ozzy has now stumbled to his feet and is forcing open the doors leading to the rest of the bus, and you couldn't see down the corridor because halfway along it was completely bent, and there was stuff all over the floor and we had no idea what was going on.

And I was vaguely aware of a strange smell, and then Ozzy is screaming at mc to 'GET OFF THE BUS NOW!'

And then I see Rudy, his hands in the air, and he's screaming Randy, Randy! And I manage to climb down from the bus, and we're on some grass, and there are people on their knees, doubled up and weeping, weeping, and I see that we're in the middle of a field, and there seems to be some kind of landing strip and some little planes dotted about, and then I see a white Colonial-style house with pillars and it's on fire.

And I'm like, *What's going on?* And I see Jake, the tour manager, and I'm shouting at him: Where's Rachel? Where the fuck's Rachel? And he says that Randy and Rachel have been in this plane crash, and they're dead, and I'm holding my shoes and I just start laying into him with a shoe. And I still don't understand. A plane? But there's this strong smell of petrol everywhere.

And then Ozzy shouted that there was a man in the burning house, and so he grabbed the fire extinguisher from the bus and began to run towards it. And I just had no idea what had happened, and as I looked I saw that there were bits of plane everywhere, and bits of body parts. And it was just so hard to take in. I kept wanting to ask what's happened, what's happened, wanting somebody to tell me, but everybody was howling and wailing. And I can't remember how many minutes it was until I finally understood, properly understood the only thing that mattered, which was that Randy and Rachel were dead. They were dead. But even then I didn't understand.

And nothing seemed to be happening, so I ran into this other house that wasn't on fire, a one-storey trailer home, to get to a phone and the door was open and there was a lady standing by a sink, seemingly washing up, and a man on the phone talking about getting the air-conditioning fixed on the bus.

And I tried to say that there was a house on fire, and they needed to call the fire service, and our bus had been hit. And this man wearing a cowboy hat carried on talking into the phone about the air-conditioning. I was pleading with them to let me use the phone, and they just seemed to be standing there, doing nothing. And this wasn't half a mile away, it was less than a hundred yards. Why hadn't he run out to help, why hadn't she run out to help?

And when finally the man hands me the phone, the only person I can think to call is my dad, and I'm sobbing into the phone and trying to explain where I am, and that we need help. And I'm saying to this woman, 'Where am I?' But she had this strong Southern accent, and I couldn't understand, and everything she said was in slow time. And I just couldn't believe what was happening. And I was disorientated and confused and trying to put all these images together in my mind to try and piece together the puzzle.

And it turns out that the bus company owns a plane company and a helicopter company as well, and this bus driver is also a fucking pilot. So he drives through the night, and gets to this place and tells someone to sort out the air-conditioning and then says to the people on our bus, 'Do you wanna go up for a ride?'

So he gets out one of these planes, starts it up and takes a couple of the guys up for a ride. And then they come down and he says, 'Anyone else wanna go?' And Randy and Rachel must have said yes. And what I have never understood about this whole horrible tragedy is why they went up there. Why ever they went up. Randy didn't like flying, and neither did Rachel.

But for whatever reason they got to go up with him, and it seems that the driver's wife was standing outside, beside the bus, watching them, and he could see her from the cockpit of the plane, and he just decided to run the plane into his wife and try to kill her. And he dive-bombed the bus. What we later found out was that they were in the process of getting divorced. Plus the autopsy showed that his body was full of cocaine. And I heard later that he'd already killed someone in a helicopter crash, yet he had walked free.

If the man on the phone had known this, then it would all make sense. And so when it happened, they were like, Oh shit, he's done it again, and wanting to distance themselves as if it might just go away.

But it wouldn't go away. It will never go away. The horror of that day and what happened to two of the people I loved most in the world will never go away.

The man in the burning house that the plane had crashed into was the woman's father. The trailer home they were in was the office part. The plane had caught the bus with one of the wings, which broke with the impact into two bits, and then it had gone into the house. And what had happened was that the old man was deaf and he didn't know that the garage of this house was on fire, and Ozzy was yelling at him to come out, but the old man couldn't see what had happened, and he was swearing and cursing at him to go away, thinking Ozzy was some kind of madman. At last he understood and found his own way out down a back stairway.

By the time the police came and the fire service came, we had worked out who had been on the plane. Just the bus driver, Randy and Rachel. And they were all in bits, it was just body parts everywhere. And all these people wanted was for us to leave town. It was one of those places in the South where everyone knows that one and this one. So they said we were all pissing around, and that we were dive-bombing the bus, that we were stupid rock and rollers. All this shit. And there was no mention of the bus driver from hell.

The funny thing was that Rachel and Randy didn't really get on. Rachel used to call him a little white bastard. We couldn't afford a wardrobe girl in those days, so Rachel looked after all the stage clothes, mended them, and washed them and ironed them. And she was a very special woman, and Ozzy and I adored her and she adored us and took really good care of me. She was like the mother that I never had. And she'd been so badly treated all her life. And it was just ironic that her and Randy didn't even like each other yet they died together. And just like Randy had said he wanted to stop doing rock and roll and go to college, Rachel too had said this was going to be her last tour. Rachel was fifty-eight when she died. She was tired and she had a weak heart, but wanted to do this one last tour to raise some money for her church: she wanted to buy an electric typewriter.

When Ozzy got back from getting this old man out of the house, we clung to each other, and we were just screaming and weeping and shaking, and we just couldn't put all the pieces together to make one good picture, because everybody was in shock.

We had to stay there for two days; although everyone wanted us gone, people had died, there were procedures to follow and we couldn't leave. And then we had to go and tell Randy's mum Delores what had happened. But first we had to call her, and her son-in-law, married to Randy's sister, came out to identify what remained of the body. His mother had three children, two boys and a girl, but Randy was the light of her life. She had taught Randy piano, taught him how to read and write music, taught him guitar, everything. And Randy, this gorgeous, talented human being, was twenty-five.

Two funerals, two very different funerals in one week. Randy's was held in Los Angeles and he was buried in San Bernardino, California. On the coffin they had a photo of him and also a picture of Ozzy and him onstage in San Francisco, which was one I had always loved. And the church was full of young kids, young musicians, his schoolfriends, all mourning this beautiful young guy taken in his prime, and his family, his mother, his sister, his brother, his girlfriend Jodie, a lovely little thing, and everyone wearing black and so dignified. All you could hear was sobbing. It was like an ocean of sobbing.

And then there was Rachel's in a very orthodox black Baptist church, and people were crying and it was like a wave of moaning. They were wearing white and all different colours and there were gospel singers. A whole different thing. They were genuine, embracing, warm, fantastic people. Rachel had talked to everybody at the church about our friendship and they all felt that they knew me.

There's not a day goes by that I do not think of them and it upsets me that Rachel never got to see my children.

We cancelled the tour for two weeks while Ozzy and I went back to the Howard Hughes house to take stock. Tommy Aldridge came with us. Rudy went to stay with his family. He was a local boy; he'd come from the same band as Randy. We were all completely wiped and in shock, yet somehow I had to get a replacement for Randy.

My father and mother had flown in for the funerals. They didn't give a toss about Randy or Rachel – well, she was just the maid, you know. I never discussed what had happened with them because they never asked. All they knew was there had been an accident and that these two people were dead. In fact, they hadn't come to pay their respects – the visit had quite another motive. The morning after Randy's funeral, my father bangs on the door of my cottage. He's wearing a white towelling dressing gown.

'How's the tour doing?'

Nothing like, Hey, kids, my heart goes out to you . . .

'Have you got the cash?'

'What cash is that, Don?'

'The cash you've been getting on the road.'

'Oh, that cash.'

And of course he meant the cash I'd been accumulating and keeping in my suede tote bag. About $50,000. Cash he owed to Ozzy.

'It's Ozzy's money.'

'Sha, give me the fucking cash.'

'We've got to get this sorted out. It's not right what you're doing.'

'What the fuck do you mean? Bring it me. Now.'

So I go into my bungalow and I bring out the bag, and walk towards the fountain and I open the bag.

'All right, you want it? You fucking get it.' And I put my hand in the bag and begin throwing handfuls of these notes up into the air, all 100-dollar bills. Five hundred notes tossed into the air in handfuls, falling into the fountain, till the air is filled with floating greenbacks, and Jet is jumping up and thinking this is some great new game, and my father is bending down, scrabbling and clawing at the tiles in the courtyard, screaming and cursing, trying to pick up bills and stuffing them into his pockets, grabbing them from the fountain, and from the other bungalow I can hear the sound of laughing, and it's Ozzy and

Tommy leaning out of the window. They'd heard my father screaming and they'd opened the window to see what was happening, and now they are hysterical with laughter, because my father's dressing gown is too short and every time he bends over to pick up the money, they see his hairy bollocks flapping in the morning air.

Although I hadn't planned it, I had known something like this would happen and originally I had wanted to burn the money in front of him, just to let him see all those dollar bills go up in smoke, but I thought it would be too complicated, too difficult to burn, and that it wouldn't work. And I was very tired and exhausted. And I knew that Ozzy's money had gone, and all I could think of was, I can't let this happen to him again. And my father must have known. Because I hadn't shown him respect in months. When I spoke to him on the phone it was like, 'Whadya want? OK. Bye.' Our relationship hadn't got back on track since 1979 and the business with Jeff Lynne and finding out about his mistress. But I wouldn't have turned against my father for that. It was because he was a hypocrite. Don Arden was the sort of man who judged people on a moral level by the way they ran their lives. One of our lawyers was called Martin Machat, and Martin had a mistress, an Irish woman, and yet he was still married to his wife and had three children. And my father would spit blood over how disgusting it was. How the mistress was a whore, and how could he do this to the mother of his children. Yet he was doing exactly the same thing.

Our relationship was fucked. And with each day that went by I would find out more things about him. Because once people saw how things were between us, they started to talk. Until then, nobody had said anything because everyone was terrified of my father and they thought that blood was thicker than water.

*

Meantime I buried myself in what I had to do: trying to find someone to stand in for Randy. You couldn't find a replacement. Most guitar players are an extension of their guitar, Randy's guitar was an extension of him. He was playing from the soul; he was never trying to compete.

We were in the middle of a huge tour; how could I even begin? Gary Moore was my first call. No dice. Then I began calling other guitar players I knew in America, and they wanted this much money, that much money, and finally I called an Irish guy called Bernie Tormé, and he said he'd come out and help.

I felt like an empty shell. I knew it wouldn't be long now before I left this place. Rachel's death had made it inevitable. Over the last few months, she had been quietly packing up the things to get ready to go into storage: my record collection, my bits and pieces. I thought with sadness of the rest of the house and everything I had bought, things I had taken pride in collecting, things I couldn't take. I just stayed in bed, staring at the walls of my little bungalow and remembering everything that it had meant to me. How I had felt the first time I had seen the house, five years before, and my disbelief at just how beautiful it was, and how perfect. And how month after month, I'd wake up to hear laughter coming from the kitchen, and I'd go in and there would be Rachel standing at the stove giving Ozzy his breakfast. And his lovely smile as he turned round from his place at the kitchen table and saw me standing in the doorway and how his face lit up. And how he always had these stories and how all three of us would be laughing. And Rachel, in her Southern drawl, always telling me, 'Miss Sharon, I don' know wha' I's gonna do wi' you!'

It was then that I noticed that something was wrong with my books. The afternoon light from the west had lit them up, and it was as if somebody had tried to squash too many in. So, being a neat freak, I hauled myself up from the bed to see what was wrong. One book looked as if it hadn't been properly closed, so I pulled it out. I was right. Squashed between its pages was a Ziploc bag full of white powder.

And I look at this stuff and I think of what it has done: to Ozzy, to that pig of a bus driver, to Randy and Rachel. And I get a yellow legal pad and then open the bag and pour the white powder onto it, a glistening, sparkling pyramid of cocaine. And then I open the window onto the courtyard and I call Ozzy, who I know is with Tommy in the guest bungalow, and I wind it right open until I can lean out completely. And when he comes to the door, he sees me leaning out of the window holding a yellow legal pad with a huge great pyramid of white powder balanced on top of it.

And he's like: 'No, no, no, no . . .' He knew. It was one of those dreamlike moments when you know what's going to happen and you can see it in your mind's eye before it actually happens, and he knew what I was going to do.

And I say, 'Are you looking for this?' I can see him coming across the courtyard in slow motion, with his hands held up in front of him, and he's waving his hands at me saying, 'Please don't, please don't, no, no, no . . .' And Tommy Aldridge is standing behind him and his head is in his hands, and he's saying, 'No, Sharon, don't. Don't do that!'

And then I just blew. It took more goes than you would think, but soon the air was thick with it, like snow coming down, and Ozzy was rushing round the courtyard trying to scoop it up, trying to find something he could put it in. And then Jet arrived for yet another new game. And first he was sniffing it, and then he was licking it, and then he'd dart to the fountain to lap up some water, and then he'd be back and licking some more. Then suddenly he started shitting, and he's running around the courtyard like a lunatic, licking this stuff and projectile shitting, yellow diarrhoea going everywhere. It must have been cut with some laxative. And to this day I don't know why, but he couldn't get enough of it, even though it tasted so awful, he kept going back.

And I laughed and laughed. It was the first time I had laughed since that terrible morning, and I was shouting at Ozzy to look at Jet. 'Just look at him, running around like a fucking lunatic, foaming at the mouth, shitting. If it does that to the dog, what do you think it's doing to you?'

In the end Ozzy wasn't so much angry as embarrassed that I had found out, and pissed off because all his money had gone to the dog and he and Tommy weren't going to be having a nice day talking bullshit to each other and sniffing cocaine. I ruined their escapist weekend. I should have got them to clean it up, but it was such a mess that I had to hose it down.

How we got through those next weeks on the road I do not know. I put in Bobby Thomson, a Scottish guy we'd had working as a bass tech, as tour manager and that was the only good thing that came out of this terrible tragedy. He was a wonderful man who was a true friend to us both to the end of his life, and whose family will always be a part of ours.

Ozzy had wanted to pull out of the tour completely. I had no choice but to say, 'Fuck you, Ozzy. Randy would have wanted you to go on.'

There were people who said they would stand in for us – AC/DC called up to see if there was anything they could do. Bernie Tormé, the Irish guitar player I found, lasted two weeks. It's a lot to ask of someone to stand in a dead man's shoes, and he just couldn't cope. When we did Madison Square Garden, he had to go out to a waving forest of placards saying 'Randy Rhoads RIP'. And it was just devastating. So he helped us out for two weeks and I am for ever in his debt, because if we hadn't gone on I don't think we would ever have picked up again.

And then a kid from San Francisco filled in. His name was Brad Gillis and he had a pop band called Night Ranger, and he stayed with us for the rest of the year, did the US tour and then Japan and Europe. Only after that did we get a proper replacement: a guy by the name of Jake E. Lee, known as Jakey.

Every 19 March we send flowers to their graves. Randy had always wanted to get a degree in classical music, so his mother set up a foundation with the money that continues to come in for him to put young people through classical training. I still find it hard whenever we go and visit his mother. She never got over it. And Ozzy is convinced that had he not been asleep, it would have been him on that plane and not Randy. He says he knows it without a shadow of a doubt.

And Randy was so good for Ozzy, they were so connected. Though he smoked like a chimney, he didn't do drugs and didn't drink. And he was always telling Ozzy to stop. And I can remember his voice – he had a very deep voice for such a slight body – saying to Ozzy, 'Why do you do this so much; you're going to die. You're fucking mad.'

And Randy's death still affects Ozzy twenty-three years later. He can't play 'Crazy Train', a song they wrote together, the song that was their first hit in America, a song that Ozzy was going to do nothing with until Randy said, 'Hey, that's good, let's work on it.'

It was the hardest thing ever. It was as if we'd entered a fog and couldn't get out. I couldn't look at a photo or hear Randy's voice for probably two years without hyperventilating. And I couldn't sleep in the bus any more because I was terrified. And I would have nobody talk to the driver. The driver just drives.

Aimee and her two very proud, very happy, parents. I came back from France to make sure she was born in England.

Aimee and her besotted mummy. It was Aimee's first birthday party and I was pregnant with Kelly.

The Osbournes, December 1985. New baby (Jack), new house (Hampstead).

A traditional family portrait.

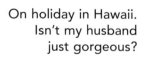

The kids at a fancy-dress party at the Hampstead house.

On holiday in Hawaii. Isn't my husband just gorgeous?

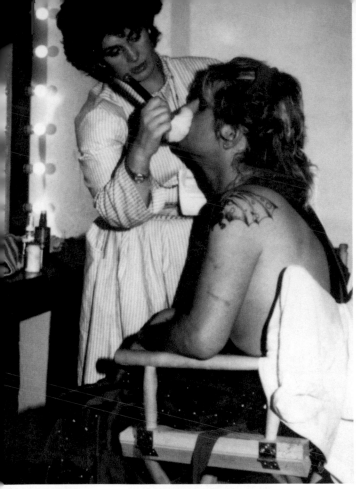

Doing Ozzy's make-up backstage, 1981. This was before we were married.

In real life Ozzy is the least scary person in the world.
(Mick Hutson/ Redferns)

Backstage with Motorhead in 1981.
Lemmy is pointing at my black eye.

Life on the road: Aimee asleep
on a bullet train in Japan.

New York, 1981.

New York, 1981.

In the garden of the first house we bought together. Outlands Cottage in Staffordshire, 1983.

Rio, 1984.

On the *QE2*, sailing to the States for Live Aid, 1985. I was so pregnant with Jack, I couldn't fly

New York, 1986.

At the WWF match in Chicago.

On a video shoot
in Dallas, Texas.

On holiday in Scotland, 1994, in search of the Loch Ness monster.

Christmas in LA, at our home in Beverly Drive. Aimee has a very young Minnie on her lap, while Jack holds Maggie. Kelly is holding Lulu.

And then there was Rachel. And it was something I never ever dealt with and I stuffed all the feelings about it deep down somewhere I thought I couldn't feel. And it felt like you had a big hole in your stomach and you would wake up in the morning and there'd be this pain, always this pain. I would just hold on to my stomach. I would moan like an Arab woman. I would wail and keen. And it was the same for Ozzy, he always had this pain. And we were permanently in fear from then on. Nobody outside those of us who had been through it could ever comprehend. Tommy and Rudy from the band, Bobby and Pete in the crew. It was just a small group, and we just used to look at each other sometimes and it broke your heart.

Since the second leg of the US tour began, Ozzy had been deep into his divorce. He had agreed to all Thelma's requests – as he should. But she still hadn't signed the decree absolute, the final bit of the divorce.

At the beginning I think Thelma had believed the pretence that I was having an affair with Randy. But at Christmas, after the first leg of the tour, Ozzy had taken her and his children on holiday for a month in the West Indies. And on the return journey she had told him that he would be served with divorce papers when he landed.

Ozzy had asked me to marry him just before we left England, when he knew that his marriage was over and that it was never going to work. I felt really bad for him. He was devastated about leaving his children, and terrified that they would turn against him and me. We were at my parents' house. And he went to H. Samuel just down the road in Wimbledon and he bought me a little diamond solitaire.

It was not till a year later, in June 1982, that the news came from his lawyers that Thelma had signed and he was now free to marry. We were in Los Angeles, about to set off for the Japanese leg of the tour, so we decided, Right, let's do it. We had a stopover in Hawaii anyway, so it was, Let's get married there!

I had hardly any time to get a wedding dress, but I went to a place on Sunset. It was very traditional, long ivory silk decorated with pearls. It was also far too big for me, but with no time to alter it, I just had to pin it in at the back. For Ozzy I got a white suit and a lavender shirt.

Only our families came out: Ozzy's mother and sister, and my mother and father. I had wanted Nana to come too, but my mother refused, saying she would only get lumbered with looking after her.

We were booked into the Hyatt Hotel in Maui, an island off the coast of Hawaii, but the moment we arrived we could see it was the type of holiday hotel where you fight for the sunbeds every morning. It was so horrible that Ozzy went onto the balcony and pissed on everybody below and then we checked out.

Luckily on the other side of the island we found somewhere small and intimate and perfect. Because this was America, we needed to have blood tests done to get the licence, but then we were set. Maui was totally different then to how it is now. The airport was the kind of place where you put your bags on the runway and only small planes could land. And it was lovely, very small, just our families, the band and the crew. Ozzy's best man was Tommy Aldridge and my bridesmaid was his wife Alison. But mixed with the happiness was a sadness: as I pinned myself into my wedding dress, I thought about how Rachel would have made it fit in ten minutes, and the absence of the two people we would most have wanted by our side was always there. It was barely four months since they had died. Ozzy and I got married on a hilltop overlooking the beach on 4 July 1982. I was twenty-eight and he was thirty-three.

And as my father was walking me down to pass me onto Ozzy, he wasn't saying, Do you love him, and I hope you're going to be happy. He was asking whether we were taking the stage set to Japan, and how big a production it was going to be. And my mother never said a word, at least not to me, though she talked to my bridesmaid.

'Oh,' said Alison, looking at my mother's hand. 'Sharon's wedding band is just like yours!'

'Hardly,' she replied. 'Mine is much bigger.'

We stayed one night. I spent my wedding night signing paper after paper for my father – it turned out to be the only reason he came. Ozzy's mother and elder sister Jean stayed on, but my parents left as soon as they could the next day. They took the few wedding gifts that the band and the crew had got us back to England, because that's where we were going to live so that Ozzy could be near his kids.

---

20 April 2005, 5.00 p.m.
Malibu

From the road these houses look like shacks; only from the beach side do you see how palatial they are. This land is not meant to be lived on, but people defy nature by building here. In the winter and spring there are mudslides and they try to hold it back with concrete and cement. And the salt from the sea spray destroys everything: plastic, metal, wood. In the summer there are constant fires, and about every five to ten years something catastrophic happens with the weather, and they keep rebuilding and rebuilding and rebuilding – people don't care, because it's so beautiful here.

The ocean sparkles with light. The surf washes over the sand in loops fringed with foam, and there's not a footprint to be seen. In California, no one can own the shore itself, but they can make it very difficult to get onto. To the right is the little town with a Victorian pier, and to the left you can see the great sweep of the bay where sky and sea merge into the same aquamarine and indigo.

Normally the first thing I do when I come to the house is light the candles, then I'll call up the general store and get some logs in and some Bonio for the dogs. But not today; I only have time to go through my dressing room for thin summer clothes.

Ozzy and I have been renting here for twenty years and I've been coming for thirty. When I worked in LA on my own I would come down at weekends and spend the day here. I have seen it grow and it's just beginning to get overpopulated but I still adore it. And just down PCH is the pet shop where we bought so many of the dogs. Minnie, Alfie, Lola, Ruby. And Sugar, who lives in England.

We had been looking for years to buy a house at Malibu, and every time there was an open house I would go, but I never found the right one: too much work, not big enough or too expensive. Then when I was living in a rental here with my cancer, I started to look properly, and found this house. A couple had bought it, totally redone it, so there was hardly anything to do. And because they lived in it full time, it had all those things I needed: big bathrooms, plenty of closet space, and it was a great mix of contemporary and traditional, and the price was good, so we bought it.

12

On the Run

The tour in Japan lasted two and a half weeks, and then we came back to England because Ozzy hadn't seen his kids in a while. Having nowhere to stay in London, we had no real option but to go to Wimbledon, and when our flight details were changed, I called my brother to ask him to arrange a car to pick us up. When we landed at Heathrow, no car. Should I have been surprised? David had never acknowledged our wedding, never sent a telegram, nothing. Even when we had spoken on the phone there hadn't been a word of congratulations. And when we got to Wimbledon and I asked if I could see my wedding gifts – I wanted to write thank-you letters – my mother said they'd been lost on the flight.

So we'd been back a day and my father and brother suggest taking Ozzy to the pub for lunch. A normal thing to do. So they take Ozzy to lunch, and proceed to tell him that I'm insane, that I am the reason ELO left my father, but that Ozzy doesn't have to worry because they can get the marriage annulled on the grounds of my insanity, and in the meantime they can put him into hiding.

When Ozzy came back and told me what had happened, he was absolutely terrified. There he was thinking he had married this woman whom he'd known for years and suddenly he discovers that, according to his father-in-law, his wife is a fucking headcase. He knew things weren't great between my family and me, he knew all about the money and all of that shit, but this was a whole new level.

'You've got it wrong,' I told him. 'You must have been pissed.' It was so extreme that even I could not believe my father would go that far. The next day we had planned to take my mother for an outing to Kent, to have afternoon tea at some country house she wanted to visit, but as I came back to the house, I walked in through the gates and suddenly I was surrounded by her dogs. And although I hadn't been around much, these dogs did know me, and I like dogs and they like me. But, for whatever reason, the Dobermann suddenly jumped up and hit me with his head, and then the two Pyrenean mountain dogs set in and knocked me to the ground and were tearing at my arms and my body, and I was screaming and trying to protect my head. And finally my mother emerged from the house and called them off, and I was taken to hospital just down the road in Roehampton. Ozzy just ran. He couldn't believe what was going on in his life, and he went up to Staffordshire on his own.

I wasn't only bleeding from my thigh, I was bleeding from my womb. It turned out that I had been pregnant, and I'd had no idea. I miscarried the next day. I was in agony from the miscarriage and from the bruising, and I didn't know where to reach Ozzy, and I just kept to my room feeling desperate. Two days later Ozzy reappeared. We took one suitcase each and took the first flight back to Los Angeles, and went straight to the Howard Hughes house. I was moving out.

It was reasonably straightforward. The things that Rachel had already crated up could be put straight into store. The staff promised me they would take good care of Jet and Mr Pook; I had been away on tour so much that I knew they would be well looked after, and I had no real option. And I'm just with the removal guys packing a few more crates with my stuff before I leave, when the bookkeeper arrives from the office up the hill. Batyu Patel.

'Sharon, there's just a couple more things we need you to sign.'

'I'm not signing another thing, Batyu. I'm out of here.'

'I promise you, this is the last thing. How can you not do this one last thing for your father?'

So just to get rid of him I said, 'Fuck it, all right.' One last and final fucking time. I signed my name at the bottom of a tax return.

And I took one last look across the City of Angels spread out before me from the terrace, and then turned to Ozzy.

'Right, that's it.' I left with two suitcases full of clothes. My jewellery, of course, had gone a year before. As our yellow cab snaked down the hill, I could feel my eyes stinging, but I didn't look back.

My instinct told me we had to move fast. We took the redeye to New York before my father could work out what was happening. He was in LA but staying at the house he had with Meredith. As soon as we landed, we went straight into CBS who did the pressing and distribution of Ozzy's records for everywhere except England. We were leaving my father's record label, we said, and we were in litigation with him. 'And we will sue you if you give him any money.'

It turned out we had only just beaten Batyu, who had taken another redeye to New York. He turned up at CBS an hour later to claim Ozzy's pipeline money, the money that is withheld by a record company from the royalties of an album in order to fund the production costs of the next.

So then, of course, the shit hit the fan. The next thing we needed was a lawyer. But as the days went by we were drawing a total blank. Nobody was interested. Nobody wanted to cross Don Arden. Not for anything or anybody. And I continued to call round my friends, asking for any information, because the secretaries were all my mates and they knew better than anyone what was actually going on. And what the girl grapevine was telling me was that not only was my father in New York but my mother was too, that he had flown her in from London, wheeled her into CBS and she'd been weeping about how crazy I was, that I was mad and deranged. And through my girlfriends I found out that they were staying at the Plaza Hotel, so I called my mother up, told her I'd been pregnant but I'd lost the baby when the dogs attacked me and how I really wasn't well.

'So what I wanted to say was could you come over and sit with me?'

Click. She hung up.

I genuinely had wanted to talk to her, but not about the miscarriage. I wanted to say to her: what are you doing with this man? He has destroyed you as a woman, he has embarrassed you, he has humiliated you, he has no respect for you, and now he is using you against your child.

I wanted to face her with the facts and ask, 'How could you go and sit in a fucking record company with people you barely know, saying that I was a terrible daughter and a thief?' I didn't want to scream or yell, I didn't want to touch her, I just wanted to say, 'How can you side with this man against your own daughter, when he's going to fuck another woman tonight, and he's lied to you your whole life together? How can you do this?'

I knew I didn't know my father. The romantic image of the loving husband, the caring father, was a complete sham. And now I realised that I didn't know my mother either. Had she forgotten what I had done for her? Those middle-of-the-night calls, using me to attack Meredith because she was too frightened? I mean, what did I care about Meredith? Yet it was as if I took everything my mother said on board. Like that time in the Polo Lounge. Perhaps it was because the Beverly Hills Hotel had always been my safe haven, special territory that couldn't be sullied. Nino the maître d' had been his usual welcoming self.

'I have reserved your favourite table,' he said.

Reserved? Ozzy and I hadn't reserved anything. We hadn't even known we were coming till a few minutes before, but OK. And this table was a big booth in a corner. So we sat down and ordered our food, and the vast bowl of salad arrived that Americans often have for lunch. We'd just started to eat when Nino walked over with two women and proceeded to pull out chairs for them at our table, and they sat down and ordered champagne while they looked at the menu. And, although the restaurant was full, the Polo Lounge wasn't the kind of place where you shared tables and I knew instinctively that this was Meredith, and that my father must have made the reservation for lunch, which was why Nino thought I had booked, and now she was here with a girlfriend. And I was rigid. Stunned. This was the first time I had seen her, and I had never realised she was the same age as me. So there she sat, across the table, smirking at Ozzy, because he had just shaved all his hair off so he was completely bald. And the pair of them were sitting there smirking, and her hand was fiddling with her glass of champagne, and I saw she was wearing what's called a cocktail watch, a black satin strap with the face all diamonds, an evening watch. I stretched across the table and picked up her wrist.

'My husband paid for that,' I said. And she tried to pull her hand away from me. 'Also,' I told her, 'it's incorrect to wear an evening watch for lunch.' Then I took her glass of champagne, and poured it on top of her head. Then I picked up my vast bowl of salad and balanced it on top of her hairstyle, but I didn't do it very well and seconds later the contents spilt down her face and over everything. Finally I emptied the ashtray over her. Then, getting up to leave, tipped the table over for good measure.

I was shaking. He was still married to my mother. My mother still came out to Los Angeles, and she still would go eat at the Polo Lounge. Why did he have to flaunt this woman on our territory?

When we got home Ozzy called my father. 'Why didn't you tell us? You knew we were in Los Angeles. It needn't have happened.'

'Die, vegetable. Die.'

And when my mother hung up the phone that morning in New York, I knew I was alone. And that from then on my life would be totally different.

Ozzy and I had virtually nothing. We had no cash, we had no credit cards. I had lost my driving licence; Ozzy didn't have one. All we had were our passports. We couldn't hire a car, we couldn't stay in a hotel. Then, in a moment of inspiration, I went to see Bill Elson, Ozzy's agent at ICM. I told him exactly what had happened: that no lawyer would touch us and that we were completely and utterly broke.

He knew from personal experience what a bastard my father was, and yet Bill gave us money and found us a lawyer. And when Don heard what he had done, he sent some of his hoods round to lean on him. But Bill wasn't the kind of man to give in to terror or threats, and he stuck by us. By now the word was

out on the streets: Don Arden had said he was going to kill me.
He wanted me gone, and he wanted his cash cow for himself. So
Bill found us somewhere to hide, an island called Hilton Head,
off the coast of South Carolina, where he went for summer holi-
days with his family, and this was such a non-place, so not
showbiz, so not Mafia, that my father would never have found us
in a month of Sundays.

Every day we were in Carolina, I would wake up and vomit. I
couldn't eat and I couldn't even drink water. Ozzy had to force
me to take tiny sips. All I could think of was: my father is stealing from my husband. Here was this man whom I absolutely
adored, who had given up everything in his life for me, and my
family was trying to destroy him. I didn't care about me. I was
crying for him. I was ashamed. Deeply, deeply ashamed.

We stayed there while the lawyers hammered out a deal. My
father wanted one and a half million dollars for Ozzy's recording
contract. We had to waive the money we were owed for merchandising, the tours, the royalties, we had to forget everything
else, and we had to do one last album. Ozzy had neither the time
nor the inclination to write. We agreed to do a live album of
Sabbath songs.

Could we have hung on? No. While Ozzy was still in litigation with my father, he could have gone on performing, but not
recording, and careers rarely survive that kind of isolation, and it
could have lasted five years. It happened to George Michael, it
happened to Prince. It would have been endless. We had every
right to sue for the money that had never been paid on the tours
and record royalties, but we didn't have the resources, we didn't
have the time. We wanted them gone. We wanted the cord cut.

CBS agreed to lend us the money to pay my father the million and a half, against future earnings, and we went into huge
debt. It took five years to repay.

And of course the contract had to be signed. And as my father was determined to torture and humiliate me, where else but the Howard Hughes house?

Ozzy and I flew to Los Angeles. We stayed at the Hilton – we didn't have enough money for the Beverly Hills Hotel. Then, in the early evening, we took a yellow cab up the familiar road. The cab driver didn't know it, and took the sharp bend at Cary Grant's house too quickly and Ozzy and I were flung against each other. The guard showed us in as if we were strangers. Nobody spoke to us. None of my old staff were there, but the animals were. They couldn't be told to ignore me. Jet and Mr Pook rushed up and began fussing over me. And then there was just my mother and father and Colin Newman.

It's the strangest things that you remember. While Colin read out this contract that was handwritten on an ordinary piece of paper, I just wanted to scratch my bites. It had been the height of mosquito time in South Carolina and I was absolutely covered.

My mother said nothing. And I felt so bad for Ozzy. He had always been very fond of my mother, and she didn't even acknowledge him.

I walked back into a house where there was nothing that I hadn't either done or bought. I loved that house. It was a part of me. Now all we had was each other. Nothing else.

Colin read out the agreement, Ozzy signed it, and we turned round and the guard led us out. It was all done within twenty minutes; we didn't even use the bathroom. Then we took the yellow cab that had been waiting for us back down the hill, past the Beverly Hills Hotel to the Hilton.

We picked up our bags and flew back to New York to record *Speak of the Devil*. We felt utterly defeated. He'd beaten us. This was his kiss-off. In our naivety we thought we would never hear from him again.

So I booked the venue, called in Rudy, Tommy and Brad Gillis, the guys rehearsed, then did two live shows, which were recorded, and it was fucking horrible. It's horrible to have to perform when you don't want to. You do it with resentment. And then for Ozzy to produce an album that he didn't love, he felt he was prostituting himself. And the album was terrible. And I felt so ashamed at how my family could be so mentally cruel to this man. That I had brought him into a family that was so corrupt.

In the past, my father had done his best to get Ozzy to sign over his publishing. While we were on tour he'd sent one of his lawyers out with one of his hoods, but we'd resisted. Always resisted. And thank God we did. Because the only thing we had to raise money on now was his publishing. When we finally got back to England we went to see Richard Branson, who was so kind and considerate and got us out of a hole by buying Ozzy's publishing for £500,000. Because it wasn't just us: there was Ozzy's first wife, his children, the children's school fees to think about. We had nowhere to live, not even a car, and I was pregnant again. But not for long: I had a miscarriage at about fourteen weeks. It was very upsetting, as these things always are, but as I'd got pregnant just like that, the doctor told me it was nothing to worry about.

During the European leg of the tour, I wanted to maximise Ozzy's profile and so set up loads of promotion. If you're working with somebody who is an addict or drinks too much, you don't take it personally. If they choose to fuck up their career, you're not responsible. My philosophy is: you're big enough and old enough to take care of yourself; I can only tell you what I think and advise you. You don't get emotionally upset by it. You walk away. But with Ozzy it was different, because I loved him, and it would completely destroy me. I don't know what it was

about Europe, but he would always be over the top. When I
look back now I can only see the funny side, but this was career-
destroying behaviour.

Take Paris. The head of the French record company says he
would like to take us to dinner. We had never met this man
before in our lives, but he's arranged three days of press interviews and it's a very positive vibe. So we go to this private club,
the sort at the end of a courtyard where there's a wooden door
with a hatch in the top that opens to check who you are. And
this is obviously The Place. Very elite. And it's full of movie stars:
Catherine Deneuve is there, Roman Polanski is there. The
record company guy is very welcoming, very courteous, and so
we sit in this booth, sipping our drinks, when Ozzy turns to this
guy, our host, and says: 'Punch me.' So the head of the record
company blinks a couple of times, hunches his shoulders nerv-
ously and does a French-type pout and says, 'I don't understand.'

'You cunt. I said punch me. In the fucking face. Now.'

And this guy is looking at me for help: 'He is joking, right?'

'I fucking told you, you French cunt, punch me in the face
now.'

So the guy's looking really worried now, as if to say: what do
I do?

'Are you deaf?' Ozzy goes on. 'I said, punch me in the face,
you French cunt.'

'You wanna be punched in the face, Ozzy?' I ask him.

'Yes.'

So I punched him in the face.

'Thank you,' he said. 'Now perhaps we can order dinner.'

So it was like GONE as far as France was concerned.

Next came Germany. Germany is a huge market for Ozzy's
genre of music, probably the biggest market in Europe. And the
German record company have organised a formal dinner,

because they are also entertaining a young American couple who have won this radio contest in the States to see Ozzy's show and have dinner with him afterwards. So we're all there after the gig, and Ozzy is out of his mind.

He strips off all but his socks and shoes. Picture it. Everything out. And he gets up onto the table, puts his right index finger under his nose to look like Hitler and with his left arm extended starts to goosestep up and down the table doing the Heil Hitler salute. Then he comes to a halt in front of the head of the record company, who was all hair and beard, and picks up this guy's wine glass and plops his balls into it, dangling them in the wine, then bangs the wine glass back on the table.

Apart from the sound of Ozzy's shoes clumping on the wooden table, and the tinkle of a glass that he'd knocked over, there was an eerie silence.

'You're all fucking Nazis over here,' Ozzy said. 'You killed six million Jews, you fuckers.' Then he climbed off the table, straight onto the head honcho's lap, straddling him, then wrapping his legs around him, bare arsed, wine all over his balls, and said, 'Kiss me, you fucker', grabbed him by the back of his head, pulled it, and stuck his tongue down his throat. Meanwhile the two kids from California, the contest winners, are sitting there transfixed like deer caught in the headlights.

By this time I was looking for my napkin on the floor because I couldn't keep a straight face. I mean, there was his little arse bobbing up and down and I could even see the pimples on his bum and I was just laughing up a storm. The band had their hands stuffed in their mouths. The record company, however, did not find it funny, and from then on this guy had it in for Ozzy, and we didn't go back to Germany for years. As for France, we never go there now. It's possibly the only country in the world where Ozzy never sells a record. He can go to Russia, he can go to Korea, but France forget it. It doesn't exist.

Anyway, it was goodbye Germany, goodbye France. On the plane back to the States I was ripping up the contracts into fucking confetti. We were supposed to be going to Italy, but I hadn't the stomach for it.

Whenever we were back in England, we'd go straight up to Staffordshire to see Ozzy's children. And constantly staying in hotels is no fun, so as soon as we could, we began looking for a house. I wouldn't have chosen to live around Stafford – my only experience was living in London – but the last thing I wanted was to be accused of taking Ozzy away from his family, so of course I agreed.

We looked at a few, but I couldn't see myself living in any of them. So then Ozzy said there was a house he knew that was on the market that was really nice. His old house. I was mad enough to agree to go and see it. He'd given it to Thelma as part of the divorce settlement, and now she wanted to sell it and move to Birmingham. So there she was showing me around the house where they'd lived together. I can't believe now that I let it get that far. I don't know if it was worse for her or for me. Thank God it turned out to be more than he could afford . . .

The only way for Ozzy to make money was by touring, and so we continued, in South America, in Japan and in Europe, and back to North America. And gradually we began to see the light at the end of the tunnel, and when we were in Jersey City, Ozzy decided it was time I had a better engagement ring, and gave me $1,000 to buy a diamond. So I picked out a nice stone in the mall and had it set into a thin gold band, a traditional claw setting.

And then I found I was pregnant again, and again I lost the baby. As this was the third time in a year I went to be properly checked out. They found out that when I got to three or four months, my cervix would open and that would be it. It could be prevented, they said, with a Shirodkar stitch, like a noose put around the neck of the cervix. But it could only be done after the baby was conceived, at around twelve weeks, and before that I would be vulnerable to the same thing happening. So the next time I got pregnant, they said, touring was absolutely out. I had basically to stay in bed and do nothing.

The timing wasn't great. As Ozzy was away from England so much anyway, he'd been advised to take two years out, where you live abroad and don't pay UK income tax. However, the rules were very strict (the scheme doesn't exist now), and he was only allowed a very few days back in England. I can't remember now why I decided on Antibes as our base. Neither of us spoke a word of French, but perhaps somebody had said the climate was like California. It was on the Mediterranean, and with Nice airport less than half an hour away it was close enough to England for friends to visit and for Ozzy to fly in and out easily.

We rented a house on the *Cap* that was fully staffed, with a husband and wife and a gardener, and it was fabulous. We would go and shop in the market in the old town, and Ozzy's family would come down, his mum and his sisters, and my niece Gina, Dixie's daughter. Dixie herself had completely aligned herself with my mother, so that was that door closed. That's the way our family operated.

But there were times, long weeks, when nobody came, when Ozzy was away touring, and I had no alternative but to rest, not allowed to drive, not allowed to do anything. And in fact it was the same for all three of my pregnancies. The first three months were always hell.

It would be nice to say that Ozzy behaved impeccably. But he was a complete and utter bastard. He was out of his mind, drugging, drinking, cheating. Ozzy was constantly with someone, if only because he cannot stand his own company and hates to be confined to a hotel bedroom. It's a kind of claustrophobia and he panics. But although I knew that if and when he did pick up girls it didn't really mean anything, it still hurt. Also he was a terrible liar so I'd always find out. I would know the signs: when I'd call he would hang up on me, saying, 'Can't talk.' And then I'd hear the receiver clattering down in some hotel bedroom somewhere and I'd look at the receiver in my hand and feel the tears well up. It was a very lonely part of my life, and I missed him terribly.

It was hard to cope on my own in a foreign country with no one to talk to. So I would just store it up and by the time we next saw each other it didn't take much for it all to boil over.

'But I don't even know her name,' he'd say. 'I don't even know whether I did the fucking act or not.' All very reassuring. We had a very volatile relationship in those days. I would always initiate the violence, and though it was wrong of him to hit me when I was pregnant, at the same time I would whack him as hard as I could where it hurt. I knew he felt dreadful about himself, always saying, 'What's wrong with me?' I knew that deep down he truly loved me, and that was the only thing that pulled me through.

Once the Shirodkar stitch was safely in place, I was free to get back on the road. And the next time I was in LA I had a meeting with the European Asian bank, who had financed the purchase of the Howard Hughes house six years before. They were based in Singapore, and this was one of the deals I had signed for my father. The loan was huge because he'd had no capital and no collateral. All he had to do was pay the interest on the loan, known as balloon payments. This unusual form of unsecured mortgage came courtesy of an 'arrangement' he had with one of the managers. In exchange, this man would come over to California every year and stay at the house where hookers would be laid on, and he'd get to meet this star and that star –

people like Tony Curtis and other friends of my father's. So for years this bank manager had covered my father's arse, but then he loses his job and the auditors go in and basically my father is busted. They told me that in the six years he had the house, he had only made one of these 'balloon' payments: $50,000 dollars on a $1.7 million loan. The unpaid interest was, of course, added to the original sum borrowed and now it was pay-up time. As my father didn't begin to have that sort of money, the bank had no option but to repossess the house, they said.

As soon as I had moved out, Meredith had moved in. As for the things I had put into store, my father found out the name of the removers, got a court order and said everything was his: my camera collection, my record collection, my books, my shit, my photos, personal letters, clothes, even down to bits of memorabilia I'd had since I was a child. Everything disappeared, though I have a fair idea where at least some of it ended up. But I never saw any of it again. My father wanted nothing there of mine, including my animals: Jet was given to Air Supply (my father's then cash cow), while Mr Pook was thrown into Benedict Canyon from a moving car. The staff managed to scramble down and find him and took him in. They were lovely people and we were still in touch, which was how I heard Dudley Moore was interested in buying the house. If my father managed to sell before the bank repossessed he could pay what was owed and there was sure to be some left over. However, there was one detail in this scheme that he had overlooked. The house was in my name.

If it had been anything else then he'd have forged my signature, no question. But in America, when you sell a house, you have to be there in person, you need a notary public and you need ID. To prevent any misunderstanding, I got the name of Dudley Moore's business manager and called him and said that I was the owner of the house he was interested in buying, and that

I would never, ever assign the title to anybody else. And then I called the broker and said the same thing. And then I called the bank. 'I will never assign this house so you might as well repossess it,' I said. So that's exactly what they did. They repossessed, my father was evicted, and he never got one single dime.

Today, even with the other houses and land sold off, the Howard Hughes house must be worth forty million dollars. I don't dream very often, but when I do I'm back there, with the children as babies, and I've bought it back. I could have somehow raised enough capital to pay off the bank myself because, as my father knew, it was worth much more than the money that was owed. But I didn't even try, because I knew he would only have burnt it, with me and my children in it. He was no stranger to arson. He'd done it before in London. It was never proved, but everybody knew.

I had crossed the line. From then on, my name was erased. I was known as the nigger-fucker. (My father came from a generation where black people were called niggers, and in his world that was the worst thing a woman could do.) It was out and out war. I'd get a phone call from Del Ferrano, the guy who still does our merchandising, saying that Don had been on the phone. 'He knows you're in New York, and says to remind you that New York is a very dangerous place. And says to tell you to watch your backs.' A few years later he tried the same thing in Los Angeles. This time I had all three babies with me, and he happened to see us walking down Sunset. As there's only a handful of hotels to ring, he found out where we were staying, called the room and the nanny picked up the phone.

'Tell them to leave town,' he said. 'Otherwise something might happen to their children.' We stayed exactly where we were. But it wasn't just bravado. That man was capable of doing anything.

*

We'd always said I would have the baby in England, and about a month before Aimee was due, Pete drove me back from Antibes and we rented a service apartment on a short let in a mansion block in Collingham Gardens, just off Gloucester Road, in Kensington. And Ozzy took some of the days he was allowed in the UK to be there with me when Aimee was born. She arrived on 2 September 1983.

New baby, new house.

We finally bought a tiny thatched cottage near Eccleshall, Staffordshire. Outlands Cottage, Offley Rock, was all we could afford. But for me it had one great plus: it was ours. However, the first day we moved in – we hadn't even unpacked the van – Ozzy set it on fire. To make me feel welcome, he'd put too much coal on the grate and the thatch went up. By the time the fire brigade had finished, it was little more than a shell, so I decided I would completely remodel it. The thing I had most disliked was the mean, ugly little modern staircase, and so I found some wonderful carpenters in Devon and they built me a huge Gothic staircase. I had antique fireplaces put in, and in the end it was amazing, with a beautiful Smallbone kitchen and two fantastic bathrooms, although it was also completely ridiculous in that you couldn't move. I spent a fucking fortune doing it up because I was determined to make the house itself somewhere I wanted to live, because Eccleshall was like hell.

Although otherwise our cottage was totally isolated, we had to pass another little house to reach it. Our neighbours didn't have a toilet, a bathroom or a television, so this old couple used to shit in a shed at the end of their garden, usually whenever I happened to be walking past. And I just found the whole thing so depressing. The woman was like the farmer's wife in *Babe*. She always had the apron and she always had the wellington boots. We were putting up a television aerial on the roof of the house when there was a knock at the door. It was Mrs Babe, wanting to know what it was we were doing. She was none the wiser after I'd told her.

It didn't bode well when I lost the new engagement ring. I went mad looking for this fucking ring and we stripped the house and stripped it again, and then two days later I was outside chatting to the builders who were having their tea. And there's this one guy with his legs crossed and there's something twinkling on the bottom of his boot. And there, stuck between the ridges of this steel-capped bovver boot with all the mud and the shit is my ring. The band was broken, but the diamond was fine, so I got it set in a thick gold band, and now Ozzy wears it on a chain around his neck.

As for village life, everything revolved around the pub, and so when Ozzy was home that's where we went. And it was bingo night, and it was darts night, and I was the Yank who had stolen Ozzy away from his northern lass of a wife, so no one wanted to know me. Even more terrible, I would openly tell him to stop drinking, that he'd had enough, things like, 'You're not driving me like that, give me the keys.' But wives didn't say that kind of thing in Eccleshall. The pubs up there didn't even stick to closing times, and these people would go on and on drinking till everyone was pissed out of their minds. I thought it was insane behaviour, particularly as Ozzy didn't even have a driving licence at the time – but I couldn't do a damn thing without drums going in Birmingham relaying it all to his first wife.

I was desperately lonely and so alienated. His children would come over and everyone knew Thelma, and I was the wife-stealing Yank. And I can honestly say that when I had married Ozzy, overlooking the Pacific a year before in Maui, I had not imagined I'd be spending New Year at the Red Lion with the ladies that picked potatoes.

But there was one shining light in all this: Pete Merton's mother Phoebe. Pete was living with us in the second bedroom and when he saw what a state I was in, with no one to turn to, he mentioned me to his mother, and the next day she was there. Everything I know about babies and bringing up children, I know from Phoebe Mertons, and I'm eternally grateful to her. Over the years, she was always there for me, prepared to drop everything and come and help when I was sick or had other problems. A few years back she won an OBE from the Queen for having fostered so many children.

In the last few months of pregnancy I had begun to realise just how difficult it would be to work with a baby. Ozzy's career didn't run itself, and I was now his sole management: negotiating his contracts, setting up his tours, employing crew, organising the merchandising, stage sets, support bands and the rest of it. So when Aimee was a week old, I got somebody in to help. Lynn Seager had always worked in the industry, so had great experience, plus a great personality, and we immediately hit it off, and twenty-something years later she still works for me. We set up an office, one room just off Charlotte Street, and I was so lonely in that cottage, I would take the train up to London, lugging Aimee around in a sling, go to the office, then get the train back all the way back to Stafford again. I can still hear the words that echoed round the station like the voice of doom: Stafford. This is Stafford. Stafford, Stafford. This is Stafford.

Then, before Aimee was four months old, I found I was pregnant again. With Ozzy away on tour, I just couldn't manage on my own in Staffordshire, so I went back to Antibes for the summer: a different house, but just as comfortable.

Then one day Ozzy went to the doctor. This wasn't unusual, because he is a terrible hypochondriac. If he has a pimple, it has to be skin cancer. He has a twitch in his back? He needs a new back. So he had just got back from America and was complaining about not feeling well, and first thing in the morning he goes to the doctor. I'm giving Aimee her breakfast, some kind of hot porridge-type cereal. And he comes back and says he's got something to tell me. I'm spooning this stuff into Aimee's mouth and I'm listening.

'I've got an infection.'

I just looked at him. Then I picked up Aimee's bowl, a thick-rimmed Peter Rabbit bowl, full of porridge, and I slammed it over his skull. And I brought it down on him with such force that it broke, and suddenly blood was pumping out of his head, and it was everywhere, and I'm like, Oh my God, what have I done?

My immediate reaction was to hold him and say, I'm so sorry, so sorry, and I'll take you to the hospital. But I didn't. Because my next thought was: fuck. Now he's going to beat the shit out of me. And I had my unborn baby to think about. So I picked up Aimee from the high chair and took her outside to the garden where Lynn and a couple of friends we had staying were sitting in the shade having breakfast. But I didn't tell them. Not a word. I just asked Pete to get him to hospital. But Ozzy refused to go. He came out in the garden and sat there, with his head covered in blood and porridge, which was his way of making me feel guilty. And he still has a nasty scar on his head where the hair doesn't grow. And I do feel guilty to this day.

Ozzy has an addictive personality even in the way of ordinary things, like food. He'll go through patches when he will drink only one brand of orange juice, or refuse to eat anything but brown rice or mangoes. This was his *escargot* period, and you'd see him sitting there, in one of the harbour bars, holding these things that looked like eyelash curlers and eating his way through twenty-five snails a day, till every part of him reeked of garlic. Whenever he was back in Antibes, he would spend his entire time at the harbour waiting for the big yachts to come in, because that was where he would get his drugs, from the guys that crewed them. And so then we'd have all these weirdos coming into the house. It was just getting ridiculous, with the drinking and the drug use and the people he was hanging with. It had been over four years since I had stopped drinking, but Ozzy was if anything getting worse. Once he used to be a funny drunk, now he was becoming an angry drunk. And however much I would plead with him – 'Please don't do this. Don't drink. Don't you see what you're doing to yourself?' – it had about as much effect as if I was asking him to learn Hindustani.

He was like two completely different people. At night he'd be the Hulk and in the morning he'd be his usual sweet and gentle self. The adorable lovely guy who would coo over his baby girl and bring me a cup of tea in bed. It was on one of these mornings when he was full of remorse for how he had behaved the night before that I extracted two promises from him: one, that we would sell the cottage and move to London, and two, that he would go into rehab the moment our second baby was born. 'I refuse to let our children grow up with a father who's a fucking alcoholic and drug addict,' I said. Because that was what I now accepted he was.

A month before Kelly was born, I went back to the same apartment in Collingham Gardens where I'd stayed before and began looking for a house. Two weeks later Ozzy arrived for the birth and I took him to see somewhere I'd found in Hampstead. It was Victorian, semi-detached with a garden, not enormous but somewhere to put the pram, and I could walk to the Heath, and walk to Golders Hill Park. It needed a lot doing to it, but the price was good and it had great potential. I've always had this thing with houses: I go in and I know instantly. A big plus for me was that Colin Newman and his wife Mette lived round the corner.

Given all we'd been through, it may seem strange that we had stayed with my father's accountant, but in those days there were very few specialist music accountants around and frankly I was scared to leave. I had lost my family, and I was scared at the idea I might lose Colin and Mette as well. I needed some kind of continuity in my life, and I had known Colin for so long, and Mette had originally worked as his receptionist, so she and I had been friends since before they were even married, and their children were the same age as mine. The idea of having a girlfriend round the corner, somewhere I could wheel the pram and have a chat, was heaven. At the cottage in Eccleshall if you tried to go for a walk, you took your life in your hands. I'd have to practically throw the pram up onto the bank whenever a car roared by. There was no pavement, no parks, nothing except overgrown footpaths. Remote countryside like that might be great if you're a rambler or even have kids old enough to play by themselves, but not for babies. And in the summer a thatched cottage is like sitting in a fucking bees' nest.

Kelly was born on 27 October 1984. Ozzy kept his promise about going into rehab and the next day he and Pete flew to Palm Springs, California. Until I began reading about the Betty Ford Center, where people went who were alcoholics and drug addicts, I had never even heard of Alcoholics Anonymous or the twelve-step programme, and I had no idea of the philosophy behind it. All I knew was that it helped people to deal with their problem. Ozzy had a problem, so that was where I sent him. And it wasn't just me giving him an ultimatum. In his sober moments he too knew that something had to be done.

20 April 2005, 6.00 p.m.
In the Bentley, heading back to LA along PCH.

On my cell.
   'Hi, Tony Macaroni, have you got my husband there?'
   'He's in the studio with Mark right now, Sharon.'
   'What time is his meeting tonight?'
   'Six thirty.'
   'And you're taking him, right?'
   'Right.'
   'Take your time coming back. The florists are delivering at seven, but they may come late and I don't want him to see. They're putting them in the laundry room, so make sure it's shut.'
   'Will-do.'
   'How is he?'
   'He's fine. Jack phoned from Thailand.'
   My darling Jackie Boy.

Tony Dennis was one of the two little Geordie boys who followed *The Blizzard of Ozz* tour. They were at that first show in Glasgow, and at the second show in Newcastle I brought them in for the sound check and got Ozzy to sign their Sabbath albums. They became like our mascots, and they were staying in train stations and bus shelters and telephone kiosks, and Ozzy said to me, 'Look, we can afford twenty pounds a night.' And so he said to Tony, 'I can't pay you anything, but if you do the bags, I'll pay for you to stay somewhere', so he used to stay in B&Bs. And then when Kelly was born, he began working for Ozzy full time. His friend joined the merchant navy. Tony is the most honest and reliable and willing person you could hope to meet. In the old days he even did the cooking. I cannot cook. I've told Ozzy, the day he learns to do the plumbing is the day I will learn to cook.

13

Palm Springs

Palm Springs is two and a half hours south-east of Los Angeles. Ozzy was booked in for an initial six weeks. Pete stayed long enough to see him settled in, but then Ozzy was on his own. He had no idea what to expect; I'd been the one reading up about it, not him, and I later discovered he thought they were going to teach him how to drink sensibly. He had no idea that there were no half measures, that he would have to give it up completely. Nor did he expect to have to share a bedroom, or help with household chores, but that's what AA is about. It was a great learning curve for Ozzy.

For the first two weeks he was allowed no contact with the outside world whatsoever. After that he could phone once a day, a five-minute call from the facility call box. But I can remember so clearly the first time we spoke. The first few weeks of a baby's life are so intense, and there's so much you want to say and so much you want to hear, it was just like an explosion. We had never been apart so long since I took over Ozzy's day-to-day

management in 1980, and even in the early stages of the pregnancies, when I couldn't travel, we were always talking to each
other on the phone. Every day, no matter where he was, we
would talk, and we still do today. So for me the overriding question was when can I come? In a month, he said. And realistically
I wouldn't have been able to go any sooner anyway. I would
never take a baby younger than six weeks on a plane.

I made arrangements to travel as soon as I felt Kelly was up to
it. She was having trouble feeding and it turned out she had
some kind of allergic response to breast milk and had developed
a fine line in projectile vomiting. My plan was to take a rental
for six months. The Hampstead house would take time to get
ready and meanwhile we needed somewhere for the band to
rehearse, and I knew Palm Springs and liked it, very artsy, full of
painters and sculptors, and in 1984 it was still a small community. I'd been there several times with girlfriends on weekend
retreats and I had always had a great time, and while England
settled in for winter, we'd be enjoying the dry heat of the
desert, which I love.

The first thing we did was to book ourselves into a hotel: me,
thirteen-month-old Aimee, newborn Kelly, a nanny and Tony.

We arrived a week before Ozzy was allowed to see anybody,
and then came a call from the facility. They needed me to come
in for a preliminary talk with Ozzy and his counsellor.

I can't remember now what I had expected from our first
encounter after six weeks apart, but I was feeling very emotional,
tired from having the baby, the travel, the jet lag and not sleeping properly, but I knew that I would have to try not to let Ozzy
down. But when we gave each other a hug, he felt strangely dis-
tant and I felt my heart speed up, though I didn't know why. I
can't remember now if he even spoke to me, which was strange,
because we'd spoken every day for the last month without any
problem. And then the counsellor began. She was sitting behind

a desk, and Ozzy was sitting to one side, facing her as well, with his head bowed.

'Mrs Osbourne,' she said. 'Your husband has some issues with you.'

What?

'Your husband wants to know where his money is.'

His money? What is this?

'Your husband believes that you and his accountant are taking his money and it is this that has led to his drinking and drug abuse.'

I stared at her, unable to speak. As I listened, my heart racing with what was now anger, she told me that Ozzy's situation would be greatly improved if we considered a separation followed by a divorce.

Just in case I had misunderstood what she had said, I repeated the allegations – not to Ozzy; he wouldn't look at me – to her.

'If I get it right, what you are saying is that my husband's drink and drug problems are down to me, that the reason he hits me is because I am stealing his money. And that although he's just left one wife with two children, you're now suggesting he leaves another wife with two children. Is that it? Well, let me explain something to you. We basically live from month to month because he lost everything in the divorce and we're starting again. And as for his money, how can I be taking his money when I don't even have a bank account?' Because of my past, I had had a prenuptial contract drawn up, because I was terrified my father's debts would come back to haunt me. In America, once you're married, your husband's debts are your debts, and your debts are his debts, and there was no way I was going to have Ozzy working his arse off to pay my father's fucking debts. If anyone wanted to sue me, they could go ahead. There was nothing to get. I didn't have a bank account. I didn't earn money. You can't take blood from a stone.

Ozzy didn't say a word. He just sat there. And I was just, What is this? Even though I knew nothing about therapy I knew this couldn't be right. I mean, the guy's a fucking alcoholic, you cow. Of course, it's not his fault. Alcoholics always put the blame elsewhere; they are the ultimate victims.

It was hate at first sight. I figured she wanted to fuck my husband. Although I knew little about the psychology of the addict in those days I knew from personal experience that they all lied. Yet here she was accepting his version of events like he was a fucking altar boy. Ozzy has always been terrified of being ripped off, and being poor, so these could have been valid areas for discussion. But accusing me? At a first meeting?

I said I would provide her with details, and left. I dropped in the envelope the next day, including the phone number and name of the fucking bank manager. 'And would you please tell your patient,' I wrote, 'that this is where his money is, and that this is the bank manager's number and he can phone him up any time to check. Or perhaps he would like you to deal with it, as it seems clear to me that you two have a connection.' Basically go fuck yourself, you cow. I never spoke to her again.

A week later it was family group week, which I had to attend and that is all part of the process. When you arrive for treatment, each person is put into a group of between five and ten people. This is called your home group. You work with the same counsellor, you have your therapy sessions together. It's the group that you hang with. You hear about their problems, and they hear about yours. So the family group is made up of the loved ones of the other people in Ozzy's home group. They could be husbands and wives, children or, for young people, parents, so for Ozzy's home group of six, we were twelve.

For the first week you just listen to everybody's story, then do group therapy.

But I very nearly didn't even last out the first day. I got so upset, I couldn't take it, and after only a couple of hours I left and began to run across the lawns to find my car, and then a woman saw me and came running after me. She didn't know who I was, and I didn't know who she was, although later I found out that she was Mrs Firestone, of the Firestone tyre company, who had put a lot of money into the project. But to me she was just a lovely, very elegant lady. She sat me down on the grass, and said, 'I know it's hard, but stay. Don't go. Come back with me, and stay.' And she was so kind and understanding, and so very different from the counsellor-bitch from hell who, until now, was the only person I had had any contact with. In the end they decided that I had so many issues that I'd bottled, I needed to stay for two weeks of family therapy.

And as the days went by, however painful it was, there was also relief. Because I had never spoken about Ozzy's problems to anybody before. And just as he got close to his group, so you get close to the other families. And it was so enlightening. Until then I knew nothing, I had no idea even that alcoholism was a disease, and I learnt so much about it and about the effect it has on the family. Because it's not just one person: the whole family gets sick.

And I'd sit there and listen to stories of kids who were affected, and it was enough to break your heart. Meanwhile Ozzy was having a blast and he made some very good friends in there, one of whom, a woman, is still a good friend of ours. For Ozzy it was like summer camp, and his body was coping fine. And it was good for him. Within a few weeks he'd stopped playing the victim, and there was no more of this I-have-a-very-evil-wife-who's-sucking-me-dry-and-because-I've-just-lost-everything-with-my-other-wife-I'm-frightened-to-leave-this-one-because-then-I'll-be-left-with-nothing sob story.

The day he came out, there was a leaving ceremony, when people got up and talked about what they thought of each other: members of the home group, counsellors etc. And when it came to Ozzy's turn, it was all about how wonderful he was, how well he'd done, how committed he was to the programme. Because Ozzy is a people-pleaser. That's the Ozzy they wanted to see, so that's the Ozzy he gave them. Only one counsellor didn't buy it.

'You're young, you're good-looking, you're talented and you're wealthy,' he said. 'And you will be back here within a year.'

He was an optimist. Ozzy didn't last two hours.

'Let's go and have lunch,' he said, as we left. We went to a café, with nice food and a nice ambiance, and the first thing he did was order a beer. And then he ordered another one, and then he ordered another one.

'So you're drinking,' I said.

'Yes.'

'Knock yourself out.' And I sat there and thought, he's just put himself through hell and back and now he's throwing it away. I'd had it all planned out, how he now had this little community of friends who were all so supportive of each other, and there were the AA meetings held twice a day in the facility. I had wanted Ozzy to have his support group so he could continue with his sobriety while he wrote and rehearsed, because I'd already brought in his band. We had commitments.

Over the next six months, to some degree he tried, because once you're educated to your problem you never drink in the same way again. From now on there's guilt added to the mix.

In January we had a huge show to do in Rio. Rock in Rio it was called, and Queen and Rod Stewart were on; one huge artist after another. And it was a big payday for us, so, as much as I was scared that Ozzy wasn't ready in terms of his sobriety, there was nothing I could do. As there was no way I could take the children with us, and there was no way Ozzy could have coped without me – Tony had only just joined us and he was still very young, just twenty-one – I brought in another girl I knew from when I lived in Los Angeles to help the nanny, so at least I knew my babies were safe.

Anyway, all the artists are on this one Varig Airlines plane, chartered by the promoter to take the LA-based performers to Rio. And soon after take-off the drinks trolley comes round and so my husband begins to drink. And he continues to drink until he rolls off his seat into the aisle. By now they're serving dinner and the trolley can't move because Ozzy is taking up the aisle. So I try to shift him. Then somebody else tries to help. But he won't budge. So I pick up a fork – this was in the days when you were still allowed metal forks on planes – and I lift up my hand and then bring it down hard, stabbing him in the arm with this fork. He got up then. He fucking jumped up then.

I was humiliated. Humiliated for him and humiliated for me. Was he really that drunk that he couldn't move? Although I will never know for sure, there's a bit of me thinks that half of it was acting, because he just loved the attention. I mean, if he really had been out for the count on the floor, then a fork in the arm would have made no difference. But when I stabbed him he was up. And I was just so fucking humiliated. All the other bands were laughing: 'Oh, here he goes. It's just Ozzy.

I would say to him, 'Don't you have any pride? Where is your pride? You wanna get stoned? Do it in the privacy of your own room. Be a closet drinker.' But no, he always made such a spectacle of himself. If there was a plant in a restaurant, Ozzy would fall into it and end up wrestling with a fucking palm tree. He liked playing the clown because it was a role he had been working at since he was at school when, because he was dyslexic, being the class clown was the way he survived.

But, of course, when we got to Rio, Ozzy delivered. It was a great show and he had great reviews. Great everything. Because he was brilliant, as he always is.

The six months in Palm Springs was basically a total waste of time – I had learnt more than Ozzy. The twelve-step programme, the backbone of AA philosophy, is above all about accepting you have a problem, and accepting that you are making other people's lives a misery. It's about honesty and commitment. Take step four: 'Make a searching and fearless moral inventory of yourself.' At that time, I felt Ozzy wasn't in a place in his life to do that. He would stay clean for two weeks, and then that would be it, until he behaved so badly he'd be plunged into remorse and the cycle would begin again.

While we were still living in Palm Springs, I began to go to meetings for relatives of alcoholics, called Al-Anon. But it made me so depressed listening to one sad story after another that I would come out feeling there was no hope and what the fuck was I doing. He would never be sober for any length of time. Unlike the family therapy group I'd gone to while Ozzy was in treatment, I didn't really connect with anybody else there. I never did it again.

When the six-month rental in Palm Springs was up, the children and I went back to England. It was May and London was looking lovely. Lynn found us a nice little house in Hays Mews, the other side of Berkeley Square to the flat in Mayfair where I had first seen Ozzy sitting on the floor with a tap around his neck. And it was perfect for the children. I could gate the stairs, and being in a mews it was safe from the fear of traffic. It was also easy for me to get to Hampstead to check on how work on the Hampstead house was coming along.

I'd put Aimee and Kelly in the double-stroller and go to Hyde Park for an ice cream by the Serpentine when the weather was good. We'd go on boat rides and we'd watch the riders in the park, the horses, and there would be the mothers and the nannies and the grannies. And it made me so sad to think that my mother didn't want to know her grandchildren; she never even acknowledged their existence. I had made one further attempt to reach out to her when I was pregnant with Aimee and doing up the cottage in Stafford after the fire. I'd phoned and asked if she'd like to help me choose a bath. She'd come on one condition, she said. 'That your husband isn't there.'

We agreed to meet at the Cavendish Hotel in Jermyn Street at two o'clock. She arrived at four. Because I'd been so nervous about the meeting, I'd asked Ozzy to wait until she got there. Finally she arrived with my half-brother Richard. My father was now spending so much time in Los Angeles with Meredith that he paid his stepson to be my mother's bring-me-fetch-me boy. So we had a coffee and a sandwich and it was a very stilted conversation, and then she came with me to Harrods and I ordered the bath I wanted. And that was that. At least there had been no argument, no shouting, so it was a beginning, I thought.

The next day our American lawyer Fred Ansers got a phone call from my father in Los Angeles. A hysterical phone call, Fred told me, saying who the fuck did I think I was and how dare I humiliate my mother by taking her to buy myself a bath. He was raving like a maniac, Fred said.

At first I couldn't understand what it was about, because it clearly couldn't have been about a bath. And then the penny dropped. It was about money. Because this was my money I was spending and I didn't have to ask their permission. If I wanted to buy a bath in Harrods with gold taps then I could, because it was my money, not theirs.

Because she always thought that I would come crawling back, and I never did. She couldn't stand the fact that I went out and I was surviving and I was living a life; that I had a house, had got myself together. I'd had my children, I wasn't a whore, I was a married woman living a decent life, and neither of them could stand the fact that I didn't need them. And Ozzy's career was going better and better, and they couldn't stand that either. My father had never been the sort of person who, when people had left and gone on to get good jobs, had praised them or wished them well. He was never like, 'You go, girl, great, I'm so proud of you.' Everything was his. 'I made Ozzy a star; she stole him from me.' And my mother was exactly the same. If I had ever come back and my mother had seen that my jewellery was bigger than hers, she would probably have stabbed me.

I weakened just one more time. It was a few weeks after the Harrods bath incident, and my niece Gina told me that she had seen a photograph of Ozzy and me and Jet at the house in Wimbledon. This photograph was a wedding gift from a photographer friend of ours, called Mark Weiss, and it was taken at the Howard Hughes house, standing in front of the living room fireplace, and it was the only picture I had of Jet. So in a moment of vulnerability, I called the familiar Wimbledon number, and my brother Richard answered the phone. I told him about the picture, and he said he'd have to go and ask his mother. If he'd had a wank, she'd want to know about it.

'Well?' I said when he came back to the phone.

'She says to tell you to go fuck yourself.'

I never spoke to either my brother or my mother again.

I got the photograph when she died. Nothing else.

What kind of woman are you? was the question I had wanted an answer to for so long, but now I had answered it myself. One I did not want in my life.

Another group of people who hated Ozzy and me at this time were Black Sabbath, because while Ozzy's band was a huge success, they were nowhere. Sandy Pearlman, the producer who had taken them on when they refused to stay under the same management as Ozzy, had lasted five minutes. And where did they go? Back to the Meehans. And when my father heard that this was going wrong – again – he went out of his way to get them back with Don Arden. He knew Sabbath would love nothing better than if Ozzy disappeared up his own arse, which was exactly what he wanted too, so he'd do whatever it took to make them bigger than Ozzy. Ronnie Dio, the singer they were so in love with when they kicked Ozzy out, had left after two records. My father put in a new singer, Ian Gillan from Deep Purple. But after a few years they split with him and went back to the Meehans and from then on, for the next ten years, they would go back and forth between the Meehans and my father like a fucking yoyo.

In June 1985 I had a call from my friend Gloria.

'Wouldn't it be great if Sabbath could get back together, just for this?' she said. She was referring to Live Aid. Six months earlier Bob Geldof had put together Band Aid and done a charity Christmas single, 'Do They Know It's Christmas', but this was much more ambitious. It would be live concerts, televised from London, Philadelphia and Melbourne.

And she was right; it was a great idea. And so, with Gloria and me acting as go-betweens, it was agreed. As nobody was being paid, we decided to say nothing to Don. It was hardly a state secret that he hated Ozzy's and my guts, and if he knew we were going behind his back, he would be sure to do something to stop it. So on 13 July Black Sabbath re-formed for Live Aid, nearly ten years since they had last stood on a stage together, and I watched them perform in the JFK Stadium in Philadelphia. My instinct about my father had been right. The day before the performance, when Ozzy was walking away from rehearsals, a man had come up and served him papers: Don Arden was suing Ozzy for enticement, saying he was trying to take Sabbath away from him. Gloria got a writ claiming the same thing: enticing her husband away from Sabbath. It was all a stupid waste of time and money. Live Aid was a one-off; it was for charity so no money was involved. My father did it because he couldn't bear to think we did something without him. It wasn't the first time Don had served papers on Ozzy. Once, shortly after we told CBS we were leaving my father, he served papers on Ozzy while he was actually on stage.

Getting to Philadelphia was a nightmare. As I was pregnant again, too pregnant to fly, Ozzy and I went on the *QE2*, and it was horrible, like a floating Butlins, and I had no idea that the Atlantic would be so rough. After all, it was mid-summer, so I'd thought I'd be lying up on deck getting suntanned, like on a Caribbean cruise. Instead I was being thrown around the deck getting seasick, my legs feeling like noodles. After two days Ozzy went to the on-board doctor, who decided he was suffering from claustrophobia and mania. The doctor was so afraid, he put Ozzy to sleep for two days. So while he's in our cabin sleeping like a baby, I'm wandering around a fucking tugboat on my own. In the afternoon, there were these idiots playing some game where they pushed wooden horses with sticks, and there would be people dancing with numbers on their backs. It didn't help that I was the size of a tank.

Not only was I five months pregnant, but since 1980 I had put on an average of a stone a year, and continued to do so till 1989. Ozzy didn't care what size I was, at least, not when he was sober, but when he had an audience and he was drunk, that was different. On one level even I had to laugh, because his jokes were funny, but deep down it was misery. I can remember being out one night with the guys from Slade and we were in some Greek restaurant in London, and Ozzy was being very funny and very witty at my expense. The way I looked, the way I dressed, the size of my arse, and I can remember looking at Slade's singer

Noddy Holder and seeing the look in his eyes and just wanting to die.

When we got back home I would go crazy and I would hit him and hit him because it was the only thing I could do. Once I cut my wrists because my hand went through a window. Another time I took a knife and cut myself in front of him on purpose. I'd had enough of being humiliated, of being a laughing stock.

'This is what you are doing to me!' I screamed, holding up my bleeding wrists. Yet it made no difference what you said to him. He would nod as if he'd understood and taken everything on board but then just go on and on like before. It was as if the alcohol had made him deaf. It was especially bad when he was making a record. I'd explain why this or that had to happen but he'd take no notice and go on and on and on about whatever it was he wanted changed or different, and it was like a dripping tap and I would literally bang my forehead on the wall above the bed and tell him to stop, to shut up.

For a long, long time after Randy's death, Ozzy could not bring himself to say he had found a replacement, and without a writing partner, he couldn't write. Now finally we had our permanent replacement. Jake E. Lee. Jakey was half Japanese – his father had met his mother in the war. He was as dark as Randy had been blond, and very, very good-looking. Of course, nobody could replace Randy, but this was the first time Ozzy had somebody of whom he could say: 'I have now found my new partner.'

And I had a new baby, born on 8 November 1985. A girl, they'd said when I had my scans. So when Jack arrived, Ozzy was so excited he fainted. He was already pissed even before the baby was born; the pockets of his jacket were rattling with the miniatures he'd been swigging throughout my labour. We were both taken totally by surprise, having been told over and over by the hospital that it was another girl and so – poor Jack – I'd done out the room with everything pink. But if you've got two daughters already, it's nice to have a son, and not only for the dad. After the delivery, we spent a couple of hours together and then I fell asleep while he went back to the new house in Hampstead and continued to celebrate by taking one of the nannies to bed. I probably would never have found out if Lynn hadn't dropped by and caught him.

When Ozzy was going through the artistic process of writing and recording a new album he was always at his worst, because then everything was on the line. And this time Ozzy was bad. His drinking was bad and his behaviour was bad. And at the same time as having to cope with him, there was a lot of work going on with the album – *Ultimate Sin* – marketing campaigns and the tour to arrange, and the crew and all the band were staying in London.

He was heavily back on the bottle, and I remember one big fight when he hit me very badly, then whacked my niece Gina with a vacuum cleaner as she was trying to separate us. I was used to the fact of Ozzy being excessively temperamental when he was writing and recording, and I got it and understood it, but I had the two girls running round and was breastfeeding Jack while trying to run a business, and I was very tired. But we got over that, we always did. We always got over that and life went on. But the drinking didn't get any better.

---

20 April 2005, 6.00 p.m.
Rodeo Drive, Beverly Hills

I have a Cartier-Bresson photograph to pick up from Ralph Lauren. So I park the car, and a few feet away is a beautiful young woman handing a baby to an older woman who looks like her mother, and she's wearing the most fabulous sandals. Birkenstocks, but sparkling.

'I just love your shoes,' I say. 'Where did you get them?'

'I designed them myself.'

'Oh really, well . . .'

'Would you like me to send you some?'

It turns out this woman hasn't customised a pair of Birkenstocks, as I thought she meant, she actually designed them for Birkenstock. She turns out to be Heidi Klum, the supermodel, and the bulge in her tummy is Seal's baby. Only in Hollywood.

When you're a celebrity, it's like you're a member of the Famous Club. During Oscar week I was walking through the lobby of the Beverly Hills Hotel and there was Jamie Oliver. And we both looked at each other and went 'Hello!' He was with Brad Pitt, and Brad and I have met a few times, but just in passing. And he is gorgeous, but I don't *know* him know him. So anyway, he and Jamie Oliver are friends, and Jamie had come over to cook for a pre-Oscar charity dinner. So that was all very jolly, and very Hollywood, don't you know?

14

Home

I always think of Hollycroft Avenue as our first proper home. There was a little Montessori school that Aimee went to for a couple of hours a day, and there was enough space for two nannies and Tony to live in, and I had a housekeeper called Anne who lived out, and she was always going above and beyond what was expected of her, and life was sweet. Ozzy had bought me a little white Mercedes. So I had my freedom, and I had my kids and I was in London and I felt human. I didn't have to sit in a pub where people called me the Yank and the Home-wrecker.

Ozzy was still spending half the year on the road, and I would be constantly flying out to set up a tour, then flying back to see the children, then flying back out again to be company for him. And staying in hotels around the world, one night here, a couple of nights there, you're always losing things. No matter how many times you look under beds and in the wardrobes and check the back of the bathroom door, there's always something missing when you get back. And in the end you have to accept it as a travel expense. But then things began to disappear in the house. I noticed little things, like my tights and Ozzy's socks that I would always buy in bulk. And, of course, because of what happened in the Sidney Sheldon house, I immediately thought it must be the housekeeper. But that was obviously just me being paranoid. And yet this little voice saying 'It's her, it's her' wouldn't go away. Then one day she didn't turn up for work, and there was no phone call, nothing. So leaving the nanny in charge of the kids, I told Tony we were going to pay Anne a visit, and Gina was staying at the time so she came too.

And so we're knocking at the door, and there's no reply. But then Gina sees a curtain twitch, and it's Anne. She pulls back the curtain and points at her mouth, saying she can't open the door because she hasn't got her teeth in.

'If you don't open the door now,' I shout, 'I'm going to break it in.' So she opens the front door a crack, but I put my shoulder to it and push. The house stank. I went straight into the living room and there was her husband, a builder with a huge fat belly, snoring in front of the TV with his great feet up on the coffee table. And suddenly I see what he's got on his feet. Not slippers, but Ozzy's stage shoes, his favourite Capezio dance shoes encrusted with rhinestones, and I go mad. And then I see that the piles and piles of what look like washing around the room are in fact piles of my dirty underwear.

She was arrested that night. There were only two bedrooms in the house and one of them was choc-a-bloc with my babies' belongings, from baby shoes and a christening gown to toys and nappies, not to mention jewellery, silver frames, silver mirrors, bed linen, cutlery and bits of my dinner service. There was mildew in all the cups, fungus on everything. The police went under the floorboards and found about £12,000 in cash. In all they took out thirteen black bin bags of stuff. When the case came up in court, her plea for clemency was that she was 'on the change' — suffering the effects of the menopause — and she got two years suspended. As I couldn't prove the cash was mine they gave it back to her. Some of the jewellery was returned to me, though I could never bring myself to wear it. As for the silver picture frames and silver mirrors, like everything else she took I gave them to charity.

I can never understand how somebody can enter into your life, into your confidence, become part of your family, and then steal. It's happened to me several times now. One woman is still in prison in LA as I write. Is it supposed to be some sort of excuse that I am wealthy? Because somebody has money in the bank, does that give these people the green light to take what is not theirs? If you work at Gucci, why not steal handbags? The guy who owns Gucci is wealthy. What's the difference? Yet these people come into your home, that you've worked your arse off for, and say, Oh that's nice. I think I'll have that. Even at my lowest times, when I had nothing, I could never have taken anything from anybody. The idea of personally thieving, of going into somebody's house is something that sickens me.

It's like with nannies. You trust these people with your most precious possessions, and so their standards should be higher than high. There was one nanny who was always offering to take Aimee and Kelly out in the double stroller. She liked walking, she said. We later discovered that where she liked walking to was the house I'd rented for the band at the time. She'd leave the children strapped in the stroller by the swimming pool, then go inside and fuck the drummer.

It seemed that whenever I came home there was another drama, and so much of it was connected with Ozzy being drunk. All his friends were drinkers, and it came as no surprise when he was arrested for drunk driving. And within a year of the Betty Ford experience, I knew I had to get him to try and straighten out again, and one morning when he was really sorry and ashamed of his behaviour, he agreed. I'd done my research, I told him, and the place with the best results was called Hazelton, and it was in the US. There was nothing remotely similar in the UK. In the UK they would detox you, give you a bit of therapy, then throw you out to fend for yourself.

The Betty Ford clinic had been like a holiday camp: swimming pool, lovely weather, everybody laughing and having a good time. Summer camp for grown-ups. Hazelton was boot camp, though I didn't tell Ozzy that. All I said was that it had been recommended, and that a lot of the literature on addiction comes out of Hazelton, which it does. But not only was it hardly the Betty Ford environment, it was also hardly California. It was two hours outside of Minneapolis and it was winter.

Just like before, there were two weeks when he wasn't allowed to phone, though I did get occasional calls from his counsellor, just checking in. They needed time to assess his progress to see what the next step of his treatment would be, they said, before we could start talking dates for the family therapy week. So I asked if I could just come visit. And they agreed.

I got a car to pick me up from Minneapolis airport as I could never have found my way otherwise. It was snow everywhere. When I arrived at the facility I was told that I was fifteen minutes early, and that I would have to wait. When finally I got to see Ozzy, he looked desperate. Like a prisoner. And the moment we were alone he just clung to me. 'You've got to get me out of here. Please don't make me stay.' The counsellor had a very different take. Ozzy needed long-term treatment, he said. A minimum of six months. *Six months?* Although I knew he was probably right, I felt my mouth go dry and panic begin to rise. I mean, six months without my crazy husband? On any level, I just didn't think I could do it. So I said that my husband and I needed to talk before we could make a decision.

Then Ozzy and I had a talk. It wasn't the six-to-a-room he

couldn't take, it was the prospect of facing the 'hot seat' in ten days' time, where you sit in front of your peer group and they tell you what they think of you. And he was fucking terrified. His people-pleasing technique hadn't worked here. I went back to the counsellor and said we would have to think about it, but that I had to go home. I was getting the next plane back.

The next time we were allowed to talk – a week later – he was begging me: 'I have to leave. I can't do the long term. I can't, I can't.'

'Ozzy, it's your decision. If you stay clean, it won't be a prob lem.' But in my inner heart I knew that he wouldn't. Pete Mertons went to get him, and he was sober for a while. Perhaps six weeks.

That summer of 1986 was the first time we rented a house at Malibu, and we did that for the next few years. We anchored ourselves on the coast of California for the summer months. It was good for Ozzy – he could come back and spend time with the children – it was good for them, because they got to see their daddy and yet had weeks and weeks at the seaside. In previous years we had taken them on the road in a specially converted tour bus. Ozzy loved it: he would take them on stage with him at every opportunity, but it was far from ideal. They would have to spend most of the day in his dressing-room trailer as backstage is a minefield for little people, cables everywhere, heavy equip-ment being lugged around, and noise. They never complained. Like circus children, they had grown up with it; it was all they knew.

Writs were a continuing feature of our daily lives. One time Ozzy was performing at Irvine Meadow between LA and San Diego and a man tried to serve papers on me backstage. Not my father this time, but a sound and light company who said we owed them money from the tour and I said we didn't. So Ozzy is on stage doing his encore, 'Paranoid'. Slash from Guns N' Roses joins him and I see this guy, but he's got all the laminated VIP backstage passes and so I think he must be with one of the other musicians from the band, because he was built like a bodyguard. And I am more on stage than off listening to Ozzy, when this guy comes up and he taps me with a rolled-up bunch of papers on my upper breast and says, 'You've just been served' – because as soon as the writ touches your body, technically you've been served. So I just yelled for our tour manager, Bobby Thomson.

'Bobby! Bobby! Stop that man,' and Bobby grabbed him and held him, and I took off one of my beautiful Maud Frizon shoes, and holding the foot part, hammered him on the head with the heel. 'How dare you, you bastard, you motherfucking piece of shit!' I screamed, jumping up and down to reach him. 'How fucking dare you. Never, ever do that again.' Because the way I look at it, it's my home. If anyone comes on your tour bus, in your dressing room, in your venue, in your house, it's an invasion. If you're in a restaurant, that's not. And the way he touched me was unforgivable. So the next day the police called and said that this man had made a charge of assault and battery. So I told them what had happened and how he had touched me inappropriately, and how my friend Gloria had witnessed it all, which she had.

But the guy didn't give up. A day or so later, I was sitting on the deck, looking out from the beach house onto the ocean, and I see this man, and he's on a pristine beach with private access dressed in writ-server's outfit, and I recognised him immediately.

Autumn 1986 was the last time Ozzy was unfaithful to me. I had flown across to spend three days with him at the Sunset Marquis Hotel in West Hollywood to check on how the recording was going. I was commuting to LA nearly every week. So I was packing to leave again, to go to the airport, when I did my usual check around the bedroom, and there was something under the bed. A stocking. One black stocking. So I asked him how he thought it came to be there.

'It's probably been there for fucking ages.'

'No, it hasn't,' I said, 'because I was here last week. And I checked and there was nothing.'

'Well, it's nothing to do with me.'

'So the maid was just cleaning the room and decided to remove one of her stockings and throw it under the bed, is that it?'

'I don't know.'

Finally he admitted he'd gone with some old tart he'd picked up at the bar.

'Well, I think you better have an Aids test, don't you?'

Aids had just begun to impinge on the world in a big way but I didn't really expect it would come up positive because it was still very much associated with the gay community and one thing Ozzy has never been is gay. But I wanted to give him a shock. And my God, it certainly did that: Ozzy was terrified of Aids. Nor was the test something you got done while-you-wait. It required a blood sample, and so we went to a doctor who said we would get the result in a week. There was a lot of slapping and hair-pulling going on that week. And then came the results. We went to get them together. Positive. So now I would have to be tested too. Ozzy was mortified, and he completely broke down.

'Right,' I said to the doctor. 'Take some blood from me, but also take three more vials from Ozzy, and I want you to send them off to three different labs and with three different names on.' Because I knew from my gay friends that in those days the test was so unsophisticated and delicate that it only had to be shaken about and you could get the wrong result. So that was another week we had to wait. All the results came back negative. But every month after that for two years Ozzy had the test done again because he was so terrified. And that was the last time he was unfaithful, ever. It put the fear of God into him and he never wants to relive it.

I never found out who it was. And, anyway, it wouldn't have meant one thing or another. It wasn't anyone of any consequence. I mean, it wasn't Princess Diana or Princess Caroline of Monaco, and it wasn't Madonna or Blondie.

Just like Kelly says, I am always looking at houses, even if I'm perfectly happy where I am. But I had nothing to do with our next upheaval, the following year. I was in LA on business and Ozzy was in London. A brochure for a house had come in the post and he'd opened it, he told me when he called for our nightly chat. 'It's in the country and it's the most gorgeous house I have ever seen,' he said. 'I'm going to see it tomorrow.'

The next day he called again. He'd seen it. He wanted it. Beel House had an unbelievable history. It had been owned by Elizabeth Taylor and Richard Burton and Dirk Bogarde. He sounded so happy and excited that I thought, why not?

'Go for it, Dadda. Do it!'

I had no idea what it looked like, but two weeks later it was his. There were deer in the garden, and it was a fabulous Georgian house in a quiet and incredibly beautiful corner of the Chilterns in Buckinghamshire, within easy reach of Heathrow and the M25. And that was it. We sold Hampstead immediately, which in retrospect was a big mistake, especially since financially things were going so well for Ozzy that we didn't need the money. Only once we'd moved in did I realise there was a pub at the end of the fucking drive.

But in terms of the children, the move to Little Chalfont was the best thing we ever did. We found a lovely Montessori nursery school for Aimee and Kelly, and later they went to Gateway School in Great Missenden. And the friends they made back then are still their friends today.

As Ozzy's star rose, Don Arden's reached its nadir. Several years before, when he still had the Howard Hughes house, my father suspected that the LA accountant Batyu Patel had been stealing money from the company. Instead of investigating whether this was true, as usual he decided to sort it out himself. So he paid a visit to the house where Batyu was living, one of the two I'd had refurbished. And he attacked him, tied him up and punched him, and did God knows what else. I wasn't there. At the time I hadn't talked to my father or my brother for over three years, so didn't even get a reported version. My brother now says he had taken two heavies with him, but it was Don himself who did the dirty work. But when I remember how he dealt with Paulita, the thick gold necklace wound round his hand before punching her in the face, I can imagine he didn't go any easier on a man he decided had betrayed him on such a massive scale as he believed Batyu had.

So then he tells Batyu that he has twenty-four hours to find the money, leaves the phone lines open, but locks him into the house. Batyu isn't stupid, so he just breaks a window, climbs out and takes the first plane back to England. My father follows him to the house in Harrow where he lives with his parents. So Mr and Mrs Patel are sitting quietly in their kitchen, enjoying a chicken tikka with their son, when the door bursts open and two Italian-American hoods and a Russian-Manchester Jew walk in and start beating the shit out of their son. And they kidnapped him and took him to the house in Wimbledon and kept him there all night until the banks opened, when he was persuaded to make a large withdrawal, about £50,000. So that was all right then.

Not satisfied with that, my father arranged for a random check of the accounts and claimed to have found a deficit of $600,000 and so – three months later – went back to the house in Harrow. This time Mr or Mrs Patel called the police. The charge was kidnapping and extortion and assault. My brother was arrested, sent for trial, found guilty and given a two-year prison sentence, though he didn't serve the full term. My father, in the meantime, had fucked off to California and went into hiding. He didn't give evidence at his son's trial; he didn't come over when his mother died. He sat *shivah* for her over the phone. Two years later he was extradited, stood trial and amazingly got off.

In 1987 it was album time again – Ozzy was about to record *No Rest for the Wicked* – and the worst time in the world for his and my relationship. We would argue over producers, we would argue over studios, we would argue over everything. Ozzy is the sort of guy who believes in luck. If he's done an album in such-and-such a studio and it's been a success, then that's a lucky studio, or a lucky producer, or a lucky engineer. His tendency has always been to stay safe, whereas I want to progress. We'd been doing a gig in Connecticut but had come into Manhattan to stay the night at the Parker Meridien. So it's late and so we decide to go to the Hard Rock on 57th Street, and they show us to a table in the VIP section, which is on a mezzanine slightly away from the general public. And we sit down – six of us – me, Ozzy, Jakey Lee, Lynn, Tony and Larry, an ex-Vietnam security guy, and the food had just arrived. As usual I had a Coke. Ozzy, of course, had a Hard Rock Hurricane, having already been drinking all day.

I was talking about the need to bring in a new producer. And Ozzy wanted the same producer he'd had before. He wanted to play safe, and he thought this producer was lucky. And I get that,

I honestly do get that. But Ozzy's way of dealing with it was not to sit down and have a debate or agree to disagree. It was, literally, let's have a fight. So suddenly Ozzy lunges at me across the table like a madman, grabs me round the neck and starts to strangle me. And it's such a shock that my chair tips back and I'm basically still sitting in the chair on the floor and Ozzy is now stretched flat across the table and his hands are round my neck. Then we're both down on the ground and other people are trying to get him off, but he's like a man possessed and it isn't until Larry drags him off that I can breathe again.

As we were away from the main restaurant, the in-house security didn't see what was happening. But Brian Johnson from AC/DC did, and he came over to check if I was OK. And it was the Rio plane thing all over again but with an extra lick of violence. Somehow when nobody else saw I could cope, but in public it was humiliating and acutely embarrassing. Ozzy once wrote a song about Jekyll and Hyde – 'Mr Jekyll Doesn't Hide'– and that was him. He would have these mad rages, and just minutes later he'd be wondering what he'd done. Tony took Ozzy back to the hotel, and I decided I would stay in Lynn's room that night. We must have been back an hour when there was this terrible hammering on her door, and I could hear Ozzy outside screaming to be let in.

Violence has always been a part of my life, and the idea that I might get hit didn't scare me. So I was like, 'OK. Fine. Bring it on.' And I opened the door. And he was still yelling and screaming, and Tony and Larry were both trying to stop him.

'What the fuck do you want me to do, Ozzy? What the—' I never got to finish my sentence before Ozzy threw a punch and we started to fist-fight, then he got me by the arm and flung me against the door, and my head ricocheted off the wall and I slumped to the ground. This seemed to satisfy him and he left.

Lynn and I got a cab to the nearest hospital. This was New York on Saturday night, and compared with what else was coming in through the door, my dislocated jaw wasn't that important. It was horrendous. There were stretcher cases, and blood, and sirens, and people crying and drunkenness. And I'm like, for fuck's sake, this is not what I signed up for. And it really wasn't.

Ozzy was now doing combinations of prescription drugs and drink, big time. All he had to do was complain of back pain and he could get any fucking thing he wanted. As for drinking, he would not stop from the minute he got up to the minute he collapsed. He had it hidden everywhere. In the cellar, in the back of the coal cupboard in the hall, in the oven – it was safe because I never cooked. Bottles of vodka, scotch, Jack Daniel's, Hennessy, whatever; he had no particular choice. It wasn't as if he was a gin drinker: he was an anything drinker.

And I would do anything to stop him.

When I found the booze I'd throw it away, or I'd piss in it, or I'd stick the neck up my arse, just as a kind of Fuck You, because I knew he would drink straight from the bottle. I wanted him to suffer. And even when I told him what I'd done, he'd still fucking drink it. And it didn't matter if I poured a case of whisky down the drain, all he had to do was find someone to take him to Beaconsfield, the nearest small town, and he could get anything. He was always drunk. And he'd say, 'Take me to the pub', because he was banned from driving.

'Why, Ozzy? The pub doesn't even open for an hour.'

'Because I want to.'

'So you'll be sitting an hour by yourself waiting for this pub to open. Why?'

'Because I want to.'

'Ozzy, I love you, but actually I can't stand this, because I am not prepared to be picking up the pieces every single fucking day.'

And of course there had been times when I'd said, 'That's it, I'm out, fuck you, I'm gone.' But where does a woman with three children, who has no bank account and no money, go? Because I was in so much trouble through my father, and so many people wanted me for his debts, I still didn't dare have a bank account, didn't dare have a credit card, so I couldn't even check into a hotel. And then Ozzy would call up the accountant and say, 'If she calls, give her nothing.' I had no family, so where do you go?

A couple of times I had gone to my niece Gina, who by that time was married, and she always said I could sleep on her sofa. But I had three babies. And I was like, what the fuck is going to happen to me? So I would stuff it, everything I would stuff. I stuffed everything about my father; the position I now found myself in was a direct result of my father. I was living with an alcoholic who had gone from being like Arthur, the funny cuddly drunk, to the fucking Hulk. Because alcoholism is a progressive disease. It changes in how it manifests.

There were times, especially when we were living at Beel House, when I was terrified. He would come into the bedroom after getting back from the pub and my stomach would knot. I would pretend to be asleep. Please God, I beg of you, do not let him wake me up, let him think I am asleep. A few times I would put the children in the car and run away in the middle of the night; I would pile them in the car and just go. I was never frightened that he would do anything to them, but I didn't want them to see or feel the atmosphere in the house.

His addiction with drink had moved into a sexual addiction as well. He wanted sex all the time, all the time. And I'd be pleading with him, 'Please let me sleep, let me sleep.' But I would never say no. I just wanted to keep the peace. It was easier to say yes.

Because I was genuinely so tired. I'd had six pregnancies in six years. Yes, I had nannies, but whenever I was home I spent all my time with the children, and I had three children under five, and so by the time they go to bed you are drained. And so you too go to bed. And then your husband comes back from a night at the pub, and he's there in the bedroom, smoking a cigar and wanting sex. Nothing to do with love. No kissing involved. Not that I could have kissed him anyway. You can't kiss and hold lovingly someone you're angry with. So I would just turn my head. I would shut my eyes tight. Mouth and eyes both closed. And I would lie there and I would cry. Not sob. I would quietly cry and I would turn my back on him. Oh God, please let him sleep.

One time things got so bad that I gave Ozzy an ultimatum. I was off to LA, working on his behalf. 'If you're drunk when I come back,' I said, 'that's it. I'm divorcing you.' And when I did get back, he'd done it. Full of remorse, he'd laid off the booze for two days. He had gone cold turkey just like that.

The next morning I woke to a terrible noise in the bed beside me. The sound of choking. Ozzy was totally rigid and his eyes were rolled back and he was choking on his tongue. So I put my hand in his mouth – my half-brother Richard's wife had been an epileptic so I knew what to do when someone has a seizure – and I pulled his tongue back, and I had to hold my fist in his mouth to stop him biting, but people's jaws are really strong. He was under for about a minute and a half, then he regained consciousness for two or three minutes. He didn't talk, but his eyes came to a normal position. But then nearly straight away he went and had another one. So Tony and I got him into the car and drove him to our doctor in Harley Street. He wouldn't talk. At this stage he was very lethargic and floppy. Across the road in the London Clinic they put him on monitors and did various tests. He'd had an alcoholic seizure, they said. If you go cold turkey without a gradual withdrawal, your body goes into shock.

One day I was talking to Ozzy's agent Bill Elson, the guy who'd lent us money and helped us when we were on the run from my father, and he said I should think about taking on other artists to manage. 'Because otherwise people will think of you as just a wife.'

The person he had in mind was Lita Ford, known by her fans as the Queen of Noise. She was originally a Londoner and joined the first all-girl rock band called the Runaways in the mid-seventies. They had split up long before, but the singer, Joan Jett, had gone on to do well with her solo career. Lita Ford was a guitar heavyweight who also sang and had done a few solo albums, but nothing had ever happened. Now she was looking for a new manager, Bill said. 'And I bet you one thousand dollars that you'll get a hit with her.'

The fact that she had once been managed by my father and had done nothing with him may have encouraged me to see if I could do better. I accepted Bill's challenge.

My main focus was her image. She had never moved away from the girl-rocker mould, so I took her out of her hokey jeans and ill-fitting T-shirts and put her in designer clothes and made her look sexy, and it worked. Her fourth solo album, *Lita*, was a huge hit, and she did her only successful US tour. She had her first Top 20 single, 'Kiss Me Deadly', and then came 'Close My Eyes Forever', a duet she did with Ozzy. He had written the song as a duet some time before and suggested I gave it to Lita. Then I said, 'Why don't you sing it with her?' It was a huge, huge hit.

Although Lita and I had our moments, it gave me much-needed confidence, and I decided I might as well continue. The Quireboys had played a lot of gigs around London.

They'd had a record on an indie label and everybody was after them for management. So I thought, OK, I'll go talk with them. It took a month of schmoozing and then I closed the deal as their manager. I signed them to EMI to a huge recording contract, and their album, *A Bit of What You Fancy*, was a huge hit in every country but the US. It was even huge in Japan.

Ozzy was not happy that I was managing another band. I was giving them too much of my time. He wasn't jealous on an artistic level; he was doing just fine, all his albums were still going platinum, his tours were doing great. But the energy I was expending on them was ridiculous, he said. And it was probably true, though I had no real alternative as their second album was now due. I'd got them the best guy there was at the time, a fabulous producer called Bob Rock, but the lead singer wasn't coming up with the lyrics, and it was dragging, and the album was way, way late.

Then there was Bonham, started by John Bonham's son, Jason, a drummer just like his father and just as good, and the living image of him. The guys in Bonham were no trouble at all – great people, and a pleasure to deal with. The Quireboys, however, were a pain in the arse because they were all drinkers. But all of it, positive and negative, took me away from home – not only the day-to-day management, but the constant travelling. And Ozzy was not happy about it at all. I did my best to balance everything. But I was like one of those variety entertainers who spin plates on top of sticks, constantly rushing from one side of the stage to another, with just enough time to give one of the plates another spin before it topples over. My stage was the world. There were tours to set up, record deals to negotiate, promo to steer. I would try never to stay away from the children longer than five working days and always be back at the weekend. If Ozzy was on the road then I would never stay longer than ten days away, just enough to get the tour going, to make sure everything was working smoothly, then leave.

There were three benefits from working with other artists. First was the boost to my self-confidence, which one way and another had had a real battering. Second, I was making money. I always felt uncomfortable spending Ozzy's money. He was the one going out and earning it; all I was doing was giving him advice and telling him what he should and shouldn't do.

If Ozzy hadn't been there, I would have stayed with my father and I would have ended up in prison like my brother. I know that. So I was very lucky to be in the position I was in, and my husband gave me virtually anything I wanted.

The third plus was that, for the first time in my life, I could be legitimate. When I started earning money with other bands, I could pay my way in tax and pay whatever else I was due to pay. There were plenty of people around me saying, Oh, there's this tax scheme here, and that tax scheme there, and if you have a Panamanian company you can have a tax shelter and all that shit. I just didn't want to go there. And I knew it wasn't necessary. Ozzy's finances had always been very straight. I wanted every-thing in his life to be correct, because I'd seen what happened to my father. So we'd pay the tax and we'd sleep at night. I never wanted Ozzy to have what I had when I went to sleep: that some time I'm going to get that knock, going to get that phone call.

One of the first things I did with my money was throw a Christmas party. Ozzy was away in America on tour, so this would be the perfect opportunity, I decided.

Historically Ozzy does not like Christmas, never has, never will. Every Christmas we have ever had together – bar the first, which was amazing – has been hell. Where it stems from, I don't know. Perhaps because he was always drunk and messed up so that people would be angry with him.

I have always loved throwing parties; the Ardens' parties had always been famous. So I told the kids that this year we were going to have a Christmas party and it was going to be the best Christmas party ever, and Ozzy won't know, and nobody's hurt.

So I had carol singers, I had caterers, I had Christmas trees, I had entertainers and I had 500 invitations printed. It was all very elaborate. We had an avenue of Christmas trees leading up to the house, and there was a huge marquee complete with chandeliers, and Christmas decorations everywhere. Everyone was welcomed with mulled wine, carol singers and a gift bag, probably fucking pearls and rubies knowing me. To eat, there was Christmas dinner with all the trimmings, then a flambé stand where you could get pancakes with brandy and lemon.

It wasn't sex and drugs and rock and roll, it was just fun, with people dancing to a big band orchestra, and we had a blast. And the kids were there, and Bon Jovi were there, and the Quireboys were there. Everybody was there. Except the husbands.

Because Gloria and I had hatched up this little scheme together. She and Terry have always had houses both in the US and England, and on this occasion our husbands were on a solo tour in the States, and because we talk to them after every show – to see how it's gone, and generally let some of the adrenalin run off – Gloria had to give Terry a reason why she wouldn't be at home that night. So she told him that she and I were going out for a Chinese.

Unfortunately the wardrobe girl on Ozzy and Terry's tour had a boyfriend who was on Jon Bon Jovi's tour. So this guy calls his girlfriend in New York – which is where they were that night – and tells her all about it. Then she goes and tells Ozzy how the party sounded amazing, and how sorry he must be to have missed it . . .

He went fucking ballistic. It was if I had fucked the Household Cavalry three times each. It was as if I had fucked every person at that party.

But the truth is that Ozzy would have hated it. Not only that, if he'd been there he would have been staggering drunk and he'd have caused a fight. There is no point in celebrating Christmas with Ozzy because he just hates everything about it, so it would have been miserable, as per usual.

I think in my gut I always knew that, one way or the other, he would find out. But I didn't care. I wanted the children to have a good time. I wanted the children to have a blast at Christmas. And they were so excited. They all had little outfits: Aimee and Kelly in matching velvet with white lace tops, and Jack had a little black velvet suit. As usual I was wearing some kind of black tent, but with beautiful jewels, probably bought new for the occasion. It just felt so exciting that we were doing something fun at Christmas. And it was even more exciting that it was a secret.

If I'd used Ozzy's money that would have been different. It would have been like a slap in the face. But this was money I had earned. In fact, I had been with Ozzy two days before in New York, and when I'd left him I'd cried, because I really didn't want to leave him. And it was Christmas time, and New York does Christmas better than anywhere else in the world, and I was going home alone and I was so sad. It wasn't like I had cried with my husband, then was going home to another man. It's not like there was anything indecent about it, or morally wrong.

However, Ozzy didn't see things quite that way. It took him probably five years to get over it. Every time he heard the word 'Christmas' he would hit me. Through every month through every year he would bring it up: 'That party, that fucking party.'

What made it even worse was that everybody we met said it was the best party they had ever been to: the food, the flowers, the bands, the this, the that. And I've got my head in my hands going, Oh God no, please.

It was terrible. The next time I saw him, he beat me. We were in bed and it was the middle of the night in Chicago, and the rat was out of the bag. Forget the cat. He went fucking insane. And it went from thinking I must be having an affair to obviously I was living with somebody. It was total paranoia, day in, day out.

And Terry was the same with Gloria, and she didn't even throw the party, but she was there, that was enough. Like little boys Terry and Ozzy wound each other up. It was as if I had fucked every Coldstream Guard and they'd fucked me up the arse. That's how bad it was. For years and years.

A few months later, we were back in LA staying at the Beverly Hills Hotel. It was beautiful spring weather so, just for fun, we hired an open-top Rolls-Royce Corniche for a couple of days. With the children going in and out of the pool, it was as remote from an English Christmas as anything could be. But the second afternoon we were there, Ozzy started ranting. Party this, party that. What triggered it, I have no idea. I had just walked in from having lunch with a girlfriend, but it was like a burst of machine-gun fire. That was it, I'd had enough. I grabbed the kids, piled them into the back of the Rolls and left for the airport and England.

A few minutes after the Corniche had swung out of the hotel, Ozzy had a call from the lobby.

'Is Sharon there?' It was my father, who we hadn't seen or heard from in years and years.

'No, she's gone to the airport.'

'Would you mind if I came over and talked to you.'

Under normal circumstances Ozzy would have told him to fuck off, but he was angry with me and so he said OK.

What followed was a rerun of the pub-lunch scenario in Wimbledon several years before, but with a twist: then my father had accused me of robbery and insanity, now he was accusing me of every sexual deviancy he could think of.

Ozzy told me later that all his anger against me melted away as soon as this diatribe got going, so whatever aberration my father accused me of, Ozzy just agreed, determined not to give Don the pleasure of any reaction. If my father had told Ozzy I'd screwed a fucking donkey he'd still have shrugged and said, yeah, yeah, he knew.

And the more Ozzy didn't react, the more frustrated my father became, until he had run out of disgusting things to say and was about to leave. Ozzy still didn't really know why, after all this time, he had come. When Don got to the door he stopped and turned back to Ozzy, his face full of fury.

'And anyway, who the fuck do you think you are, driving a Rolls-Royce?' he said. It turned out he had seen me driving around Beverly Hills and had followed me like a stalker. And he thought this Corniche was ours, and it was killing him, it was fucking killing him. He was so eaten up with jealousy that he'd decided, yet again, to try and destroy our relationship.

I was a whore, a nigger-fucker, I took his money and his artists. Now, my father had exceeded anything he had done before. His own daughter even wanted to have sex with him, he said. Where do you go from there?

The problem with working, whether I was managing Ozzy or somebody else, was always the childcare. The very first nanny we had came from Birmingham and had just graduated from her two-year nanny course. This girl was nineteen but very naive. The idea of all that travelling didn't put her off, she said. Aimee was just a baby and we were on the road in America and I needed a nanny so that I could do my business at the theatres and when Ozzy was on stage, and at that time we were seeing a lot of Ozzy's children by his first marriage too. Jessica must have been about fourteen and Louis ten, so we needed someone who could handle all ages.

So we were on the road, going all across America and Hawaii and Japan. Then out of the blue she handed in her notice. She'd had enough of travelling, she said, and she'd found this nice family in Birmingham, where she came from. Naturally, I understood. Being on the road the whole time isn't easy, though it made things difficult for me: she had been very good with Aimee and I was now pregnant with Kelly. And who was this nice family in Birmingham? None other than Jessica and Louis. This girl left us to go and work for Thelma. Oh, and it also turned out she had been fucking a member of the crew.

Then there was the one shortly after the business of the nanny who liked fucking the band member (and Ozzy). I wanted to see what kind of a girl she was before I employed her. Her hobbies, she said, were sewing and reading. Dating anybody? No. Married? No. The only question she asked me was where the nearest public library was. And, of course, she showed me her diplomas and all that bullshit.

So we were just getting ready for Christmas and she asked for a couple of days off, and I said fine, although at that stage I only had one nanny. Then came the phone call. She was calling from the local hospital.

'What's happened? Are you all right?'

'I've had an abortion.'

'But you don't have a boyfriend.'

But she did.

The next thing is a man is screaming down the phone, demanding to know where his fucking wife is. *His wife!* She wasn't pregnant by the husband, but by the boyfriend.

Then the 'nanny' phones me again.

'Are you coming to get me?'

'Absolutely not. I never want to see you again.'

'Can I come and collect my things?'

'Of course.'

It was Christmas Eve, so by five it was dark. She arrived with the boyfriend, but I had no intention of letting her in the house. I'd got everything out of her room and had it waiting by the front door, then, when she arrived, I threw it onto the drive in armfuls: clothes on the car, on the gravel, in the flower beds, in the bushes. As for her stereo I threw that on top of her car. Then I turned out the lights and locked the front door. This person I brought into my house to take care of my children was a liar and a cheat and a fraud. I never heard from her again.

Then there was the nice young English girl with ruddy cheeks and bright blonde hair, a hearty girl, with dungarees, who had previously cared for sick children. When I got back from Japan one time, I arrived at the house to no sign of her or the children, though the car was out front, which was odd. I called up the school, and the children were there. But she had just packed and left. What would have happened if the plane had been delayed? Later it all came out, how she was throwing dinner parties in the house, and when the children came downstairs she would scream at them to go back to bed.

In America we had one who wanted to go to Disneyland for the day with Aimee and Kelly and another nanny. I had arranged the limousine to take them, and the tickets. But in Disneyland babies are only allowed to ride on the baby rides. So these girls left my babies with total strangers when they went on the big rides. Aimee told me everything when they got back.

It's incredible how stupid they were, thinking they could do all this stuff without anyone finding out. Aimee might only have been five, but very little got past her. It was Aimee who found one nanny in the downstairs toilet straddling a chef we'd brought in for a party. A female chef. This girl was horribly drunk, so I decided I had to do horrible things to her. That night, after I'd put her to bed, a friend and I got Pedigree Chum, coffee, sugar, Marmite, butter, peanut butter and ketchup, mixed it all in a blender and poured it over her when she slept. In the morning when she woke up, she thought she'd been sick. And then she left.

The hardest thing in the world is to find a decent nanny. They come into your house, and you ask them to look after this gift from God, these unique things, your children. Then they lie, they cheat, they steal, and above all they want to fuck your husband. My advice to any mother is never ever have a young girl to look after your children, however normal she may look. The list of stories of nannies who run off with the fathers of the children is endless. I have had dozens of nannies – when you need two at a time, then the numbers add up – and I can honestly say there have only been a very few I had good relationships with: Clare, a friend of Tony's, who was wonderful, and Kim, who came from Cumbria and the girls were her bridesmaids when she got married. She was a genuinely good person who now works at a school for special needs kids. And, of course, Melinda.

One week in 1989 the tension in the house was really bad. It was September, just after Aimee's sixth birthday, and Ozzy was clearly on edge, wandering back and forth from his studio in the coach house, taking beer from the fridge and then going back. And he was very argumentative. It didn't help that I was biting each time. Instead of just ignoring him and getting on with my life, I was on his case. We were snapping at each other. He was in a very punchy mood, and so he would punch. He had probably punched me about five times that week. I only had to say something he didn't like and he'd lash out, punching my head, my chest – anywhere that was close.

I don't really know what the staff must have thought. But it's very difficult when you're in somebody's home. And it wasn't like he was beating me to a pulp, and it wasn't like he would attack me with a knife or a gun. You'd say something and he'd just slam you one, basically. So what's the housekeeper going to do? What's the nanny going to do? They're scared stiff too.

Every night that week he'd ended up punching me, and I was covered in bruises. I bruise easily anyway, and when Ozzy punched me it would be navy-blue purple, and then it went green.

It was a horrible week. I'd dread it when he came back from the pub in the afternoon, and then I'd just have to wait till he got Tony to drive him back to the pub for the evening session.

One night he was really drunk and stoned from other things he'd been doing, and he passed out on the bed. I was downstairs reading. Tony and the nanny were at the top of the house, three floors up.

It was an old house with thick walls and very well sound-proofed, so I didn't hear him come down until the sitting-room door opened. My husband came in and sat on the sofa opposite me. There were three identical sofas around a square coffee table. And then he started to talk.

'We've made a decision.'

We? 'And what have you decided?'

'That you have to die.'

And I looked in his eyes. And when Ozzy was really stoned his eyes would be void of any emotion – I used to say, 'Oh God, the shutters are down.' They were still eyes that could see, but there was no one behind them. They were like a dead man's eyes. I could have been begging him on bended knee, I could have had a gun pointed at my head, when Ozzy was that stoned nothing penetrated, nothing at all.

When I saw that look in his eyes, I thought, Jesus Christ.

He moved to the middle sofa, to the one directly on my left.

'We're very sorry to have to do this to you,' he continued, 'but you see we don't have an option.' He was speaking very quietly, very politely. Not ranting, no 'you bastard' or 'you cow'. It was very, very calm. I had never seen him like this before. Never. And I was absolutely terrified. I was used to the other; with the other I knew what to expect. But here I was on the edge of an abyss.

And then he just lunged. I was sitting cross-legged on the sofa, as I always do, and he literally lunged at me. My legs were tucked up and I had no time to disentangle them before he had all his weight on top of me, and he had his hands round my neck and we both rolled off the sofa and fell onto the floor. He bent his knees and straddled me. I couldn't scream because his hands were round my neck and I was choking. I could feel myself going, but at the same time I was reaching out my hand, my fingers desperately searching for the panic clicker on the coffee table. Because either me or the nanny were so often alone in this huge house, we had them in every room. It was a mobile thing that I knew was somewhere on the table. And there was a huge alarm on the roof that we used to laugh at because it was so loud. Somehow I got the clicker and squeezed it in my hand and the alarm went off, its clanging ringing round the house and in my ears. My last memory was of just squeezing this thing.

When I came to, Ozzy had gone and I dragged myself into the kitchen. Then came the banging at the front door. We were wired up to the police station and they arrived within minutes of the alarm going off.

'My husband,' I managed when I let them in. 'My husband tried to kill me.'

My heart was pounding, my neck was aching.

'Do you know where he is now?'

I shook my head. I had no idea and my throat was too sore to speak, and I realised I'd wet myself. A detective walked me back to the kitchen, and the uniformed men went upstairs. And then

I heard yelling and crashes. They found him up in our bedroom, and they were trying to put him in handcuffs, and he started to fight them. All I heard was his voice echoing around the hall.

'This is my fucking house! Get out! You can't do this in my fucking house.' They handcuffed him in his underwear and took him away.

The detective drove me to Amersham police station where I was photographed. I was naked to the waist, because they needed to see how he had beaten me that week. The nanny had stayed behind to look after the children while Tony had put some clothes together for Ozzy and taken them to the police station. Both of them were utterly terrified. There was not a word said between us. By the time the detective took me back, the house was quiet again. I went upstairs to check on the babies, and they were still sound asleep. Thank God, they had slept through it all, and I sat outside their bedrooms on the floor and I felt free for the first time in my entire life.

---

20 April 2005, after dinner
Doheny Road, Beverly Hills

The end of a happy evening, a happy day. Billy Morrison is one of those guys who seem never to grow old, perhaps because he still has that post-punk Gothic look he had when he was bass player in the Cult. Billy and his wife Jen live just down the road, and Billy's band is even called Doheny. Billy is Ozzy's sober sponsor on the AA programme. A sober sponsor is someone who is in recovery and takes their recovery seriously. And Billy has been sober now for fifteen years. It's because he has been so important to Ozzy staying sober that we invited him and his wife here for our celebration dinner. It was just the four of us, and David Withers, our chef, had pushed the boat out: we had salmon ballantine with fennel marmalade, trio of chicken, and four of Ozzy's favourite desserts for everyone: a little coconut cake, a mini mango trifle, raspberry soufflé and berry jelly, and the dining room was over-flowing with balloons. And Ozzy talked about how he never thought he would ever go a year. The longest he's stayed sober before is 120 days. 'Each time I came out of rehab, I'd do one day more than the last time, and then get fucked.'

15

Free

All night long I just sat there, in the dark on the landing, outside the babies' rooms. Never moved. Never cried. I just felt calm. Something had been lifted from me. He's gone. He can't hurt me any more. I don't have to be frightened that he's going to come in and punch me or abuse me or fuck me in the middle of the night.

I honestly felt like a ton weight had been lifted from my body. It was as if this spiritual thing had entered into me and cleansed me, and I sat on the floor outside the babies' rooms for hours, with a blanket from the spare room wrapped round me.

All I could feel was this lightness and spirituality. The house was calm. No noise, no disturbance, and the babies were sleeping peacefully, their sweet breath no louder than a murmur, a fluttering of warm air on my cheek.

In the morning, I got them up and took them to school. The first moment I knew that this was not simply a terrible family tragedy was when the electric gates opened and the kids asked, 'Who are those men, Mummy? Why are they taking pictures?'

I said I didn't know. As news must already be on the wire services, I decided I had to tell the headmaster and his wife what had happened and ask them to please watch out for the children, to make sure that nobody got into the school.

I returned to the house by a back route and a back gate. And even before I got in I could hear the phones were ringing, and it was on TV. And that's when I actually cried. I cried and cried and cried. And Ozzy was in court that morning, but was then taken back to Amersham police station and kept in the cells where he'd been since the night before.

He had a lawyer, Colin said when he called to see how I was, but he refused to tell me what Ozzy was saying to the lawyer. 'It will destroy you,' he said. 'Just take my advice and don't go to court. He's talking a load of gibberish. I'll get you a lawyer.'

I didn't need a lawyer. I'd done nothing wrong. And I had no intention of going to court. I wanted nothing to do with it.

The next day the detective came back to ask if I would press charges. If I agreed, he said, my husband would be charged with attempted murder. I said I would think about it.

He wasn't as reticent as Colin was about what Ozzy was saying in his defence: that I'd been having affairs, that I bullied him, that I had all these other men, and that basically I just used him as a workhorse. And I'm like, OK, fine, whatever. Whatever he says, it doesn't matter. Because I know in my heart, and the people who know me and who know my children know the true story, know how it really is.

Looking back now, from the perspective of over fifteen years on, Ozzy was obviously very, very frightened and he had to have a 'reason' for what he had done, so he'd conjured one up. He wasn't going to turn round and say, 'I was so fucking stoned I didn't know what I was doing.' But back then I just had to think about what I was going to do. Was I going to press charges?

And then Colin called again. 'Guess who's trying to contact Ozzy to offer help.'

Yes, the Arden & Son double act was in town. Every time Ozzy would appear before the judge, my father and brother put a heavy in court to try and talk to him. It hadn't worked. So they'd sent him a telegram, and Ozzy gave it to Colin, when he went to visit, and Colin gave it to me. And I took it upstairs and put it in Jack's potty, and got Jack to shit on it. Then I wrapped it up and had it delivered back to the office, to my brother.

He'd given a line to one of the papers saying that he didn't blame Ozzy for what he had done. In actual fact, he said, he didn't know how he'd stood me for so long.

I got up, took the kids to school, got the kids back from school. Dinner, homework, that was it. I never went anywhere. I just hibernated. I was under pressure to make up my mind. They couldn't hold Ozzy in the cells indefinitely, they said. I was just going back over my entire life.

One night in 1978 I'd been out partying with Britt Ekland at a private drinking club called On the Rocks, above the Roxy on Sunset Strip, a club for the elite of the music industry. Apparently Britt and I left at about two thirty in the morning, and I was driving the Rolls-Royce. Britt told me that I was driving very erratically and, sure enough, we were pulled over by the police. In California, at that time, to see if you'd had too much to drink they would get you to stand on one leg or walk a straight line. I didn't even manage to get out of the car. I poured out of the car and my legs couldn't hold me up and I was just a big crumple on the road. They then arrested me, handcuffed me and took me to West Hollywood police station. I was screaming and swearing like a fishwife. Apparently they kept me there till seven in the morning when Britt bailed me out, took me home and Rachel put me to bed.

I say apparently because when I woke up later that day, I had no idea anything had happened. I had a couple of freeze-framed pictures in my mind: in one I was looking through a wire cage from the back of a police car – there to prevent you attacking the driver. In the second I was a prisoner with just my underwear on and screaming. Then a girlfriend called me and said, 'I'm so glad it happened to you. Maybe now you'll behave yourself.'

And I was like, what? It was a complete and utter blackout. Apart from these two vague freeze-frames, I had no memory of it. None. Apparently I was screaming so much and so loud that the women police officers had taken my clothes off to humiliate me, to make me shut up.

I could have killed somebody. I could easily have killed somebody. And I hadn't thought about it for years, but at the moment I needed it, the memory came back. Ozzy was me. I was Ozzy.

I couldn't press charges. He was so stoned, so gone, that it just wasn't Ozzy any more. If he had been sober or just ordinary drunk, then I would have said, 'Absolutely. Off with his head.' But in all good conscience I couldn't do it. He would have been put away for years, and I loved him, and our children needed him.

I don't remember how it was arranged in the end, but he was charged with some lesser offence. Perhaps assaulting a police officer, I don't know. But there was a court order to prevent him coming to the house or seeing me or the children. But I never went to court. Never had to give evidence. They couldn't make me, because I was his wife.

The rehab he was sent to was Huntercombe Manor, near Maidenhead. I told the kids that their daddy was on tour. They were used to him being away, though I kept checking in case they'd heard anything at school, but nothing. Until one day Jack said his friends had been talking about his daddy.

'And what did they say, Jackie Boy?'

'They say that Daddy eats people.'

'And what did you say to them?'

'Well, I counted everyone I knew, and there's nobody missing, so I know he doesn't.'

The only person missing was my husband. And when I was out somewhere, I'd think, Oh God, if I'm late Ozzy will kill me. But then I would realise that he wasn't there, and that I could stay out if I wanted. That I could do whatever I wanted. And gradually I began to think about putting my life in order. Getting a divorce, losing weight.

For the time being the money situation was OK. I would get cash from the accountant in the usual way; my husband hadn't put a stop on that, and I had my own money. But it felt so strange not talking to him. And he had begun to send me letters, letters that would melt your heart. Full of remorse and repentance and promises that this time he would change.

'I know I have a problem, but I never want to hurt you' – that sort of thing. And so I decided to phone him. And we both cried, and I told him that I loved him, and he asked to see me and asked me to bring the children, and I said that I would have to think about it.

As much as I loved my husband, I found I was beginning to enjoy being single again. My social life was blossoming and I would have dinner with girlfriends. The last few years had been like a desert. First I would want to spend as much time as I could with my babies, and then there was the embarrassment of Ozzy's drinking. When I first knew Ozzy, he was the quintessential life-and-soul-of-the-party drunk. Everyone had to invite Ozzy, because he was Mr Funny, so entertaining, singing along to all the songs. But gradually he had turned into Mr Nasty.

Truculence turned to anger, to picking a fight. And I would always be the butt of his jokes. I didn't laugh any more, and friends would get embarrassed. And then I was embarrassed because they were embarrassed, so basically we stopped going out. That was just how it was. Although I had an office in London, most of my work was done on the phone to America or Japan in the evenings and way into the night, and I had accepted that this was my life. Suddenly, here I was not having to make excuses. I was enjoying that the girls at the office were saying, 'Come on, Sharon, we're taking you for dinner.'

And at last I had a nanny I could trust. The nanny who had been with us the night Ozzy tried to kill me had fled a few days later. And I don't blame her; there was a lot to deal with. Then Tony suggested a friend of his from Newcastle. Clare was a lovely girl who wanted to be an air hostess, but luckily she was persuaded to come down to Buckinghamshire and work for us. She was pretty and young and the kids adored her. And they adored Tony, who they had known all their lives, and so we were all fine. And when Clare needed a break, or I was going to the States and she needed another pair of hands, Lynn would move in. And I could go to see a movie that wasn't Disney. And I could go out with my friends. And I was OK.

'Well, of course, you must divorce him,' people said.

'Well, of course I will divorce him,' I repeated. But the truth was that I didn't want to, but it sounded so pathetic I couldn't say the words, not even to myself.

Finally I went to see him, and I knew I had been right not to press charges. The person who did that to me wasn't this man, the man I'd married. And I understood why the situation had got to the point that it did. But although I missed him terribly, I knew he wasn't ready to come home. And he knew it, and anyway the court wouldn't have let him – he couldn't even leave the grounds. But he was doing all right and he needed time to think. He needed time with no work pressure, with nothing to do except think.

Huntercombe Manor didn't use the twelve-step programme, it had no connection with AA, but there were still parameters. Although phone calls were rationed, Ozzy had his own room, and Tony would go and take him things, and his sisters went to see him, and I think he had other visitors too. Eventually, after about three months, I took the kids to see him, and after that they would go twice a week. And then after five months away, he came home, and I said that if he ever laid a finger on me again, that was it, I would have him arrested. And I meant it. I never wanted to be hit again. I never wanted to be frightened again. And so he came home.

And I'm trying now to think how long it was before he started on the bottle again. Weeks. Just fucking weeks.

It started off with a little tipple here and there, and that was it. Because people think that an alcoholic is just somebody who drinks too much, but it's gone way beyond that. When you drink or take drugs, chemical changes are wrought in the brain. Some are obvious and don't last long, like thinking you're witty or funny, but other changes are permanent. And the police had made it clear that they didn't like him, especially the detective who wanted me to press charges. Ozzy had always been used to wheedling his way into people's affections and making people like him. But it didn't work with them. They were having none of it. To them he was just a spoilt little rock star.

For the second time in my life, unhappiness had resulted in weight loss, not the other way around. By the time Ozzy came home, I was down to eight stone, the same size I had been when we were at the studios in Monmouth nearly ten years before.

My relationship with Lita Ford began to slide. I had taken her on when I was very big, and as I began to get slimmer our relationship got worse. Then one day she asked to have dinner with me. So we went to have dinner, and she fired me.

'If you wouldn't mind waiting while I go to the bathroom,' I said. 'We'll finish this conversation when I get back.' But I never did go back. I just got in my car and left. Never saw her again. She owed me God knows how much in commission, but I didn't give a fuck. I had never liked her, and I didn't respect her, so it was like, All right, luv, forget the fucking money. See ya. I was relieved to get shot of her. After all, I'd only done it for a bet, and I was exhausted. It was one less person to worry about.

Yet I couldn't stop that thought at the back of my mind: what if something else happened? I have to take care of my children, I have to work . . . But in the end Ozzy was right in what he'd always said: that I was spreading myself too thin. Even though I was now down to only two bands, what with him and three young children it was ridiculous. So I told both Bonham and the Quireboys that I was retiring from management. 'God bless, good luck, just go.' They both got other managers, but neither of them did much after that. And neither did Lita, the old cunt. I can't say it was because I wasn't there; it was just the way it panned out.

Half the problem, I realised, was my insistence that we live in England although Ozzy earned his living in North America and Japan. I had tried as long as I could to keep the kids grounded at the same schools and with nice friends but it was making us live apart, and as much as I wanted my children to be brought up in England, I wanted to keep us together as a family. I felt so guilty it was destroying me. If I didn't spend time with Ozzy then I wouldn't have a husband, because you can't keep a husband like that. So I would go to Ozzy, and then come home to the children, and then out to Ozzy and back again. It was just insane. As much as Ozzy was travelling, I was having to do three or four times more.

So we decided to move to Los Angeles, and we found a rental in Pacific Palisades, just down the coast from Malibu, because the children so loved the beach and it's a well-heeled suburb, very family-orientated, and they went to a Calvin Christian school with strict uniform, and we were very happy there.

---

21 April 2005, 11.00 a.m.
Doheny Road, Beverly Hills

Ozzy was very sweet when he found his roses this morning. He brought one up to me and laid it on the pillow, and I found it when I woke up. I still haven't told him about the party, and just hope Howard and Dave can disguise the preparations.

I pull up outside the Beverly Hills Hotel. The door of the Bentley is opened for me.

'Hi, Chris!'

'Hi, Sharon, howya doin'?'

I have known Chris for over thirty-five years. When I first stayed here in 1968 he was a parking boy. Now he owns the parking lot. In all that time, barely a month has ever gone by when I haven't been here. When we lived across the street, it was like our neighbourhood diner. We'd come here for all our meals, including breakfast. They even did packed lunches for the kids to take to school.

It's also my local beauty salon and I've been coming here for years. Kay, who runs it, is Korean and a true character. She will hug you half to death. Sometimes she'll come to Doheny, washing my hair at the kitchen sink because we've got this amazing spray attachment there; then while Kay does her magic with the hairdryer, Fariba, a lovely lady from Iran, will do my nails or wax my legs. But I prefer coming here. There's always some drama going on in the salon, and everybody knows me and Ozzy, and Kay will tell me all the gossip, who's been in, who's had a terrible face-lift.

16

Pacific Palisades

In many ways, although we had changed continents, life continued much as before. I was that mum who got the kids up and took them to school, I was that mum who made sure they had their lunches and picked them up from school and sat with them and tried to make them do their homework, and gave them parties and made sure that Christmas was always great and that they had a stable lifestyle.

I tried to shield them from the worst of Ozzy's drunken or stoned excesses, and Kelly and Jack were really too young to understand. But Aimee did. All I was able to do to balance it was to give them as normal an upbringing as I could while Ozzy would disappear from time to time, on the road, or into rehab.

One time I was visiting Ozzy in the latest rehab and Aimee was with me. I was just looking for my car keys when this man came up.

'Mrs Osbourne?'

I smiled.

'I think you should know that your husband has Parkinson's disease.'

'Excuse me? You're a doctor and you're telling me this in a car park in the facility, with my daughter stood here? And, for the record, he does not have Parkinson's.'

'I'm telling you. I'm a fully trained doctor.'

'And I'm telling you, you're a twat and fuck off.'

I was furious. Here I was on the fucking gravel in a pissy car park, and he's saying, 'Oh I think you should know that your husband has Parkinson's.' How fucking dare he.

I'd had this at two other detoxes. When you're an alcoholic you sweat and you shake until you get your next drink. So he would go into rehab. And that's how they would see him. So that's what they thought it was.

Ozzy had always had a weird body language, and over the years I'd got used to it. But one day he woke up and his foot was like a dead foot, it just flapped, and there was no muscle tone in his calf. So we went to a sports injury place, and they couldn't fix it. 'Neurological'. So then we went from one neurologist to another and nobody knew what it was. We had every test in the world, brain scans, cat scans, dog scans. Finally we went to one guy who did a spinal tap, and he said, 'He's got MS.' I didn't know what MS was so I looked it up. Multiple sclerosis. I freaked.

I didn't dare tell Ozzy. For six months I went to an MS support group at UCLA, just twenty minutes back down Sunset in Westwood, trying to understand the disease, trying to work out what to do for the best. The dead foot thing never happened again, but the long-term prognosis was very scary. Ozzy was forty-four. I would take long walks around the Lake Shrine in Pacific Palisades, ten acres of lake and park in celebration of spiritual enlightenment, beautiful gardens filled with religious symbols and quotations from the Bible and the Koran. And it was there, on my own, that I made up my mind.

Ozzy's latest album, *No More Tears*, was the biggest he had ever had, and the huge follow-up tour was happening and it was sold out everywhere. So we talked and I said I thought it was time to call it a day. The constant touring and the constant abuse of his body with drink and drugs had finally taken its toll, I told him. But he would be going out on a high. And so he agreed. And we turned his No More Tears tour into the No More Tours tour. And I was just talking to Gloria about it – the only person in the world I could trust with the MS diagnosis was my girl-friend – and we thought, wouldn't it be nice to end where Ozzy began, which was with Sabbath.

We put it to them and everyone agreed except Ronnie Dio, who'd gone back to singing with them. So the other guys in the band said, OK, we'll find another singer. Rob Halford was from Birmingham, just like they all were, and he had no ego problem. He was in a band called Judas Priest, a very big band at the time, and he was overjoyed to step in and to be there with everyone on this special occasion. So Sabbath performed a set with Rob singing, then Ozzy took the stage with his band and did his set, then Ozzy came back on with the three original guys from Sabbath for four songs, and it was great, and very emotional.

Just before these last few gigs, the head of Ozzy's record com-pany said he wanted to talk to me alone. CBS had by then become Sony, and it was run by Tommy Mottola, a great music man who managed Hall and Oates. *No More Tears*, the album, had done such great business that he couldn't understand what all the talk of retirement was about. So I had no option but to tell him about the MS.

'Are you sure about this, Sharon?'

'Sure I'm sure. I had it from his neurologist.'

'Have you had a second opinion?'

'No.'

'For this you need a second opinion. I'm going to find you the best neurologist in America and you're going to go see him.' And he found a man in Boston at a place called the Caritas St Elizabeth's Medical Center, where they do a lot of research on neurological disease, and Tommy organised a plane from Detroit where Ozzy was playing. And this MS specialist looked at Ozzy, looked at his brain scans and basically said, 'Fuck off. You're wasting my time. He's not got MS.' Ozzy had no idea what he was talking about. He was dumbstruck when I told him the situation. He wasn't angry I'd kept him in the dark, he was thankful. He said that if he had known, he would probably have killed himself.

St Elizabeth's was involved in joint research with the John Radcliffe Hospital in Oxford, and this guy suggested we saw a colleague there for a third opinion. And so when the last two gigs with Sabbath were done, we went back to England and saw this man: 'Nothing, go away.'

But Ozzy's symptoms were still there, and as years went by his body language got more and more bizarre, especially when he was drunk. Alcohol seemed to enhance it: some nights his body would be totally arched over and his hands would come up, like he was begging like a dog, and I thought it was the drink. It wasn't until ten years later, in the summer of 2003, that we came any closer to discovering what was wrong. By this time, Ozzy's body language was fucking ridiculous, but then so was his drinking. However, alcoholics shake when they don't have drink, not when they do. I had come to realise that it wasn't just the drinking, that there must be something neurologically wrong.

Michael J. Fox had just been diagnosed with Parkinson's, and I read an article in *People* magazine about the neurologist he'd gone to see, and how great this Dr Roper was and how he'd put him on certain medication which hadn't stopped the Parkinson's – you can never make it go away – but had stabilised it, and minimised the symptoms, which meant he was now living a really active life. I called up Dr Roper and asked if he'd see Ozzy, not because I thought it was Parkinson's, but simply because he was a good neurologist. So Ozzy went and was put through a whole series of tests. They sent his DNA away and then sent him to someone else and somebody else. And finally Ozzy was diagnosed.

Although it's quite normal for people to have one chromosome that's damaged in some way, the chances of two people meeting, falling in love and marrying who both have the same damaged chromosome are about one in a billion. But that's what happened with Ozzy's mother and father. But then, nothing with Ozzy is straightforward – that's what makes him so special. Right now, there are only three people in the world who have what he has. There's no name for it. Whenever you have something with your body that is shaky and is neurological in origin, they call it Parkinsonian syndrome. But it doesn't progress like a normal Parkinson's and you don't have all the things that you get with Parkinson's disease. They're now writing medical papers on him. Yes, one day Ozzy Osbourne is going to be famous in the medical world.

But back in 1992, I was faced with another problem: Ozzy's career. He couldn't just say, 'Oh, I thought I had MS, but it turns out to be some other weird shit.' Because you can be a drug addict in this business, you can be a murderer, but if you're sick, forget it, you're written off.

So we decided that Ozzy should have a year out. At least he came off a huge record. There were rumours in the industry – there always are, people talk. Is he well? Is he not well?

After Ozzy was misdiagnosed with MS, it put me off everything in America. All that certainty, that aggression everywhere you looked: Dont Walk, Dead End, Wrong Way, and I decided

I wanted to go back to England. By this time we had already sold Beel House. I had enough bad memories not to be too sorry to see it go. Also it had reached what the builder called the domino point: mending one thing only triggered something else that needed to be done.

So it was back to house-hunting again. My requirements were specific: it had to be in the Chalfonts, to be near the children's friends and schools; it had to be off the road; it had to have a lot of land. Suitable properties were few and far between.

The first thing I liked about Welders was the address: Welders House, Welders Lane, Jordans, Bucks, and – in what I took as a very positive sign – Jordans is a Quaker village, that is, not a pub in sight, so I flew over immediately to have a look. It was November 1992 and Lynn came with me. The approach was very romantic – an ancient road no wider than a cart track that in summer is so closed in by trees it's like driving through a green tunnel. When you come to a gap you know you've arrived. Leaving the car, we walked the rest of the way on foot, through the five-bar gate then down the drive, and there was Welders. It wasn't particularly pretty from the outside – it didn't have the elegance of Beel House – but this was a strong, handsome Victorian mansion.

Inside, however, it began to improve, and felt very warm and welcoming. The lady of the house showed us round. She told us how it had been built by Disraeli as a wedding gift for his daughter. This lady's husband built special effects for George Lucas. He had recently gone over to California and so they had decided to move there permanently. The dining room was full of the awards he'd got for the *Star Wars* series, including a Golden Globe.

Once you moved through the house to the other side, everything changed. The surprise was nearly as great as the Howard Hughes house. The terraced garden sloped down to a huge area of open grassland, and beyond it were trees stretching away as far

as you could see. So Lynn and I walked right down to the edge
of the forest and then looked back at the house, set up on its hill,
looking stately rather than elegant.

'This is just too good not to take,' I said. 'With this land, and
this situation, it's just too good.'

On the way back into London, all I was thinking was: how
can I make this house work? Because inside it was all over the
place. What I'd really wanted was somewhere we could move
into right away, but realistically I knew that was not possible. So
I called Ozzy.

'Get Colin over, and see what he thinks.'

So Colin came over. Stood, looked and said, 'If you don't buy
it, I will.'

Within three weeks it was ours, though Ozzy hadn't seen it
because he was still in California with the babies.

I was a bit worried that he'd freak when he saw it because of
the state it was in inside. By the time he got back, the builders
were already working on the roof, then the whole house needed
rewiring and replumbing. The kitchen area was a jumble of small
rooms: butler's pantry, larder, flower room and so on, so I
knocked everything out and made one big L-shaped room,
because we had to keep to the footprint of the original building.
Several rooms couldn't be touched at all as they were listed,
including the downstairs cloakroom, which is covered with fabulous hand-painted antique Delft tiles and has a lavatory that is
antique in itself. Upstairs I changed the configuration entirely.
The top floor had been used as model-making studio. Great
light, but no water and no heat. I turned this into the children's
floor, with three bedrooms and a bathroom, and painted the
whole landing area like a sky with fluffy white clouds. The children were still children then: nine, ten and eleven.

We put in a gym for Ozzy next to the kitchen, copying the
original roof design of the house, and doing the façade in old

bricks; now it looks as if it has always been there. Tucked in behind it we added a little courtyard with a fountain. In the meantime we rented a house in Gerrards Cross, a couple of miles away from Welders, so that the kids could be near their school and their friends, in an area they were familiar with. And it all worked out great. They settled straight back into the same schools they had left two years before, back to their old friends, their old life, as if they'd never gone.

1993 was one of the best years of our lives. We were neither of us working; we were together with our children in one of the most beautiful parts of England with a garden that seemed to stretch on for ever, where we could do what we liked when we liked. Even before the house was finished, we'd come over at weekends and go off on our quad bikes to explore the grounds, and I'd put together a picnic: French bread and salami, apples and bananas and fruit juice in cartons, and individual cheeses that the children loved to unwrap.

And we'd go down into the forest, find a grassy spot in the sunshine and lay out the rug, the kids would pick flowers, and Ozzy would help them climb trees or make little dams, and it was just idyllic. There was one long hot day in summer, I remember, where we stayed out till late. The bracken was as tall as Aimee and they played hide and seek, and everywhere were spires of purple foxgloves in patches of forest sunlight, and they would put them on their fingers and dance up to show us. And there wasn't a sound, except their voices ringing out and the birds singing and cawing, and butterflies dancing along the paths and the sun streaming golden through the beech trees, and we watched the sunset. Ozzy said it was one of those days he would never forget.

And sometimes, during those first few months before Welders was ready, we'd load our bicycles in the Range Rover then drive to the heart of the Chiltern hills, and go miles and miles along cycle paths, coming home with our picnic basket filled with bluebells. In the early summer we went up to Scotland to Inverness to look for the Loch Ness monster. We had the best time ever. Jack and Ozzy would take a flashlight out at night and go sit by the loch. We stayed in a little local hotel, and although the whole of Scotland seemed to be filled with American and Japanese tourists we never got bothered. We were allowed to be totally anonymous, just visiting old castles, having picnics by fast-flowing burns and being a family.

By the time Welders was ready to move into, our dogs were ready to come out of quarantine. There was Sugar, the boxer we'd bought at the pet shop in Malibu; Baldrick, a bulldog Ozzy absolutely adored who'd been given to him by Zakk Wylde, his guitar player, and a Cairn terrier called Toto. In the meantime we had bought Sunny, a German shepherd, for Aimee. It was her choice, so we asked for the most docile in the litter.

In our naivety we had both imagined that the quarantine kennels would be like a farm where the dogs could roam around. How wrong can you be? It was like a concentration camp. It was a concrete prison. They were never allowed out onto green grass, never allowed out of their cell.

Six months to the day we all went over to the quarantine place to collect the dogs. It was a Sunday, and it was closed. We stood there and couldn't believe it. So I went in and pleaded with the security guard to let us in and let us have our dogs, gave him the form showing when they'd arrived. And he said no, that it was more than his job was worth, and I went back to the car. So Ozzy basically said, Fuck this, and he started climbing over the fence. The security guard came rushing out shouting what the hell did he think he was doing and the rest of it. Then the guard recognised Ozzy as he was perched on top of this barbed-wire fence and he relented, and let Ozzy go in to get the three dogs. There are some occasions where being famous has its advantages, and this was one of them.

They were never the same again. For the first time in his life Baldrick lived up to his name: he came out with barely a hair on his head. It is the cruellest, cruellest thing, and I would never, ever do that again to any animal. Thank goodness there are now animal passports.

The idyll couldn't last. After a year Ozzy was itching to do something. At the time I did think that I could have just melted into domesticity, though I don't know how long it would have lasted. So I thought, Let's just go on a festival tour next summer. At a festival you have nothing to look after but yourself and a few of your crew. It's like taking a package holiday compared to organising a transpolar expedition.

When you take your own tour, as I had been doing with Ozzy ever since the beginning, the pressure is enormous. Each night you have to go into a different venue and do everything. You have already employed a tour manager to get you there in one piece, a production manager to take care of the production lights, sound and union crew, and a stage manager to run the stage as the show starts. But that still left a lot for me. The first thing I had to do was make sure everything was there on the 'rider' of the contract: these are things the promoter has agreed to provide.

First there was the technical rider, meaning what the band needed in terms of lights and sound if they were not taking their own: follow spots, operators for the follow spots, lighting rig with 200 to 500 multicoloured lights, breakdown of the sound system. If the building is new enough, then it would have an electrical supply powerful enough to maintain all the lights and sound. If not, the promoter would have to bring in an outside generator. All that would depend on the building. Then there would be all the stuff concerning the union: in most of the buildings you have to have union crew because they're union-run. This applies to some venues in England and all venues in America. In practical terms, this means they have to help you unload the trucks, they have to help you put up the lights and sound, even if you don't need them. Some of the buildings are so strict you cannot even bring in outside caterers. You can't even bring in your own dresser without having a union dresser in the building too. Because you have to pay them anyway, you get them to do something useful, like the washing or whatever. Then there's the crew food: the promoter will need to know what you need for your crew to eat. Some might be vegetarian, so they'll need to be told that. All this is on the technical rider.

Then there's the artists' rider. These have become notorious over the years, but I never played that kind of game. It was started by spoilt American rock bands in the eighties and was utterly childish – they did it just to see how far they could go. I've seen it all. Everything from rock bands who were on heroin so would need adult diapers because they were incontinent, to a prima donna who wanted a hundred Jo Malone candles in her dressing room and rose petals strewn everywhere. You would get people in Bumfuck, Idaho, who'd want sushi and yellowtail on their rider. You're never going to get sushi in the middle of the country, and if you did you'd probably get food poisoning.

Our artists' riders were always basic: clean fresh towels, a mirror, a couch, a carpet. We didn't have lavish backstage areas or food requirements, because ultimately the artist pays for it. It all comes out of their money. There's one rock band who, after the gig, likes to have chefs come and cook chateaubriand. So those caterers are staying late, they're probably working until two in the morning, and all that just to cook steaks and have some very expensive red wine. It's got to cost three to four grand, for just eight people. And if you imagine it's the promoter who's paying, dream on.

Axl Rose of Guns N' Roses would have huge parties back-stage after the show, catering for five hundred people. And that number of people backstage after a stadium concert is not so difficult. He'd have a big marquee put up and he'd have it catered, and there would be lighting, and a theme, like a disco night or a Southern night. He was not getting it for free, any more than he was getting the lighting rig free. It gets knocked off the profit. But Ozzy and I would look at all this and think, You idiots. We'd get on our old tour bus and stop at a truck stop to eat.

And as for the drugs and the women . . . Bands would send crew out into the audience to find good-looking girls to bring back. And the word would spread: this band had hundreds of girls and they were all blonde and they were mud-wrestling blah, blah. And then in the nineties it was all very gay, and there were all these young bands coming up and they were all fucking each other, and they thought it was so daring. We'd gone through all that in the seventies. They were so stoned they thought they were shocking. But we were, 'Oh dear, sorry, we've been there, seen all that.'

This was exactly what I was trying to avoid by joining somebody else's festival. Like Lollapalooza, which was *the* festival at the time. It was very hip and paid very well. If Ozzy went on a festival he would save half his crew: no lights, no sound, just his techs and the monitor guy. A handful of people; the saying is 'clean money'. And so, for six to eight weeks in the summer it's a gift: turn up, play, get paid, fuck off. Ozzy could have headlined for them: his audience was such that he could pull an audience of at least thirty thousand in any town. Some towns he could pull sixty or seventy thousand.

Lollapalooza was run jointly by the William Morris Agency and a singer-songwriter called Perry Farrell. So I called William Morris and said, 'How about Ozzy?' And the guy I spoke to basically said fuck off, or as he phrased it: 'Oh please, we don't take harder-edged bands, it's not cool.'

This was at the time when grunge was at its height, and in musical terms grunge turned out to be the least creative of any genre of music ever. The only band to survive the grunge fever is Nirvana, and then tragically the singer committed suicide. Back then if you didn't come from Seattle, you lied and said you did come from Seattle. The music industry is like that – full of small, blinkered peons. Bon Jovi came from New Jersey, so when Bon Jovi was big, everyone had to come from New Jersey. The same was true when Detroit was big. And in the early nineties, if you didn't come from Seattle and you weren't grunge, you were dead. You were over. The record industry is run by Yes Men who follow the bouncing ball, and if the bouncing ball is bouncing in Detroit or New Jersey and you're not from there, you're fucked.

There are so few pioneers in the music industry, people prepared to take a chance. Ahmet Ertegun is one of the great pioneers with the foresight and the gift to understand music. He went out on a limb and signed Led Zeppelin. Clive Davis is another one, the same as David Geffen – they didn't stick to one genre of music. But the majority are pampered, untalented also-rans who have no musical ability at all. I don't even know an A&R man these days who can play an instrument or read or write music. All they have is an ear for what is current.

So we were turned down, but it got me thinking. If Ozzy was having this problem, what about the rest of our genre of bands out there? What about the fans? If Lollapalooza didn't have 'hard-edged' bands, who did? True, they were very wholesome: Greenpeace would be there, and you could sign up to save the rainforest, and you'd go from forty singing monks on one stage to a hard rock band on another and Tom Jones on another. It was a mish–mash.

And then there was Lilith Fair, which was all women, the Greenham Common of the rock world, all long skirts and hemp and henna tattoos. So I decided what was needed was something that was not wholesome, not saving a fucking rainforest or any other charitable cause, where you didn't run the risk of any monks moaning, just hard-edged music from morning to night without a break.

And that was Ozzfest.

But it would take some time to organise, and in the meantime Ozzy was fretting to get back on the road, so that summer we did a three-month tour called Retirement Sucks, and there I was back in it again, doing all the work I had hoped to avoid.

One of the biggest problems I ever face is dealing with the support bands. Not the band members themselves, but their tour managers, the great majority of whom are fools, pumped–up, bumptious fools. Half of them are there by default, yet when they're out on the road they become bolshie little shits with the power to make life very difficult and niggly. They're like an insect bite you keep scratching that just gets more irritating. But when they get too big for their boots, I keep them in line.

We were playing a big arena in LA called the Forum, home of the LA Lakers, and the support band were called Korn. They were on the Epic label, as Ozzy was, and Tommy Mottola had begged me to take them and so I did; Tommy had been so fantastic to us with the MS business. And it's fair to say that the band was good musically speaking, but the people around them I called the Ship of Fools. They were all young guys who hadn't come up through the business and they didn't know shit from piss.

As I am running the tour I expect to be treated in a certain way, and I expect my headliner to be treated in a certain way, and I put down rules and regulations. For example, when Ozzy comes down the hallway to go on stage, I don't want to see anybody there. Not one single body or face. Because of course each band comes with its own posse of people: a friend of a friend, your next-door neighbour, your kids, people from the management company, people from the publishing company, merchandising people, girlfriend, drug dealer. A whole sea of people.

And there is nothing worse for an artist coming out of their dressing room, psyching themselves up to go on stage, than to have some idiot come up and say, 'Hey, Oz, this is my neighbour, can I have a picture and can you sign my girlfriend's tits . . .' I always make it a rule that I don't want to see any fucker for that five-minute period from when Ozzy leaves his dressing room until he gets out on that stage. It's his. The only people with him are the stage manager, the production manager, Ozzy's security and Tony. And they walk him nice and slowly to the ramp. He can psych himself up, do whatever he does before he hits that stage. I think to myself, he's fucking earned that time. And people should be respectful of that.

With Korn, we had a couple of times when there'd be some wanker doing this and doing that. And then a couple of times the band didn't turn up to the shows. And that is really disrespectful, not only to Ozzy and me – I would have to pick up a local band – but it's not what the kids have spent their hard-earned money for, and you want to give them a good show.

So one day I was talking to one of their managers – yes, it took two idiots to manage one band – and this guy was telling me how Korn were going to be making a video, so we were talking about the pros and cons and how horribly expensive it was.

And the next day they didn't turn up. This arsehole hadn't mentioned that the video shoot was the next day nor that they weren't planning to turn up for the show that night. This was the third time they hadn't turned up, so I called Epic and said, 'You can keep your band, they're off my tour. They can fuck off. They're not coming back.' The record company are begging and pleading. 'You can't do this, they're a young band, it's not their fault, it's their managers', and the rest of the bullshit. And I even get Tommy Mottola on the phone. So I go to Ozzy and explain the situation.

'Look,' he says to me. 'I feel sorry for them, they're young guys, let them back on to finish the tour.' So OK.

So they come back, and I'm backstage, going down the horrible metal and concrete staircase at the Forum, and the manager is coming up. And as he passes, he stops and he pats my arm. And I do not like being touched at the best of times.

'I'm so glad that Ozzy made you see sense,' he says, still patting.

Then I say, 'Take your fucking hand off me. Never touch me. Ever.' And his hand was still there. 'I fucking told you, take your hand off me,' I said again. He was a big man, six foot four and broad, and I kicked him in the knees with my foot, and he stumbled down the stairs.

From that day on there was very bad energy between us. Another time, one of their bands – again, let's call them the Two-headed Twat – wanted to leave and come with me. In the end it didn't work out, but a year or so later, one of the two original idiots called me up.

'I'm warning you,' he said. 'Stay away from the Twats, otherwise you will have no career in this industry.'

'Listen, kid,' I replied. 'When you were sucking on your mother's tits, I was working with artists that were selling millions and millions of records. Go fuck yourself.'

Backstage at Ozzfest, in 1999, with my 'baby-band' scout.

Taken at the Olympic torch ceremony in London, 2004.

Launching *The Osbournes* TV show. Kelly with Lulu, Ozzy with Maggie and Crazy Baby, Jack with Lola, me with Minnie.

Ozzy is one of the funniest men alive.

(*Right*) This was taken during the last photo shoot for the last *Osbourne* sho

During the hard weeks following my operation, Minnie never left my side.

Left to right: Jack, Kelly, Justin Timberlake, Barbara Davies, me, Elton John, Natalie Cole and Tony Bennett. They were helping to launch my charity.

Ozzy at the Queen's Golden Jubilee with Tom Jones, Rod Stewart and Paul McCartney. Only Ozzy would get to meet the Queen along with Kermit the Frog.

I was so thrilled to be on *Parkinson*, but it was a special honour to share the stage with Dame Judi Dench and Dame Edna Everage.

It was Michael who first suggested that my life might be worth writing a book about.

DAILY Mirror
Tuesday November 23 2004
www.mirror.co.uk 35p

GET ME OUT OF AIR!
NATALIE'S TERROR IN JUNGLE: PAGES

I WILL F***ING KILL YOU!

Naked Ozzy's rage as he fights £1m jewellery robber at his home

By NATHAN YATES

Osbourne was furious. He screamed at the raider, 5ft 2 being £20,000 of gem from his mansion yesterday.

They came inside John Ozzy's home while he and wife Sharon were asleep – hours after he went to a birthday party at London's The restaurant.

FULL STORY: PAGES 4&5

TOUGH GUY: Ozzy bares tattooed torso before the raid

EXCLUSIVE

DAILY Mirror
Tuesday December 9 2003
NEWSPAPER OF THE YEAR 32p

Sweetest chariot

By ALUN PALMER

OZZY Osbourne had quad surgery yesterday after a quad bike crash.

The rocker broke six ribs, collarbone which was left peaceful on a machine was left...

FULL STORY: PAGE 11

OZZY IN QUAD BIKE HORROR

Six ribs and collarbone broken, blood in lungs

The 55-year-old rocker had emergency surgery following the smash in which he broke his collarbone, six ribs and a neck vertebra.

He had an operation to ease bleeding in his lungs and surgeons lifted his collarbone which was resting on a major artery.

The former Black Sabbath frontman, who suffers minor injuries, crashed the machine while he was riding around his vast estate in Chalfont St Giles, Bucks, where he has been taking he spent off from his busy timetable.

His publicist Cindy Guagenti said: "The accident occurred while he was taking a day off from his promotional schedule surrounding the UK release of Changes, a song duet with his daughter Kelly.

"Doctors revealed Ozzy had broken his collarbone, six ribs and a vertebra in his neck." Guagenti said the injuries were not life threatening but confirmed Sharon had rushed to the Wexham Park hospital in Slough, Berks, to be at her husband's side.

A family friend said: "Ozzy is fine and in good spirits. He wasn't going at all that great a speed but suffered some bad injuries.

"He is just grateful it was nothing more serious."

Ozzy, who owns several quad bikes, managed to struggle free.

CRASH: A quad bike

and staggered from the manor house to raise the alarm after the crash. He was taken by ambulance to hospital.

The accident happened just hours after the singer claimed he was cured of a debilitating condition which he blames on a singing career.

He said he was now walking and talking normally after firing the doctor who prescribed him copious amounts of valium, dexedrine, myorine and other drugs.

Over 15 months he spent £36,250 on prescription drugs and more than £900,000 on doctor's fees.

Ozzy said: "I was wiped out on pills. I couldn't walk. I could barely stand up. I was lumbering about like the Hunchback of Notre Dame.

"We got to the point where I was scared to close my eyes at night afraid I might not wake up." He condition got so bad he even had tests for Parkinson's Disease.

Ozzy started filming the third series of The Osbournes – MTV's hit reality show about his family – a month ago.

The programme was scheduled to begin on January 13.

An MTV spokesman said it was not clear how the accident would affect production or whether it might even be included in the latest series.

alun.palmer@mirror.co.uk

SHARON RUSHES TO SIDE OF INJURED OZZY

Rocker has surgery after accident

By ALUN PALMER, EMMA BRITTON and TOM PARRY

OZZY Osbourne's distraught wife Sharon last night raced to his hospital bedside after he was badly hurt in a quad bike crash at his country mansion.

The 55-year-old rocker had emergency surgery following the smash in which he broke his collarbone, six ribs and a neck vertebra.

ROCKER: Ozzy shows off his motorcycle at home in Los Angeles

OZZY WIFE IN FIGHT FOR LIFE

Agony of cancer op

by ROBIN HUTCHISON

ROCKER Ozzy Osbourne was in shock last night as his wife was fighting for her life.

Dour soap star Sharon had hoped for an all clear after an operation for colon cancer.

But she's now been told the disease has spread to her lymph nodes and will need chemotherapy. Shattered Ozzy had to be woken after learning his wife had cancer it has emerged.

The former Black Sabbath singer said he "completely lost it" when he heard Sharon had been diagnosed with cancer.

"I've done a lot of praying believe it or not," he said.

INJURED: Jack Osbourne

OZZY Osbourne's teenage son Jack had a call trauma, Jack yesterday. The 18-year-old was suffering from exhaustion. He's now with pals being filmed by a TV crew at the time. Osbournes said he was going to show son that he was a man.

THE Sun
30p
www.thesun.co.uk 30p
Tuesday, November 23, 2004

BATTLE: Ozzy with Sharon, who ne

Kerry: Nat's so like me

I'M a Celeb cheeky Kerry McFadden last night backed Natalie Appleton to win the hearts of millions. The reality TV star says Natalie Appleton, who could soon win...

PAGES 6 & 7

Sophie: I'm still nutty!

SINGLE mum...

FOILED: 9/11 ON LONDON

By DAVID WOODING, Whitehall Editor

AN al-Qaeda plot to fly planes into three skyscrapers at London's Canary Wharf and nearby Heathrow has been foiled. The 9/11-style plot to attack Britain's tallest buildings is shown up in fire from bin Laden...

Target . . . Canary Wharf

Continued on Page Nine

EXCLUSIVE: STAR'S 4am TERROR

OZZY: I had £2m gem raider in headlock

By JAMIE PYATT and SUE EVISON

REVISED Ozzy Osbourne desperately grappled with a masked £2MILLION gems raider inside his Buckinghamshire mansion.

Unarmed Ozzy, 56, wrestled the armed raider to the ground before he fled after one of a gang threatened both him and wife Sharon. The angry star said he wanted to protect Sharon, right, who was staying with them.

Continued on Page Four

DAILY STAR
THE NEWS THE GOSS THE PICS THE SPORT
TUESDAY, December 9, 2003 NOW WE DO IT EVERY DAY 30p

OZZY BREAKS NECK AND SIX RIBS

by ANTHONY WALTON

OZZY Osbourne was seriously ill in hospital last night after breaking his neck in a horror quad bike smash.

The 55-year-old former Black Sabbath frontman also suffered multiple internal injuries.

Last night he was undergoing emergency surgery. Doctors were trying to stem the flow of blood into his lungs, his spokeswoman revealed.

The accident happened as Ozzy was racing around the grounds of his 18th century manor house at Chalfont St Peter, Bucks. He is thought to...

Turn to page 11

Rocker in bike smash

Just when life seemed too good to be true, fate decided to put the boot in.

(Credits: Top left: Mirrorpix; all others: John Frost Historical Newspapers)

Kelly and I collected the Emmy award for *The Osbournes* on behalf of us all. I was still having my chemo at the time.

It was Simon Cowell who made my TV career in the UK possible.
(Rex Features)

(Overleaf) Our love for each other is unconditional.

The last thing in the world anyone should do is threaten me. Because I don't threaten well. I was weaned by the King of Threats. And not only threats; somebody that actually would carry out those threats. So for people to get heavy with me it's like, You have no fucking idea who you are dealing with. Because I would bite your fucking head off and stick it up your arse. Nobody can frighten me.

---

21 April 2005, midday
Beauty salon, Beverly Hills Hotel

I'm sitting in Kay's salon, looking like an extra-terrestrial, my hair in silver-foil-wrapped spikes, waiting for the colour to 'cook'. Another client is talking to me, a woman in her thirties, a comedian. I don't know her except from seeing her on television.

'You know what, Sharon? This isn't bullshit, this is really straight talk. You should write a book. You are always so honest, and as a woman you could answer those questions about what to accept in a man. How do you know what you can work through and get past? How do you know you can overcome certain things?'

'You don't. But I learnt many, many years ago that if you're with a man and there are things that bother you, you can't change them. You think you can change them. You can't. You have to accept them.'

'It's intriguing to me how you can love them, and accept them. And what do you accept? But when do you walk? And how do you know when something can not just be safe, but can flourish? Like you made your relationship better. How do you know? How do you know when to walk?'

'I would walk, and walk over the other side and be more unhappy without him than with him. Nothing is perfect: this relationship was given to me for a span of time, and I was just better with him than without him. It's hard when you suddenly wake up and you're old enough to realise you can't ever change people. But that's just how it is. You can't.'

'But every woman is always wondering what do you take, and what don't you take? When do you stay and when do you go?'

'I was just better with him than without him.'

'I want an Ozzy,' the comedian said, laughing. 'The later years! And definitely you should write a book. It'd be a bestseller.'

17

Ozzfest

From the moment it began in 1996, Ozzfest was a huge success. That first year, we did only two dates, Phoenix and Los Angeles. It took the same format as the other festivals, in the sense that it started early and went on all day, but it was a completely different vibe. You could get your tongue pierced, your tit pierced, and no way could you sign up for a good cause. But I had no idea when I started that we would still be doing it in ten years' time. The following year, it really took off. In 1997 we went to twenty-two cities around America.

To give an idea of the scale of the operation, we travel with about sixty crew, all employed directly by us. There are two stages — one the permanent stage at the venue, plus a second stage that gets put up when we arrive. Ozzy always headlines, playing last, and there are twenty other bands, again, all paid by us. The total number of people on the road ranges from 500 to 600, depending on how many are in the bands and their entourages. To put that in perspective, every day we cater for 550 people, three times a day, with extra food to take to their buses after the show.

In addition there is the union crew, locally employed. There are the buses for the bands and crew and then there are the trucks for the equipment. And then there are the carnies. The carnies are like the fairground part of it: they do a climbing wall, 'Aunt Sally' stalls, that sort of thing. The same people travel around with the tour. I have nothing directly to do with the carnies. All I do is approve what they do: one of them spray-paints topless women, one does tattooing. I don't pay them; they buy space on the concourse area.

We play in 'sheds', what in England are called amphitheatres: outside venues of about sixty acres of ground, with permanent stages, permanent backstage facilities, and permanent facilities of toilets and drinks and food. The roof over the stage covers about ten thousand seats – these are the premier seats, which cost more. Then you have the lawn area that has no shade or cover, which can take another 20–30,000 people. And there are towers and PA systems and screens so people can see and hear. Then there's the area when you first enter the building where you can get refreshments and get into the carnie concourse.

When it comes to the Ozzy official merchandise, the T-shirts, the CDs, although we provide everything, the facility actually sells it, using their staff and taking a percentage, and they make shitloads of money because we open the doors at nine thirty in the morning and close at eleven at night.

The area we use for the second stage is usually a portion of the car park. As soon as we arrive, our crew put up the stage with the help of the local union crew, with a sound system and tents to change in. In order to get it up and running by nine thirty, when the first band starts playing, they have to have been working for two and a half hours. Usually our crew have loaded and

packed the trucks from the previous night by three in the morning. So it's very, very tight. As our main stage doesn't start until
four, everyone works first on getting the second stage up and
running.

This second stage is used for what I call the baby bands, the
new, untried bands. When we first started out, I was ten years
younger than I am now and I was still on the street, still very
much into new bands, but Jack has done these now for years. At
the age when most boys were doing a paper round, he knew
every band, every label, every producer. At thirteen he was an
intern for Virgin. He has a very good ear, and some of the bands
that Jack put in ten years ago are still out there. I don't get
involved; the thing is, if I am into these bands, if a fifty-plus
woman connects to their lyrics, then there's something terribly
wrong. But you know what's good and you know what's crap
instinctively. It's something that's born into you.

Putting a festival together is a bit like putting an outfit
together, or a fashion show. It has to be the same genre. Other
festivals mix and match, especially in Europe. You get a lot of
people now who will go out with hip hop bands: they want to
be cutting-edge, they want to be cool. But you wouldn't put
Celine and Pink together, you wouldn't put Gwen Stefani and
Barbra Streisand together; it wouldn't work. So many people try
to fix it when it's not broken and we don't. We just stay true to
what we are. Hard core.

Ozzfest is a huge undertaking, bigger than anything I had done
before. I had my LA office to back me up – Michael Guarracino
and Dana Kiper were already with me – but if I wasn't travelling,
I was on the phone till four in the morning. I was already in my
forties, and it just wasn't fun any more. I remember being in a
state of permanent exhaustion; I even looked forward to the
flights as that was the only time I would have people looking

after me and not the other way round. But if I hadn't done it, I wouldn't have had a marriage – it was that simple. Ozzfest was everything I had ever wanted: big money coming in and Ozzy topping the bill. And in the end it got too much for me to do from England. Not only the sheer scale of the organisation, but with the newer bands, these were just kids, they had to be US-based, and I had to see them.

We talked about it and said, 'Oh fuck it, let's give it a couple of years, let's go over there again, let's do whatever Ozzy's career's going to do.' There was never any question of selling Welders. We were coming back in two years. And the kids were fine about it. All they ever wanted was for us all to be together, they didn't care where.

So there we were, back in Los Angeles, looking for somewhere to buy and living in a rental house off Coldwater Canyon owned by Don Johnson, who made it big in *Miami Vice* in the eighties. It was the early summer of 1997 when September Films, an independent English TV production company, asked if they could come and film Ozzy and his family at home – that was the kind of docu-entertainment programme they did.

Ozzy is one of the funniest men alive and I always knew he was a TV natural, it was just nobody ever got beyond the Prince of Darkness thing, and it would give us great family footage to look back on. And the kids were eleven, twelve and thirteen at this time, so they would enjoy it. We said yes. But in fact when I saw the finished thing I thought it was really corny. But what do I know? *Ozzy Osbourne Uncut* went on to win the Rose d'Or at the Montreux International Television Festival in Switzerland. It was repeated five times in one year on Channel 5.

About a year later, MTV called to ask if they could come and do a *Cribs* episode at our house. *Cribs* was a regular series of glimpses into celebrities' homes and private lives, and again we said yes. Just the kids and Ozzy, though; I didn't want to do it.

By then we had bought a house. The good news was that nothing needed to be done to it. The bad news was that Beverly Drive turned out to be the LA equivalent of the North Circular. It doesn't look like a major highway, but the traffic never stops.

There's this saying that inside every fat person there's a thin person trying to get out, and it is so true, at least for me. I started dieting when I was fourteen; I went to my first health farm when I was fifteen. Through my fat phases I knew I was bloody fat and when I was thin I knew I was thin. Sometimes I would feel that I had spent my entire life dieting.

However, the only thing that really made me lose weight was serious trauma: my father's betrayal in 1979, Ozzy's murder attempt in 1989. I was in my mid-forties, and I had everything in my wardrobe from a size 4 (American) to a size 22 and I would get more and more disheartened, and when I saw myself in the mirror I would just weep. Weep on the inside, never on the outside.

Now it was coming up to 1999, but there were no traumas in sight. In fact, quite the opposite. Ozzfest was doing great, and we were more secure financially than we had ever been in our lives.

Ozzy was in hospital in LA trying out yet another detox procedure, this time one where they changed his blood. And I was visiting one day and talking to this doctor about how coping in the heat was so difficult when you are fat, and he said he had a friend, a Dr Phoby, who did a medical weight-loss procedure. A diet trains your stomach to shrink; this procedure shrinks it surgically. They cut your stomach and make a new pouch in your intestinal tract, so you get rid of the food you eat very quickly. Also, you can't eat much anyway because your new stomach isn't big enough. Ozzy had no objections. 'You know I love you as you are,' he said, 'but if that's what would make you happy, you go for it.'

People who have never been up to a dress size 22 have no idea just how miserable everything becomes when you're that big. I had gone up and down and I had seen the difference in the way people treat you when you're big and when you're skinny. When I was skinny, people would wonder if I was Ozzy's sister. When I was big it was, 'Are you his mother?' So when I had the opportunity put in front of me, I took it and never looked back.

How you look is the emotional burden you carry around, but there's a physical burden as well. When you're large, you have to wash a lot more because you smell. Your body is having to work harder, so you sweat more and it gets trapped in the layers of fat. Just getting around in the heat is like climbing a mountain. And for me, actively working, having to run around a facility in Texas or Nevada in the height of summer was a fucking nightmare. I couldn't wear heels any longer because my feet couldn't take the strain. My back was beginning to give me trouble: just the weight of your bra straps carrying around vast 40GGG breasts. And things like going on a plane and having to ask for an extra belt to attach onto the end of the normal-sized seat belt. It's a permanent scourge, self-humiliation the whole time. People who say that their weight doesn't bother them are in denial. I used to say to people, 'Look, I'm married, I've got my children, what do I care?' But I cared that I couldn't go up stairs, that Jack had to push me from behind.

When I was large, I avoided having my picture taken. I would die at functions – just finding an evening dress I could get into was difficult enough, but when you're well over 14 stone in a long dress you look awful whoever it's made by, and I would always feel conspicuous, even though I would be underdressed. You can't go looking like a Christmas tree. And whenever the big awards ceremonies were coming up, it was torture, and I wished I could have gone as a head on a plate. As it was, I went big on handbags – I'd spend thousands on handbags – or a great piece of jewellery. I would shift the focus, hiding behind my jewellery and my handbags and my meticulous hair and make-up and nails. I would spend two hours doing my make-up every day. Not a lot, but it had to be perfect.

So I was booked in to have this operation with Dr Phoby when another doctor friend of mine said they were doing a brand-new procedure at Cedars-Sinai and were looking for guinea pigs. And then he paused, before he told me that you had to fit the criteria. What criteria? You had to be obese, he said. Obese is a hard word. But I went, and I fitted the profile: age, weight, history of yo-yo dieting, and they took me, and it was free. I felt happier with this procedure than the other one because it was far less invasive. No cutting your intestinal tract – they just bind your stomach with a plastic band. I was in hospital for four days.

My surgeon was Dr Phillips, and I call him my guardian angel. He is an amazing man and he gave me back my life twice, because he also removed my cancer. The procedure itself had been tried out in Europe but hadn't been approved for use in America, which was why they wanted guinea pigs. It does now have the stamp of approval, but it's still only available to people classified as obese. Where women are concerned this means over 200 pounds in weight. Insurance companies have finally realised that to be obese is a danger to your health, and you're less at risk if you're not fat, and therefore you're less of a risk for them.

When people say something changed their life, it's usually an exaggeration, but this did change my life. Utterly and completely and in every way imaginable and unimaginable.

I could eat exactly what I wanted, all my usual crap food: chocolate, milkshakes and fries, but suddenly, I'd have a plate of chips, eat four and couldn't face any more. I wasn't hungry. I didn't know how much I was going to lose. This procedure hadn't been done before, so there wasn't a brochure saying, 'This is what you can expect', or any before and after pictures. It was slow at first, but I was losing weight steadily every week, and then the momentum picked up and the weight fell off and I loved it, loved it. I felt rejuvenated and had so much more energy, and my feet didn't hurt any more and my back didn't hurt any more. You don't realise till it's gone how hard it is just lugging all that weight around all the time, especially when we were on the road, when it could be over 100 degrees and I'd have to work.

In a year I lost 125 pounds. I started out at 225 and went down to 100. From 16 stone down to just over 7. But I wasn't the sylph I had been in 1979: the fat might have gone, but the skin lingered on. So the next thing was plastic surgery to have the excess skin removed, and the fat that hadn't shifted. I hadn't realised this would be necessary, and nobody had warned me because nobody knew what would happen, how much weight I would lose; I was a guinea pig.

I had my breasts lifted, I had my legs lifted, my arse lifted, I had a tummy tuck, the top of the thighs done. Liposuction everywhere. And it wasn't only my body. My face was hanging from the sheer loss of weight. I didn't have my nose done, or my eyes, or my lips, because they weren't where the extra weight had been. But I had a full face-lift, including my neck. Each operation had to be done individually. If you had that much work done together, you'd die.

It took me a year to throw out all my big clothes, as if I didn't really believe those days were gone for good, but I did keep a couple of outfits as a reminder of why I never want to go back there again. Trousers with legs so wide I could now get my whole body into them, and a bra like two fucking bowler hats. Now, when I look back at the pictures, I don't recognise myself. Like the pictures of Ozzy's fiftieth birthday party, in January

1998. Just because I'm fat in them, though, I'll never try to hide the picture away in some drawer – it's part of my life.

It was about three months before I bought anything new. And then it was like being given the key to Aladdin's cave. There were all these clothes I could never have dreamt of wearing before, things with colour and texture, things with sparkles and beads, pleated fabric, embroidered fabric, quilted fabric – it was a complete luxury. And so I began to buy, not fashion pieces, but glorious, timeless pieces that you can hand on to your kids, vintage pieces that will go on and on. I could finally wear clothes by Vivienne Westwood. I first knew her years and years ago when she was with Malcolm McLaren. She designs for women who have women's bodies, not for stick insects – but when you're really big you can't wear clothes like that.

Children never like change, even though it might be for the better, and particularly if it concerns their mother. They all took it differently. Kelly used to complain that she didn't like to cuddle me any more because I didn't feel the same. Aimee didn't like my new way of dressing; she missed the flowing, flowery summer tents I used to wear. And Jack didn't have to push me up the stairs any more. But for me, being able to go upstairs without even thinking about it, to run to separate two dogs that were fighting – it was unimaginable.

There is a downside. I still eat the wrong foods and, as a result, I get terrible reflux, acid bile. And when I eat too fast, too late at night, if the food won't go down, the only way is up, and I'm sick. It's not like I'm throwing up from my stomach; it hasn't had time to get that far. So I just have to eat terribly slowly and in tiny bits. I was told that a glass of wine would help to relax the muscles, so for the first time in nearly twenty years I began to drink again. Not much, a glass or two with dinner, and that's it. But never, ever in front of Ozzy.

The children want me to have the band taken off; they think

that my stomach is trained now, and that I won't put the weight back on. But for me that isn't an option. I know myself too well. I would just eat it all back again. But it's a problem. Ozzy may want to eat late, but I just can't. I keep hoping that one day, when I'm calmer, I will stop eating shit. But that's a long-term hope.

The moment I realised that everything really had changed was in May 2002 when *People* magazine included me in their list of fifty most beautiful women, and they gave me a double-page spread. I had never ever considered myself beautiful. That word was never used for me. Ozzy called me beautiful, but then he loved me, so I could never accept it as fact. And for the shoot I wore this fabulous red evening gown. Red! For years I had the choice of only one colour, black. Black made shape invisible.

With all this excess energy at my fingertips, I decided to go back into management. I mean, I was only forty-five, what was I supposed to do with my life from now on? My first signing was a young band who'd debuted on Ozzfest, called Coal Chamber. Their manager was a nice guy but young and inexperienced. So they had a big hit album with me, and then they were making their second record and they fired me. The same old story. History repeating itself, but by now I honestly didn't care. I didn't give a shit, and I promised Ozzy I would never do management again.

But then I heard that Smashing Pumpkins were looking for a manager, and I decided this was different. I really loved their music. I was a big fan. And it was like a game to me, because every big manager was after them. Bill Elson bet me about Lita Ford; this time I was betting myself. The lead singer, a guy called Billy Corgan, had a bad reputation in the business for being difficult. But I always judge people on my own radar, so I flew into Chicago, and it was loved me, loved them. We got on great. And when he told me he wanted me to manage them, I cried, because he had so much talent and he'd seen everybody.

He was a dream. He was a complete doll. Then slowly, like an illusionist's trick, he turned into a fucking alien in front of my very eyes. He wasn't even ordinary horrible, he was one of the meanest, most twisted people I've ever had the misfortune of working with. He would be openly nasty to people. Journalists, record company people, you name it. And he basically did not need a manager, because whatever you suggested he did the opposite. All he needed was a glorified secretary, which he already had, a nice girl who used to work for a Chicago promoter, and she would do all the bring-me-fetch-me, book-me-a-fucking-massage shit. And nobody could get to him without going through her, his human buffer. What she ever saw in him I shall never know. If it had been the Brad Pitt vibe I'd have got it. But this man was a light bulb in trousers, Yul Brynner's mutant brother. The band was named after a Halloween vegetable and it suited them.

We were doing the first video for the album and Billy had these outrageous clothes made. He put himself in a long black dress and he looked like Uncle Fester from the Addams Family, and his whole band was in dresses.

'You can't do this,' I said. 'You're spending fortunes on these clothes and they're crap and you look fucking ridiculous.' He wanted to do all his interviews for this project in the character of another person and, on his rider, he wanted that the promoter should find the ten ugliest people in each city to be in the audience.

'If that gets out in the press you're in big trouble. What is it for?'

'It's art.'

So we were touring Europe, and the tour opened in Germany and the head of the German record company was going to be there. So I asked Billy if he wanted to meet this guy before or after the show.

'They're cunts,' he goes. 'I don't want to meet them.'

'You know what, Billy,' I said. 'It goes a long way when somebody is personally involved with you. People have to do their work, but if they like you, if they're personally involved, they put that little bit extra into it. Be nice, they're doing their job.'

He agreed, and the next day we all went to dinner with the record company executives. And it was very strained and I was overcompensating with my silly chat. And Aimee was there with me, and Billy Corgan had a Russian girlfriend. And this young girl and Aimee would talk together. So Aimee got up to go to the bathroom and she came back and said 'Excuse me', to Billy to get back to her place at the table. And he said, 'Go fuck your-self, I'm not moving.'

So I'm like: OK. All right-ee. OK. And he continued to be belligerent throughout dinner. It was the same thing at the show: he wouldn't have anybody come backstage, wouldn't meet and greet, and I'm like, This is just fucking ridiculous. So finally I asked for a meeting, and the answer came back through his assistant.

'Billy doesn't do meetings after shows.' So I'm sitting in the hotel and it's snowing. And I'm there with Aimee, and I think: What the fuck am I doing? I said I would never do this again. So I got on the phone to Michael in LA, where it was mid-morning.

'Michael, I want you to put out on the wire service a press release saying: "Due to medical reasons I have to resign as Billy Corgan's manager. Because he makes me sick."'

Then I went downstairs and got the barman to get every single person in that bar a drink, and charged them to Billy's room. Then I got three first-class tickets to LA for Aimee and myself and the tour manager, a lovely man called Nick Cua, somebody with whom I'd worked on and off for twenty-five years. When I'd told him Aimee and I were off, he'd said, 'Don't think I'm staying. I'm only here because of you.' All three tickets I charged to Billy Corgan's room.

And he became a laughing stock, because his reputation as a pig had gone before him, and every manager in the industry called me and was like, YES! Finally a manager has turned on an artist. Because it is always the artist who fires the manager, as I had been fired before. And it was always 'my record wasn't a hit because of my manager', or 'my tour wasn't a success because of my manager'. It was the first time the tables had been turned. Very wisely his publicist told him not to comment. The band split up the following May. He was so talented that it turned round and bit him in the arse. From that day on I swore to myself, never, ever again. And I never will. It is the worst job in the world. As for what to do for the rest of my life, I would just have to find something else. Nothing ever goes as planned, never has. I can never plan. I try to but it just never works out.

We were soon hearing on the grapevine that our episode of *Cribs* had become the most requested thing on MTV. The MTV demographic is young people between the ages of twelve and twenty-four, and kids can call in and ask to see things they particularly like again. And if they get enough calls, that's what happens. And these fly-on-the-wall *Cribs* were always being asked for, but ours more than anybody else's, it seemed. So then I called MTV and said, 'Let's talk. I want to know what we can do together.' I had a couple of lunches with the people who do programming on the west coast, gave them a video of the September Films *Ozzy Osbourne Uncut*, and what I was basically suggesting was an extended version of that. And they bought it. Three shows.

Naturally, as nothing could work without our children's co-operation, they had been involved right from the start. And while Kelly and Jack couldn't wait, Aimee declined, which she had a perfect right to. I suggested she might like to take on a producer's role.

It took a long time to get going. Since doing the *Cribs* episode we had bought a new house; in the end the traffic on Beverly Drive had sent me insane. I wanted out. So we sold it before buying anywhere else. I bought the house in Doheny Road because it was the only one that came near to fitting our requirements and by then I was desperate. But it was like, love the location, love the road, hate the house.

The owner was some African potentate/king/president. But the price was good because he was having to get out quick. His taste in interior design and mine did not coincide, so I decided the only thing to do was to rip everything out and start again.

We gutted the place and reconfigured it. Downstairs we made two rooms – Ozzy's and my sitting rooms – from one. Upstairs it was the other way round: our bedroom used to be two rooms. By the time we finished everything was different. The hallway was different, the staircase was different: I had it copied from a picture I found in a magazine. The doors were all changed. The hinges on the front door were taken from moulds of Kelly's hands. The chimneys stayed in the same place, but I hated the surrounds. Pillars? Imported. Beams? Imported. The wonderful old wooden floors we have now? They didn't exist. Mr Potentate had had disgusting carpet. The wood of the floors is old (though not original to the house) but the shine is nothing to do with age, just layers and layers of marine varnish, repainted every three months. The pool was originally immediately outside the games room, a horrible bright-blue thing that dominated everything, and I wanted something that would blend into the landscape.

Everyone has nightmare builder stories, but this was the worst.

We found one – highly recommended, as they always are – paid him a deposit and never saw him again. We found a second, he gutted the house and then, when it was down to a shell, disappeared with more of our money, and it was like, this place is cursed, let's just sell it.

But we didn't, because by then MTV were involved, so at least we could put their needs into the rebuild. There had to be a control room, permanent security. It had to be wired up for twenty-four fixed cameras in all the rooms except toilets and bathrooms. A long, long procedure, which took most of the summer, while Ozzy and I were on the road with Ozzfest. Shooting began in October 2001 and the first shows have us moving in, unpacking, getting our lives settled – and still decorating. The children were back to school, Ozzy was writing, I was going into the office, Melinda was there, the house staff were there, and it just had us living a life.

So after the third week, MTV said, 'You know what? We're getting such classic stuff we're going to stay another couple of weeks. Let's make it six weeks.' So they stayed six weeks. At that stage it was nothing more than a gut reaction; they hadn't even put together the first show.

And so life in the Osbourne household continued as usual. There's always a lot going on and it didn't really affect our day-to-day lives at all. You got used to the crew being there. It was a bit like being at school: there are all these other people around, but you're not really aware of them, you just get on with your work. Then the six weeks turned into six months.

The real work was being done by the editors, who had to look through hours and hours of footage every week and try and make some sense of it. It took six weeks to turn one show around. The first series was ten weeks, and that took a long, long time, and so it was six months before the first show was aired on 5 March 2002.

The following weekend, I took the kids to Venice Beach. It was just something we did as a family every so often – a day at the seaside, and this was a nice spring day in California. But this time Ozzy wasn't with us; he was away in Canada on his first solo tour since Ozzfest had taken over our lives. And on Sunday there are lots of little cafés, and everybody takes their dogs, and it's a bit like Covent Garden in London, with mime artists and people singing and roller-blading and little stalls that sell hand-made things, clothes, jewellery, artisan stuff.

So we're on the beach, wandering along with Minnie and Maggie, our Japanese Chin, and all these people kept stopping to talk to us, and I'm like, Jeez, this is really weird. I mean, the show has only aired once. It was six months since the cameras had first started rolling, but that was the first inkling we had that things were never going to be the same again.

---

21 April 2005, 3.00 p.m.
Doheny Road, Beverly Hills

My parents used to say we were 'cosmopolitan'. Our staff in Doheny are about as cosmopolitan as you can get. Saba is from Sudan, Dari who helps with the ironing is Russian, David the chef is from Essex, Tony is from Northumberland, Melinda is from Australia and Howard is from New Zealand. Howard is like our estate manager: he looks after the houses and the staff. And when our labrador Beau was here he would take him to his home in Pacific Palisades every night and have him sleep there, then take him for a run every morning on the beach. Howard is young, athletic and reliable. Not qualities that Ozzy or I can lay claim to any more.

'Howard, do you have Jack's number in Thailand?'

'Sure. Want me to give it to you?'

'Do you know what time it is there?'

'I can soon find out.'

'Would you do that for me?'

'Sure.'

Jack has been sober now for exactly two years. The fact that Jack, a kid then aged eighteen, could give it all up and stay clean for one whole year was what shamed Ozzy into trying just one more time. So I just want to tell him that I have remembered that it's his anniversary too. And to tell him that I love him. I miss him, but it's only a few days now before we see him in Thailand for his kick-boxing match.

18

Making It

We had barely got over the shock of the success of *The Osbournes* when two totally unexpected honours came Ozzy's way. The first was an invitation to the White House Correspondents' Association dinner on 5 May 2002. This event happens every year, and this was the eighty-eighth since it began. The President is the guest of honour, and the tables are all bought by newspapers and magazines who have White House correspondents, and each table invites a celebrity. Ozzy and I were invited by Greta Van Susteren. She is a lawyer-turned-commentator, and she covered the O. J. Simpson trial for CNN and did such an amazing job she joined them as their legal analyst. She then went to Fox news and is credited with turning the channel around. Her husband John is a lawyer in Washington. We met when she came to the house to interview us on the surprise success of *The Osbournes*, and we just got on – she adored my ragdoll cats, so I sent a kitten as a gift – and basically she and her husband are an amazing couple who, luckily for Ozzy and me, have become friends.

Neither Ozzy nor I had ever been to the White House before, so this was a big deal for us. And for me it was another milestone: the first time in my life that I didn't dread thinking about what to wear; that I could go to an event this special dressed in something that wasn't an exercise in camouflage. I had a fabulously elegant dress made in navy blue silk with matching coat. It was very tight-waisted with a corset back and I wore diamonds borrowed from Van Cleef.

Although it was only two months since *The Osbournes* had first aired, when we walked down the red carpet the place erupted, the press surged forward and broke down the barriers, and we didn't understand what was going on. We knew from the ratings that the show was a hit, and not just in America, but it was aimed at young people and these people were even older than we were! The four of us were quickly removed by White House security, as we were causing a disturbance, and taken straight into the dining room, ahead of the President and bypassing metal detectors, and all the time we kept looking at each other with expressions that said, What The Fuck Is This?

So the evening began and President Bush came out and did his speech, thanking everyone present for turning up – 'members of the press, movie stars, TV stars and Ozzy Osbourne'. Ozzy was the only person he singled out. And then he started into how his mom loved Ozzy's music, and even named a few of the songs. At which point Ozzy stood up on his chair, and the President goes, 'Get down, Ozzy. Ozzy, get down!'

All these people that run our lives and tell us what's going on in the world started coming up to us. Four-star generals, senators, editors of every influential newspaper in America were asking to have their pictures taken with Ozzy, saying, 'Oh my son's a fan, or my whatever's a fan.' People were even standing in line to get an autograph. We were just blown away. The whole evening was one of those magical once-in-a-lifetime moments.

After the dinner we went on to the party, and Glenn Close was there, and her arm was in a plaster cast. And after the hello, how-are-yous, what does Ozzy say?

'You must be on painkillers. Can I buy some off you? I don't mind paying.'

Glenn, Greta, John and me, we all just cracked up, clutching each other in hysterics. He was trying to score drugs in the White House!

Ozzy had been in and out of rehabs and detox clinics over a dozen times since that first experience in Palm Springs, the year Kelly was born, and eighteen years later he was no better. If anything he was worse.

The previous year, we were in Dallas with Ozzfest. I was at the venue, doing my stuff, when I got a call from Tony back at the hotel to say Ozzy was in a bad way. Apparently he had called a doctor, spun him some bullshit, claiming he had a bad back, and this idiot had prescribed over the phone.

Tony always has the room next to Ozzy, and the first he knew about this was a knock on Ozzy's door. So he went into the corridor to find out what was happening, and was just in time to see the bellman handing Ozzy a paper bag, clearly from a pharmacy. The moment Ozzy saw Tony, he undid the top and threw the whole bottleful down his neck. Twenty-five Vicodin all in one go. Vicodin are very strong painkillers. 'Give him coffee,' I told Tony. 'Do whatever it takes to keep him awake. Do not let him sleep. Whatever you do, do not let him sleep.' I called his doctors in LA immediately.

'Did you see him do it?'

'No, but—'

'There's no way it could be twenty-five Vicodin. There's no way he could still be alive. You must have got it wrong.'

But I hadn't got it wrong. I knew Ozzy, and I knew Tony.

And Tony would call me every half an hour with another update. So I called another doctor who told me he was going to need one of those injections in his heart. 'If not,' he said, 'you're going to lose him.'

By this time Ozzy was talking to Tony. 'He's very disorientated and drowsy, but he's still awake,' Tony told me. I told Tony to get him down to the show. By then it was between six and seven o'clock, and Ozzy would go on at quarter to nine.

And it was like, was I his manager or was I his wife? Ozzy had a crowd of 20,000 young kids waiting to see him and Sabbath, who always closed the show. They'd been out there in the Dallas heat all day, standing and drinking and waiting for Ozzy.

I didn't know what to do, and I tried desperately to think it through. If I cancel, if we don't go on, there will be a riot. The last time Ozzy had been sick and couldn't make a show, I'd taken the decision to say nothing until the last minute, until just before he was due to go on, and the kids just wrecked everything. They destroyed the box office, they ripped up the seats, turned over cars – they utterly destroyed the place. It hadn't happened that many times with us but historically it had happened over and over again with other artists. You cannot keep a crowd in a facility for hours on end and then tell them they have to go home before the main attraction, because you know what's going to happen.

And Dallas in the summer is boiling hot, and Ozzy's crowd drink a lot, and we're not talking Pepsi here. I knew they weren't going to take kindly to being told to go home now, because Ozzy's not going to come.

Where do you draw the line between being a wife and a manager? I was scared people were going to get hurt. What about kids who might be killed in a riot? Could I have that on my conscience? So do I let the show go on? Yet how could I let anyone see Ozzy like that?

*

When Tony and Ozzy arrived and I saw the state my husband was in, I was heartbroken. I was just like, What are you doing? This was insane behaviour. I threw him into the shower in the trailer, got buckets of ice and poured them over him and let the cold shower run on him. He was curled up in the corner with his head in his hands, his hair plastered to his head. I was so angry, and panicked, and terrified. What do I do? Whichever thing I did, I couldn't win. If he didn't go on there would be a riot. And if he did go on he would be terrible.

And the children were there; they saw it all. Kelly and Aimee were crying and weeping and pleading with him, saying things like, 'Please, Dad, please don't die.' Because they're not stupid. By now they knew what he had done. And I was screaming and yelling at him. 'You have to go on stage, you have a responsibility to the audience, to the band, to everybody.'

By quarter to nine, he was standing and talking. And as the audience began clapping and chanting his name, he made his way from the trailer up the ramp to join Sabbath on stage, Tony by his side, and our production manager, and me. No one else in sight. And the crowd were on their feet cheering and chanting, but the moment they saw him there was a hush. It was like they had seen a ghost, a phantom walk up there on the stage, and they were in shock.

How many hundreds of times had I stood there at the side of the stage and felt my heart surge with pride and happiness? How many times? Watching this wonderful performer, who gave everything he'd got, who the moment he stepped out on the stage was on fire. How many times in the thirty years I had known him? I couldn't watch. It was pitiful. I just went back to the production suite to sit down. And I was numb. Exhausted, from the emotional turmoil, wrung out, finished. By the time I got there, the monitors showed the awful truth. Nobody was standing, the entire place was seated, which they never do when

Ozzy is on stage. They were simply stunned. And then I saw what they were seeing. Ozzy's face, as high as a house on the big screens, was like a ghoul, and the adrenalin pumped in again.

'Get the cameras off Ozzy,' I yelled. 'Just focus on everybody else. Don't put Ozzy on the big screens, don't put Ozzy on the screens.' I didn't want the kids to see him fifty-foot-high in that state.

He could barely sing; the best you could say was he mumbled. He couldn't clap his hands – or rather he went to clap them, but they missed. He had to hold onto the microphone stand simply to keep upright.

It was a disaster. I think they managed forty-five minutes and then Tony Iommi walked off. And I don't blame him. I thought it was pretty amazing that he stayed that long. And Ozzy staggered off, and he said, 'I'll never do that again.' And he never has. But I still don't know whether I did the right thing in letting him go on, and it continues to haunt me.

With drugs as powerful as that, and with that dose, any normal person would have been dead: their organs would have packed up. It was only that he had built up such a high level of resistance over the years to massive amounts of drugs and alcohol that he survived.

The next extraordinary thing that happened in 2002 was being asked to perform at the Queen's Golden Jubilee. It was such an honour to be a part of history, because it won't be forgotten, and each generation of kids at school will learn what happened when Elizabeth II reached the fiftieth year of her reign. Being part of the history of your country was so moving for both of us.

What was even more extraordinary for me was that I would be there in my own right. I had been asked by VH1, MTV's grown-up sister channel, to host their coverage of the jubilee concert. It would be the first time I had ever done anything to camera, but nothing fazed me because I had seen it so many times from the other side. Casey Paterson, the producer of the show, was so supportive and nurturing, and she said I was a natural and couldn't wait to work with me again.

Because of *The Osbournes*, everything was so easy. When you're the new biggest thing, everyone wants to be a part of you, and also I was on home territory. Being instantly recognisable gave me access to people I didn't know, like Bryan Adams, Baby Spice, Shirley Bassey, French and Saunders, Lenny Henry and Ruby Wax, and there were old friends as well, Brian May, Paul McCartney, and Richard Branson, who saved our bacon in 1982.

And it was an unbelievable day. There was all the build-up, the fly past, and Brian May, my old friend from Queen, playing 'God Save The Queen' on the roof of Buckingham Palace. It was amazing to be a part of it, to be in the gardens of Buckingham Palace. And backstage there was a great atmosphere, and the artists could go anywhere and there was a special cocktail party for them inside the palace. We had the best time. I wanted to savour every minute. I was determined never to forget a moment, and I did what I always do and took mental snapshots of everything; it's like my little Rolodex in my mind.

Ozzy absolutely stole the night – and I say that not just because he's my husband, he really did. He had Tony Iommi with him, and Phil Collins was on drums, and he had Paul McCartney's bass player and keyboard player. For Ozzy to work with his hero, and the guy who had entertained us all those years on the tour buses, was something he could never have imagined. His early inspiration was the Beatles, and now he was sharing a stage with Paul McCartney.

It was twenty, fifty times better than Live Aid. The people arranging the show for Her Majesty did a great job, and it was well rounded musically: from Paul McCartney to Shirley Bassey,

Rod Stewart, Stevie Winwood, Elton, even Cliff Richard. Ozzy and Ray Davies. It really was the best of British. The whole of England that week was so happy, and the weather was perfect. As for the audience at the palace, it was as if someone had sprayed fairy dust over the place.

That night, after finally leaving the party, when Ozzy and I were in bed, we were just marvelling at how surreal it all was. Ozzy had always been famous, I had always been a name in my business world, but the girl from Brixton and the boy from Birmingham were never top of anybody's list. It was always, 'Oh, she comes from that gangster father. And he's from that awful heavy metal group.' We were hardly Sting and Trudy. We weren't the aristocracy of the music business, like Bono, Paul McCartney and Eric Clapton. You would hardly see us sitting on the front row of a fashion show in Milan Fucking Fashion Week. Nobody had ever invited us to anything like that. And now we were on everybody's list.

The next day it was business as usual and we flew back to LA. I was longing to see the kids and tell them all about it. None of them had been able to come because they were all busy with other things.

The first thing in my diary was a medical. As a signed-up hypochondriac, Ozzy is always having medicals, and he'd just had a colonoscopy and they'd found a polyp, nothing serious, but Ozzy had begged me to have a full medical. And I hate all that stuff. I was never ill anyway. Apart from the monthly checks I'd had after the stomach band was put on, I never went to the doctor's.

So I had everything done. I was horribly anaemic, they said. And it was true that when I'd been in London I had felt very tired and drained, but I had put that down to the strain of doing something like live television. And I am always tired, always have been. But they said I was so anaemic that I must be bleeding from somewhere, either my bum or my stomach. So I had this procedure done where they give you a general anaesthetic, then put tubes down your stomach and up your bum with miniature cameras on them. The stomach one was clear, but they found two lumps in my colon. The doctor who performed the procedure showed me a picture he'd taken, and I was like, what the fuck are those two giant mushrooms doing up my arse? Because that's what they looked like, complete with stalks, minus only the little leprechauns sitting underneath. He'd removed them, he said, and they'd do a biopsy and I'd get the results in a week.

A bit of me was thinking, fuck, that can't be normal, but another bit was thinking, well, Ozzy had his polyp, perhaps this is what a polyp looks like. And I was preoccupied with getting Kelly together to go to New York to make her first album, *Shut Up*, and we were gearing up for the start of Ozzfest 2002, and Jack was just breaking up from school, so basically I didn't think any more about it. Of course, I showed Ozzy the picture, and he said, 'Eurrrrrerk', as anybody would.

So Kelly and Jack and Aimee and Melinda and I fly into New York. And because it's a charter plane we can take the dogs. If we'd gone on a commercial plane, we would never have got out of the terminal, because by this time *The Osbournes* had gone manic and MTV had asked us to do a second series. So we had the film crew with us, and I was feeling so up. The last few months had been like a dream. The success of the show, the White House, the Queen's Golden Jubilee, and I said to them, 'Life is too good. Everything my whole family touches turns to gold. I feel like something's going to happen to kick me in the arse because I cannot believe that life is this good.'

I just said it. And they have it on film.

So we get Kelly sorted in her apartment in Trump Towers,

getting the kitchen filled up with groceries, and it's a six-week let because that's how long the record will take to complete. This was going to be a real holiday for us. We were going to be doing Manhattan. That night I was starting by having dinner with a girlfriend called Michele Anthony, one of the very few women who has really made it to the top in the record industry.

She and I have very similar backgrounds. Her father was Dec Anthony, who managed Peter Frampton. He was the first man I ever saw wear a diamond earring. He was like a benign American version of my father.

Her father wanted her to work in the office, but she wanted an education. So Michele put herself through university. Now she's a brilliant lawyer and second in command at Sony. She has a great knowledge of music, a great musical background to draw from. She chose education, and I didn't, and that's one of the few things in my life that I regret, but I could never have gone her route. You have to be corporate material, and I'm not. I cannot keep my mouth shut, and I would just say Go Fuck Yourself if I didn't agree with something. I like to think of myself as a really good quarterback. I can get people motivated, and get them to go beyond what they would usually do. In that way, perhaps, I might have been good in a big company. But no big company could risk having a loose cannon like me around the place.

So Michele and I had a lovely dinner together in a restaurant in downtown Manhattan, just chatting and catching up on each other's lives. It was a warm summer's evening and I wanted to walk back to my hotel, but Michele had her driver so I didn't. That night it seemed that everything in life was perfect, even the weather. Our entire family was happy and good and healthy. Everyone was in a good place. Ozzy's tour was huge, Kelly was doing a record, everything we did was 'fucking brilliant' – it wasn't just good, it was 'sensational', it was 'groundbreaking'.

You would go to a newsstand and *The Osbournes* would be on the cover of every magazine. And this was not just America, this was worldwide. Life was good, life was sweet.

When I got back to the apartment, the MTV guys were still there, and I remember thinking, God, don't you have homes to go to? Then I went in to see Kelly, and the phone rang, and it was Dana from my office.

'Sharon, are you sitting down?'

I was sitting cross-legged on Kelly's bed as I had just come in to say good night.

'Go on, Dana, give it to me.' Dana is such a drama queen. She can make you feel like a cannibal for eating a fucking oyster.

'The doctor's just called and the results have come back from your colonoscopy. And you've got cancer. Colon cancer. You've got to get back here as soon as possible.'

I put down the phone, and I could hear that the television was on next door, that muffled sound of canned laughter and bad music that Melinda and Jack were watching. Aimee, I knew, was in her room because I'd just put my head round the door. And I said, 'Sorry, guys, I've got to go to the bathroom', because the MTV crew were still filming. Because my stomach had floored, my stomach was in my fucking shoes. You've got cancer. Whenever I'm really nervous, or in great shock, the first thing that happens is my stomach drops, and then I shit. So my stomach was like BANG, in my shoes, and I ran to the toilet, and I shat.

And the MTV crew were always very good; they knew us so well they knew when it wasn't appropriate to stay, and by the time I came out of the bathroom they had gone. And then I start running up and down the hallway, up and down, up and down, and I hear Kelly calling to Aimee to come quick. And I can't stop, and I'm just moving, moving. And they're like, 'Mummy, Mummy, what are you doing? What's the matter?' And I sat in the corner in the hallway and held out my hands to them and pulled them to me and I said, 'I've got cancer.'

The kids were just hysterical and we all sat on the floor, the four of us, and held and cuddled. And then I called Ozzy. He was in Doheny getting ready for the start of Ozzfest, and I just said, 'I'm getting a plane and I'm coming home now.'

'But what's happened? What's the matter, darling?'

And I told him, and you could hear him collapse onto the floor. His knees just crumpled.

'I'm coming home, Dadda. I'll be home tonight.'

We got a private plane, didn't take one piece of luggage, just left as we were, Kelly, Aimee and Jack and the dogs. During the flight I kept falling asleep then waking up again. Kelly was sitting beside me, and Aimee and Jack would just hold my hand, stroking me, holding me. And when the plane touched down at LA, a golf cart came up to the steps of the plane and there were Tony and Ozzy. And Ozzy had put a suit on, and a silk shirt and a tie and a beautiful coat. He had dressed himself up to meet me. And he looked gorgeous. And he smelt gorgeous. And I came out of that plane and my legs were like rubber, the children were all hanging onto me for dear life, and we all got in the golf cart and went to the terminal building, and then we all came home, all got into bed together and stayed there.

Next morning my surgeon, Ed Phillips, came round. He'd seen my video results. They stick a camera up your bloody arse and take a tour. He brought with him a cancer specialist, Dr Barry Rosenbloom, who was so reassuring, a fabulous man. He made me feel so safe, so calm, so don't-even-worry-about-this, this-is-nothing. I was in stage two, of four stages. As I was otherwise completely healthy, he said, I was going to be fine. In these two doctors' opinion the cancer hadn't spread anywhere else. It was nothing to do with the stomach band. I wouldn't need chemo, unless it had spread, which they thought was unlikely. But although the tumours – because that's what they were – had already been removed when I had the colonoscopy, they would need to take more of the surrounding tissue out, namely a couple of feet of my colon.

'But if you need time,' Dr Phillips said, 'you can wait a week.'

No. I wanted it done immediately. I felt foul. I had to get this thing out of my body. If I could have got a brush and put it up my arse, or a vacuum cleaner and put it up my arse, I would have done. I would have swallowed bleach. I felt like I had an alien inside my body and I wanted it out.

I was taken in at seven the next morning. There was no need to tell me not to eat; I hadn't eaten since I'd heard the news. The kids were giving me ice lumps because I couldn't even drink. I couldn't brush my teeth, I couldn't even wash. I was stinking.

I didn't want the kids to come into the hospital, so only Ozzy came with me, and Tony. Bobby drove. Dear Bobby, who was going through throat cancer at the same time and, as it turned out, hadn't long to live.

I was taken straight into the operating theatre. The rest of that day is only a haze. Ozzy and Dr Phillips were there and took me back to my room. They gave me a pain-relieving pump for morphine that you operate yourself, but I wouldn't use it. And Ozzy kept saying, 'Use it, Sharon, just fucking use it.'

'No. I hate this shit.' And I did. I'd had it before and I get nauseous. I would rather suffer excruciating pain than be sick. For me, vomiting is the worst thing in the world. But in the end, I had to, and even then Ozzy would complain.

'You haven't used enough, darling.'

'I have.'

'I'm telling you, Sharon, you've used nothing. Bloody use it.'

The pain was like the most terrible burning, burning through your crotch and your bum and between your legs, it was unlike any other pain I had ever had. Four days later I was allowed home. And then came the phone call. The cancer had spread. I had to start chemotherapy in three weeks' time. Again, my stomach floored. But then it was like, OK. We'll deal with it, we'll get through this. But I was fucking terrified.

Because all my life it wasn't cancer itself I'd been frightened of. It was always the chemo. I have known so many people who've gone through it and I was petrified. Charlie, a man who had a field opposite Welders where he kept horses, had had chemo for colon cancer, and sometimes he'd come in for a cheese sandwich and a cup of tea, and I'd see what it had done to him. And a girlfriend of mine, Michele Myers, who I'd known in the seventies, she'd gone through a lot of chemo and I saw her die, and I saw the agony she went through.

And lying there, feeling like shit, I kept thinking about all the good things I'd had in my life, and I thought: now it's time for your pain. It won't last but you have to experience it to become a well-rounded person. And then my attitude to the chemo changed. Far from being frightened of it, I welcomed it. I couldn't wait to get there. I was like, Bring It On. I want this shit out of my body.

Meantime the cameras were still in the house, because I decided early on we should carry on with *The Osbournes*. I could have said that's enough, leave us alone now, but that would have terrified my children because they'd have known how sick I really was. If I'd asked the cameras to go, they'd have had no distractions.

I knew that I needed my own space away from the beehive that Doheny had become. So Ozzy had rented me a house in Malibu. Usually you can't take dogs to rental houses, but this place was very big and the owners were planning to knock it down and do a total rebuild, so they said we could take the dogs, that we could do whatever we wanted. And it was so quiet there.

The phone didn't ring every five minutes, and the camera crew would come just every other day. I had made Ozzy carry on with the tour, and Kelly was back in New York doing the record, just as we'd planned, with Melinda to keep an eye on her. Jack and Aimee would go back and forth between Malibu and Doheny. And Maryshe, our housekeeper from Welders, came over to take care of me, and to give her a break there was a lady by the name of Simone, whose boyfriend worked for us. Dale Skjerseth, always known as Opie, has been our production manager for years. Sadly 2005 will be his last year with us: he's been headhunted by the Rolling Stones. Simone wasn't working at the time, so she had all the time in the world to spend with me.

It was a very weird journey.

---

21 April 2005, 3.30 p.m.
Doheny Road: my bedroom

I am in bed waiting for a conference call to be put through with our lawyers. Not for the first time in our lives, Ozzy and I are being sued. However, it is the first time that two totally unconnected people are suing us for the same thing at the same time.

Our attorneys are led by Howard Weitzman. We have known Howard since Ozzy was sued by the parents of a boy who committed suicide in 1986. Howard got the case thrown out, and he and his wife Margaret have been family friends ever since. He's one of the highest-profile lawyers in California, and has represented Courtney Love, Michael Jackson, O. J. Simpson and John DeLorean, and if he'd been around at the time probably Jesus Christ could have done with his services. His team are just as extraordinary. Orin Snyder used to work for the district attorney in New York City. He really cares about the vulnerable people involved – in this case, the kids and Ozzy – and he's spent two to three years of his life on this case, dedicating hours to it. Elise Zealand started out as a criminal lawyer, and successfully defended two innocent murder suspects, and Ashlie Beringer has got balls of steel and is spot on in her judgement of people. These two women are both total powerhouses. If that wasn't enough, they look like two girls from *The Practice*. We couldn't be better represented.

Even so, it has been three years of torture. It's overshadowed everything. It's been unbelievable pressure on the kids, and the thought that after everything they've gone through in the last three or four years, somebody wants to come in and take their money is grotesque. Jack was fifteen, Kelly was sixteen. Who would think of taking a fifteen-year-old's money?

So what did we do that was so terribly, terribly wrong? Answer: we had a hit show.

America is litigation heaven. From passengers in the back of taxis claiming they will never work again because their driver pulled up too quick and they banged their thumb, to fathers of teenagers claiming that ten minutes at a rock concert turned them deaf. Anyone can sue, and if they think there's a pot of gold in it for them they usually do.

In our case we're being sued over *The Osbournes*. Two separate lawsuits. Two totally unconnected people are claiming that it was their fucking idea. At one point there was even a third, but he pulled out when it emerged that MTV had already started filming by the time this arsehole said he met with me. But even to get to that point we needed lawyers, and so we still had to pay. The other two cases are still ongoing, though.

The nightmare began in July 2002, nearly three years ago now, when I was quietly lying in Cedars-Sinai having a blood transfusion, less than a month after my operation for cancer. I'd collapsed at Doheny and been rushed by Jack into hospital, and this moron comes into my room while I was semi-conscious having three pints of plasma dripped into my body, prods me with the envelope and then leaves it on the table. That was me being served. The doctors went fucking insane.

Appropriately enough, that's what they call these people: ambulance chasers – law firms that take on cases on a contingency basis. In other words, no win, no pay. They're basically gamblers. They can afford to lose nine out of ten cases for that one big payout that will cover the rest. It's a numbers game. The more cases these people take on, the more chance they have of winning.

So what are these two claimants actually saying? One is a production company called Threshold TV and they claim that I 'engaged in a deliberate and wrongful rip-off of the property'. I have never denied that I talked to these people, but what I was discussing with them had nothing to do with us as a family, it was simply about TV deals relating to Ozzy and Ozzfest. They have requested a trial by jury.

The other is a film producer called Gary Binkow, who claims he came up with the idea of *The Osbournes*. In fact, he came up with the idea of a scripted sit-com about a retired rock-and-roller trying to get back to a normal family life. I was never going to be in it. He was going to have Ozzy surrounded by actors and the story lines were going to be loosely based around Ozzy's activities. A year after our first meeting we received a script. It was predictable hokey. At the meeting that followed, we unanimously agreed that we didn't like it. The kids went along because there was talk of them playing themselves if they proved capable of acting and learning lines. It never got to the proposed screen test.

Until I saw the script, I gave this man the benefit of the doubt. It could have been groundbreaking TV. It could have been like *The Office*. But it wasn't. It was generic bullshit. And so we said no thank you and moved on with our lives.

At no stage was *The Osbournes* ever a sit-com. It was a reality show. So these guys talking about writing scripts are talking out of their arses. There were no scripts. Never. Not one. How could anyone ever script Ozzy? Or what about my cancer? Great plot line that.

If anyone can take credit for what became *The Osbournes*, it should be God.

19

Crisis

When I went in for my first bout of chemotherapy, a month since the day I had my cancer removed, I had no idea what to expect. Yes, they give you the literature, and they're very kind, but you don't really have any idea what's going to happen to your body once they hook you up. And hook you up is exactly what they do. Before I started, I had a port put into my chest where the cocktail of chemicals would go in, and this port is a hook, and the nurse who would hook me up was called Gabriel, and I called him my Angel Gabriel.

There were three different drips going in at the same time. Gabriel would just turn the tap, and that was it. This cocktail of acid would begin moving like a glacier, trickling down through my arms into my fingertips, through my legs into my toes, and I would embrace it. I was like, Yes, thank God.

I went once a week for three hours and the staff at Cedars-Sinai are beyond praise. The MTV crew filmed everything, so there was always someone to talk to. Then I had my work to catch up on and Michael would come in and we'd go through my messages, and I found that if I worked through it, I didn't think too much about what was going on.

The day after the chemo was always the worst. That's when you heave, barf, throw up and shit. Even the smell of orange juice would be enough. I would gag at the sourness of it. By the second week of treatment I was so weak I was urinating in my bed, just because I didn't have the strength to make it to the bathroom.

I would drift off to the sound of the surf crashing on the shore outside the window. The sea is so close in Malibu, it drowns out every other noise, and in a way it even drowned out my thoughts. Its rhythm never stopped. It would lull me to sleep, and it would be there when I woke up. Timeless. People would send books for me to read, but I read very little, because I was so, so tired. Most of the time I slept, and had to be woken up to drink and eat. If I'd been left to myself I would have just lain there and rotted.

The children would come and go. Maryshe and Simone would take turns looking after me. Ozzy would come when he wasn't performing but I made him keep to the schedule because I saw that he was frightened, terrified that I was going to die, so that it was better for him to go and do his thing and be away from it all. There was a period when he did take time off, and other bands were really kind, covering his spots. This was when, four weeks into my chemo, I slipped into a coma. Because getting the balance of chemicals right is all trial and error, and depends on your individual metabolism.

It turned out that my white-blood-cell count was on the floor. I had just had my fourth treatment and was staying at Doheny overnight before going back to Malibu. I couldn't move, I couldn't do anything. I could sense people around me but I couldn't communicate, and it was like I was looking down on everything from above. I could see my husband crying and I could see my children crying, but I didn't feel emotion. I just felt calm and at peace. An ambulance came and they took me to Cedars and I would float in and out of consciousness. They had to rehydrate me, so they put me on a saline drip, and then my blood pressure plummeted. I was aware of the panic around me – 'Take her to intensive care.' 'No, there's no time. We'll do it here.' – and I was given three pints of blood. Ten days that have vanished from my memory.

I always knew that I might lose my hair, but unlike the chemo you get with breast cancer, with colon cancer it isn't inevitable. But I'd wake up in the morning and I'd be covered in it. I'd get up to clean my teeth and the basin would be full of it. I'd have something to eat and there would be hair in the fucking food, so I'd be picking hairs out of my mouth. I found the tightest hat I had, and kept that pulled on. Not for vanity, just to stop the bloody stuff covering everything in sight.

Even Minnie's beautiful pale blonde fluff was covered with it. She refused to leave my side and her body kept me warm. Although it was July and then August, I was always freezing cold. My bones would ache through the shaking.

And then it happened again, and I was rushed back into hospital. This time for eight days. And the first time I was strong enough to walk to the bathroom, I looked into the basin mirror when I was washing my hands, and I just sobbed and sobbed. That was the first time I cried. I never particularly liked my hair, but at least there had always been lots of it. Now the little there was was dead and lifeless.

'It come back. Don' worry,' Kay would tell me, on her way to the salon in the Beverly Hills Hotel. Every day I was in hospital she came. Every day, for a couple of minutes, maybe five, just to say hello. I learnt not to study my face.

It was Kay who called Jude and suggested he drop in. And just his being there was like having a blood transfusion – he made me feel good, even though I didn't look it. Ostensibly he came to give me a bit of make-up, but what he really did was make me laugh. Jude Alcala is six foot four, handsome and Hispanic, and a true Angelino, the youngest child of fourteen. To Jude I am always 'Sharone'. We met on *The Osbournes* when he was working for MTV, since which time, whenever I have a function to go to in the States, or an interview or photo session, Jude will do my hair and make-up, and Ozzy's. And however stressed out you are, Jude's just being there is guaranteed to calm you down.

When I came out of hospital I had two wigs made, by the lady who makes Cher's. Well, why not? Meanwhile Minnie had become dehydrated too, maybe in sympathy. The vet had had her on a saline drip while I was in Cedars-Sinai.

Finally they got the levels of chemo right. All the time I continued to work, doing whatever was necessary, including hosting the American Music Awards. I was still really sick, but I felt I had to keep up the morale of the family. It was then that I got the offer of doing *The Vagina Monologues* in Chicago. Suddenly life was much shorter than I realised, and I wanted to take in as much of everything as I could. But Ozzy said no.

On 14 September the first series of *The Osbournes* won an Emmy in the Outstanding Non-fiction Program (Reality) category, the first Emmy in MTV's twenty-year history. Americans don't take to individuals as they do in Europe; they like to follow the bouncing ball. You have to be safe, have to be like everyone else; if not, people are wary of you. Through *The Osbournes* people got to see Ozzy as he really is, not the deranged rock god who bit the head off a bat, but the normal, regular guy that everyone could relate to, like him or not. And that was all I had ever wanted. The show broke through people's misconceptions.

I wanted people to see how funny and loving my husband was, and through *The Osbournes* they did.

Seven of the MTV team got an award. Mine was as producer, because that was the one sure way I'd had of retaining creative control. At the beginning I would watch the edited tapes to see if there was anything we wanted taken out – just because some-times you say things you don't really mean – but it was never to change the storyline or make us look better. By the end, how-ever, I got so bloody bored that I didn't bother. Ozzy has only ever watched two episodes in the whole thing. But it's there, part of the family legacy to hand down to future generations. Kelly and I accepted the awards on behalf of us all, and my speech was just one sentence: 'I love you, Ozzy.'

It was when I was still having chemo that we decided to renew our wedding vows. I'd met this great rabbi, who'd written a book on marriages between different faiths, and I'd told him how my own wedding day had been tainted and how I'd always wished we could do it over again. His name was Steven Reuben, and he said he would do it: why not? Rabbi Reuben was a lovely man, and whether he was a Catholic or a Muslim I would have felt just as good. It would be a New Year's Eve as we'd never had before.

It was a wonderful occasion. Everybody who had meant something in our lives was there, and I felt so blessed that we had the money to do it, and we were able to have it at the Beverly Hills Hotel. In all about three hundred people came, everyone from my doctors to the Newmans. And we had the Village People perform, and this time I had a dress that fitted. But it took it out of me, and two days later, on 2 January 2003, I was taken into intensive care again. I'd overdosed on the anti-nausea medication I'd been given and had had a seizure. All the so-called nurses who were supposed to be looking after me could think to do was to throw water on me. An MTV security guard carried me downstairs and I arrived at Cedars-Sinai in the MTV van.

Ozzy was cursing himself that he let me go through with the ceremony, but he knew how much I wanted it. Because I honestly didn't know if I would come through, and I wanted my children to see our marriage being blessed. I wanted our children to have that memory.

Among the three hundred people who came on New Year's Eve were, naturally, our families: Ozzy's sisters and brothers were there, and Louis, his son by his first marriage, and Louis' fiancée Louise. There were also three guests no one within my circle would have expected: my father, Meredith and my brother David.

I owe this change of heart to my husband. We had been in New York fifteen months earlier, in September 2001, just before *The Osbournes* had started shooting. As usual, we were staying at the Peninsula Hotel. I was in bed when Ozzy woke me up. He said the World Trade Center had been hit, and that we had to get out because it had to be a full-on attack. He had been doing a crossword and Tony had called from the next-door room to tell him to switch on the television. Kelly said, 'Let's go to the roof,' so we did. We looked south towards the Battery and there was nothing but this vast mushroom cloud that looked like an atomic bomb. And there was a man lying on top of the roof sunbathing, and he told us to get out of the way because we were blocking the sun.

Somehow we got hold of the crew, and they brought the tour bus up to 55th Street. All we wanted was to go home, but planes were all grounded. It took another two days before the bridges off the island were open. Until then, Manhattan was a ghost town. There wasn't a soul in the streets, not even any birds, just newspapers blowing like a scene from a western. So we set off to drive across America to LA, the old route 66. We were afraid, and just wanted to get home. It was then, lying in bed, driving through the night as we had done so many times before, that Ozzy began to talk.

'Listen, Sharon. We've all done stupid things, but there comes a point where you either carry on doing stupid things or you change. And I know in the bottom of my heart that if you have any feelings for your father, any feelings left at all, you have to make it up with him. Whoever decided to invent us got it wrong. We should have been born with all the common sense we have now. By the time you get old enough to realise how dumb you've been, you're too old. And as I get older I realise I've got to learn to forgive. I'm not suggesting we hold hands round the table and try to contact your mother. But when he's dead it's too late.'

My mother had died just before Christmas 1999. My brother called and told me she was dead, and I said, 'Oh what a shame', and put the phone down.

I never shed a tear, never had a twinge in my stomach, never dreamt about her, nothing. And there has never been a moment when I've thought: Oh God, if only I could see her again, if only we could have made up, if only I'd been able to hold her hand and say, 'I love you, Mum.' I couldn't because I didn't. If I ever thought about her, it was just as a sad bitter old woman with a fag in her trap and a diamond on her finger worth over a million quid. Emphysema got her in the end; she was still smoking till the day she died.

I didn't even feel relief. I knew what was going to happen, that the remaining family members would descend like vultures trying to get hold of the antiques, paintings and her jewellery, and fighting each other for it.

By 11 September 2001, I was already looking after my father financially. Shortly after my mother died, David had called again to tell me that Don was sick. He needed a pacemaker fitted. He was down on his luck and friendless. Almost everything had gone. I paid. A few months later I discovered he'd been diagnosed with Alzheimer's several years before. Meredith and he had parted and were no longer living together. I decided I wanted to take care of him.

When my mother died, my father had moved back to England, but as the house had been in her name – naturally – he now had nowhere to live. I put him in a serviced apartment on Park Lane. I asked him and Meredith to come to the palace for the Queen's Jubilee as my guests. They were still friends. But the old man hadn't changed. I discovered that even with Alzheimer's and a fucking pacemaker, he was also fucking the cleaner of the apartment block. She was married with two kids and a punch-happy husband. With the little money he had left, he bought this woman a brand new car, clothes, and the rest of it, so I decided I had to get him away from there and bring him over to Hollywood, which I did. But then he persuaded me to bring her and her two kids over to LA to live with him. It didn't last long, but I put them up in the Beverly Hills Hotel, I took them to Vegas. Why? Because I wanted to make my father happy. And because I could.

Somebody that New Year's Eve asked me when I had stopped hating him. And it's very weird, but I realised that I had never hated him. There were things about him I couldn't understand: I couldn't believe how mean he was, how callous, how he had used me – just as a human being, forget being his daughter – and how he put my life in danger, physically, financially, every which way, and seemed not to have a conscience about it. I was angry that he could do that to anybody, and I was angry with him for not being the upright, moral man I thought he was, for his having hoodwinked me. I was angry with him because he had lied to me his entire life. And he was responsible for so much unhappiness. I don't think I forgave him, but I blanked it. I did what I always do, just carried on. As Ozzy said, 'You're a long time dead.' Now he was just a sick old man.

'You need your own chat show, and I'm going to get it for you.' This was Casey Paterson, the producer I worked with on the Queen's Jubilee. I thought she only said it to cheer me up, as I was then deep into the chemo. But she meant it, and – with herself as executive producer – she took me to Kingworld, who do *Oprah*, and then took me to Telepictures. Telepictures came up with more money, so we went with them. This soon proved an important lesson: it isn't necessarily about the money, because the first thing they did was turn on Casey and cut her out of the picture. I like to think that if I'd been thinking clearly, I would have stuck by my friend and never allowed this to happen. And there were plenty of signs, like they wouldn't deal with my agent. I should have said fuck off.

Although I did get lots of experience, the show was basically crap. They changed producer, changed director and the show runner (the person who holds everything together) three times. It was a complete and utter shambles. Whenever I wanted to bring somebody in creatively, they'd say they had somebody already. I didn't realise they had a whole screw of staff on the permanent payroll and would plonk whoever it was onto me because they just wanted to give them a gig.

It was a talk show, an hour every day, and it went out in Los Angeles at eleven in the morning, which meant it was two in the afternoon in New York and everything in-between across the country, depending on the time zone. It was put out as though it was live, although each show was recorded the day before.

There were guest celebrities and Oprah-style interviews. At

one stage they wanted the more Jerry Springer-type confronta-
tions, full of emotionally dysfunctional people screaming and
shouting, and I wouldn't do it. I wanted to talk to people who
were dealing with things that had happened that were beyond
their control; I wanted to help people. They wanted to have
people fighting.

The best thing about *The Sharon Osbourne Show* was the location, at KTLA, down on Sunset, a great old studio that had been
there for years, and the set was a mock-up of Doheny which, of
course, everybody knew from *The Osbournes*: the kitchen, the
sitting room and a little library section, and I felt very comfortable there, and Minnie and Maggie would always come with me
and would regularly attack the guests.

One of my first guests was Little Richard, one of the biggest
American artists my father brought over to Europe in the early
sixties. He was such a great character, and I still had strong memories of him from my childhood. My father was the one who
got him to stop singing gospel and go back to singing the devil's
music: rock and roll. In forty years, it seemed to me that nothing had changed about him, still with his beautiful skin and his
outrageous clothes. When he first came over to London he'd had
Billy Preston with him, who could only have been about fifteen,
and who was on keyboards that famous time the Beatles played
on the roof of the Apple headquarters in Savile Row.

I had some old friends on, like Elton and Rod Stewart, and
over the year I got to meet people like Quentin Tarantino,
singers like Josh Groban, Dido, Donna Summer, Sheryl Crow.
But the people I was most interested in were the non-celebrities.
There was a family of eight kids who had lost their mum and
dad within eight months, and because they were on my show a
makeover show saw them and gave them a whole house. I went
to a women's prison for lifers in LA. This was one of the only
ideas of mine they took up. I wanted to highlight the fact that

women who murder get longer sentences than men, because women 'aren't meant' to be violent, and when they are, then the law comes crashing down on them, even though most of the time they killed in self-defence.

What was fabulous about working with a live audience was that we built up a library of inside jokes. On one of the first shows there was a woman who was very large, and I could empathise with her, having been like that myself, so I asked about sex and how she coped with that.

'Gurrrl,' she said in a rolling Southern drawl. 'I jus' take it from the side.' And I cracked up, and the audience cracked up, and from then on, whenever I got bored with these celebrities – and I often got bored – I would say, 'I jus' take it from the side.' And, of course, the audience would be killing themselves with laughter while the poor celebrity wouldn't have a clue.

The best people were the ones who were prepared not to take themselves seriously. I had an in-bed-with-Sharon slot that I stole from *The Big Breakfast* on Channel 4, and Dame Edna Everage joined me in it in her ballgown. She was fabulous. And how bad a job could it be to lie in bed and cuddle Alec Baldwin in his pyjamas?

But it meant I hardly spent any time with my family. Every morning I was leaving my house overrun with TV people to go to another version of my house overrun with TV people, and the few times I was at home, they were always on the phone saying, 'Call all your friends, get all your friends in.' And I said no.

But doing a five-day-a-week show is a slog for everybody involved. There are only a finite number of celebrities available, and that's why these shows bump things up with cooking sections and nonsense, because they need fillers. You want to ask me what to do for a fucking Superbowl party? Get a caterer. They made me interview this taxi driver dressed as Elvis. It would have been all right for two minutes, but no, they wanted to give him a whole fucking segment. So then he was dancing like Elvis and they wanted me to do an Elvis impersonation. I don't do Elvis impersonations. It was all so childish and such floss, and there'd be this voice inside me saying: why is a fifty-year-old woman doing this shit?

I wanted to do stuff on kids who get pregnant and then dump their babies, social issues that at the beginning they had told me I could do. Nobody cares that there are all these kids abandoning their newborn babies in dumpsters, and it goes on all the time. In America there's a format that works in the morning, in the afternoon, in the evening. And they follow it. If it's experimental TV you want, that's in Europe. Their answer was always the same: 'The advertisers don't like it.'

There were over a hundred different networks buying this show. And the comments would come back: we need this, we need that, and every one would be different. So you get a network in Greensboro, North Carolina, saying they want more jokes, but New York wants more serious stuff, San Francisco wants more music, and Cincinnati wants more sport. Every network wants the show moulded to them, but you cannot be all to everyone. You have to stick to your guns: 'This is what I'm about and take it or leave it.'

And I'm not going to spin plates, and I'm not going to do belly dancing, and I'm not going to do fake horse-riding. I have my own form of humour, which you would think was why they wanted me in the first place.

And as for the effing and blinding, I had to watch it all the time because they don't like to bleep on daytime TV. So I would be introducing someone and I'd get the name wrong, so I'd go, 'Fuck, cunt, shit, bollocks', which, of course, was why they would never let me go out live.

*

On the morning of 8 December 2003, I was dozing in my bed at Doheny. Aimee and I were doing a photo shoot for *Vogue* at midday, and any minute the florists would be arriving to make the house look delightful, so this was a brief moment of peace before the engine cranked into life, because the volume of people who come through the house in any given day is unbelievable. So I was lying there, thinking about Christmas at Welders, and about going to Ireland for my stepson Louis' wedding early in the New Year and what I was going to wear. We had banked up a few shows, and I would have two whole weeks off. Ozzy was already over in England with a small MTV crew doing promo with Kelly for 'Changes', a duet they had done, a cover of one of Sabbath's early hits.

At seven o'clock, the phone rang. It was Tony. Ozzy had had an accident on the quad bike, he said, and they were on their way to Wexham Park hospital now.

'I think he might have broken some ribs.'

Ozzy has a selection of bikes at Welders, dirt bikes and four-wheelers, and he was forever falling off. It had happened at least three times before, so I wasn't particularly concerned. I said for Tony to call me as soon as they got to the hospital and we could get a doctor on the phone.

An hour later the phone rang and Tony put the doctor on. I was with Jack; we'd just been laughing about how Ozzy was always crashing around, and we were like, Whatever will your father do next!

They were preparing Ozzy for surgery, the doctor said. And I'm like, Surgery? For what?

And then he ran down the list of injuries: cracked vertebrae in his neck; eight broken ribs, all at the back; collarbone totally shattered; and he had punctured a main artery which was stopping the blood supply to his left arm; a bruised heart; blood on his lung; and he was in a coma. The most serious injury was his arm, the doctor explained. They had seventy-two hours to get the blood back, otherwise they would have to amputate.

I cancelled everything. There was one seat left on the next flight to London. I didn't tell Jack or Aimee the full extent of their father's injuries. I didn't want to frighten them, and they had their own commitments. The entire time I was in the air I knew Ozzy was in the operating theatre. I couldn't eat, I couldn't sleep. I just stared out of the window into that deep, unending blue that, in the past, I had always found so full of hope.

The first thing that happened was that two policemen boarded the plane at Heathrow and walked me off. And then we emerged into this sea of film crews and photographers. Roger Moore and his wife were on the flight, so I assumed they were for them. So did they, until they were mowed down in the rush and the cries of 'Sharon! This way! How is he?'

I knew less than they did. I'd heard nothing since I had boarded the plane. The headlines in the papers were enough: Ozzy Osbourne In Coma. I felt like I was sleepwalking. The police took me through immigration, through the airport to a car where Kelly was already waiting. They had pulled her out of the recording studio. She was like a little lost girl, vulnerable and frightened, all wrapped up in scarf and gloves and little hat, because it was freezing cold. We didn't talk much, we just hugged.

It took us half an hour to get to Wexham Park hospital outside Slough. The police gave us an escort all the way there, and they couldn't have done more — it was as if they were genuinely concerned for my husband. There were police everywhere because photographers had tried to get into the intensive care unit. They took me in the back way.

Tony and Bill Greer, Ozzy's tour manager, were waiting. Somehow with the shock and the panic, I had imagined that

Bobby would be waiting for me. My darling Bobby. He had been with us through every emergency, from Randy and Rachel to my cancer. It seemed impossible that he wasn't there. But he wasn't. Dear Bobby had finally lost his battle with cancer. He died on the road, as he wanted to. We'd said, why don't you take a job in the office but he just wouldn't hear of it.

'Now, please, Sharon,' Tony said, 'don't panic when you see him, because it looks worse than it is.' Tony stayed with Kelly in one of the doctors' rooms the hospital had given us to sit in, while I went in on my own.

There were about thirteen people in the trauma unit. They were all on respirators or had tracheotomies, and they were all out. Nobody was moving. Just bodies attached to wires, and machines bleeping and buzzing. One of these was my husband.

They gave me a chair next to Ozzy, and I looked at him. He was on a respirator, unable to breathe on his own. There were tubes everywhere, coming out of him, going into him. The doctor explained how they had taken a vein from his right arm and put it into the left arm to replace the damaged artery. All they could do now was wait and hope that it would 'take'. His lungs were being drained. As for his heart, that would just take time; the same with his ribs. They could only determine what damage had been done to his neck, they said, 'when he was up and walking'. When. If.

His left eye and that whole side of his face were black. There was still dried blood and dirt in his hair where he had fallen, big lumps of dirt, and the pillow was all covered in dirt and dried blood, and there was congealed blood at the corner of his mouth, and his nose was all swollen down one side. As for his arm, there was no pulse. It was like a dead thing. When I took his hand it was completely cold.

I couldn't cry. I just took my coat off and curled up on the chair. And from time to time I would try to clean him up, pick out the dirt from his hair. I felt utterly empty. I'd fall asleep, then wake up to the same rhythms, the silent flashing lights, the beeps, the hum. They offered me a bed, offered me food, but I said no to everything. I still didn't cry. I stayed there all that day and the following night and went back to Welders at about six the next morning. I didn't go beyond the kitchen. It was days before I went upstairs and unpacked. I just stayed in the corner of the sofa in the kitchen by the phone, and would sleep, wake up, sleep, wake up and call Ozzy's security for any updates. There were no updates. All I kept thinking about was the seventy-two hours for Ozzy's arm. Every so often Tony would drive me to the hospital – it was barely twenty minutes from the house – and there were always photographers everywhere. The response of the public was extraordinary. There were crates of letters and cards and gifts sent to the hospital, chocolate and rosaries and prayers on little cards and get-well flowers. And Ozzy and Kelly's record went to No. 1.

As for the staff, I have never seen such dedication. Not just to Ozzy, but to everyone in the trauma unit. It was so humbling seeing everybody else's journeys as well as my husband's. A lady next to Ozzy died. She had only gone in with flu, but it had turned to pneumonia, and every day you would see the same family members come in and there would be little exchanges. How's it going? How are you coping? And then you'd see them sob, and it would get worse and worse and there would be more family members, and then the next time you got back the priest would be there. It was heartbreaking to watch.

Ozzy's arm took, thank goodness. The operation had been a success, though they still didn't know about his neck because he was unconscious. The next worry was the respirator. It was connected to his lungs by a tube down his throat and, because of the danger of infection, could only stay in for a maximum of ten days. After that they would have to do a tracheotomy. After eight days they would try to see if he could breathe on his own. And I was desperate for him not to have the tracheotomy because of the damage it would do to his vocal cords. I wanted my husband to live, but I wanted him to be Ozzy.

---

21 April 2005, 5.00 p.m.
Doheny Road: my bedroom

I'm packing for Thailand. Out goes anything man-made, in comes cotton in light colours. Will it be cool in the evening?

A knock on the door. 'Who is it?'

'Robert.'

'Come in, Rob, don't just stand there!' Robert Marcato is a handsome young man of nearly twenty-one. 'Everything all right with the apartment?'

He nods.

'And still all right with school?'

'Yeah.'

'What's the project?'

'Just editing a film I'm doing.'

Robert is an old schoolfriend of the kids. When I got cancer we heard that Robert's mother had been battling with colon cancer for three years. She had been in the last stages when she found out, but she didn't have the money and she didn't have the insurance, and she was dying. Ozzy and I would go over and visit her, and Ozzy held her in his arms and he swore that we would always take care of Robert, and that she didn't have to worry about her boy.

So after his mum passed away, Robert moved in here for a while. He's a normal teenager, not an addict or an alcoholic, so he would drink and want to party, and it was just when Jack had come out of rehab and we couldn't have that going on. We asked Rob to stop drinking and doing his dope, but he wanted his friends, he wanted a normal teenage life. So we found him an apartment, which we pay for, and we pay for him to go to school, and he's two years into a four-year course. He's doing well, and hopefully he will come out and pursue his dreams and be fine.

This year colon cancer has overtaken breast cancer as the biggest cancer killer in America. But still nobody talks about it because it's not romantic, and people don't like to go on TV and say, well, actually yes, I had a huge tumour up my arse. Yet it's something that affects men and women and all ethnic groups, and it is one of the cancers that, if it's found in time, you can survive. But it is a killer.

When I was being treated in hospital I had a huge support group. For every visit I would have Bobby and Melinda at my side. But when I would leave in my chauffeur-driven car, I would see these other ladies sitting on a bench, waiting for a bus. And you knew that when they went home there would be no one there to help them. And I'm thinking, how do these people cope at home when they're feeling so bad? Because the chemo really knocks you on your arse. And if you've got a baby, how can you possibly take care of your baby? How can you work? If you don't work you can't pay your rent, so you get thrown out. That was basically what had happened to Robert's mum. She couldn't pay her rent, she wasn't working, she didn't have insurance, so there she was getting thrown out of her apartment, and then she died, aged thirty-four. And so I set up my charity. Every year Elton and I do a joint party, and we split the proceeds, with half going to his Aids charity, and half to mine. And at each of Ozzy's shows, 50 cents of every ticket sold goes to the hospital. I can't help every person out there, or every Robert, much as I would like to. But I now raise enough money each year for a programme in Los Angeles where there's a car to pick up people who don't have transportation to and from treatment, or if they need somebody to do their shopping, or if they need somebody to baby-sit, or if they need somebody to give them hydration at home. Because you get very dehydrated, and if you have to come back to the hospital to get rehydrated it wipes you out. So now there are a few people who can have the luxury of that at home, instead of getting on a bus. It's not offering a cure or anything. It's a programme to do little things that help make life more bearable.

20

The Knock on the Door

Only gradually did I piece together what had happened that morning. Ozzy had gone out with MTV on his quad bike to show them some of our land, and he'd been riding over some rough grass when he just went over. There was a dip in the field but it was covered in leaves. The crew had been filming at the time, but as soon as it happened, the guys threw their cameras on the ground and ran to help. He fell off the bike, he landed on his face, and then the bike bounced off his back. It weighed 650 pounds. Ozzy was in such a state of shock that he got up and was staggering around the field. They tried to stop him, but he wouldn't, and kept saying, 'Take me home, take me home.' So the security guard heaved him up on his shoulders, then drove with him back to the house on another bike. He'd had to revive Ozzy twice; he was in a terrible state. But as much as he saved Ozzy's life, moving somebody after an injury like that is the worst thing you could do, and he could have broken his spine. It was adrenalin that was making Ozzy stand up, brought on by the shock.

The children were now all at Welders; with the scare stuff in the press, Jack and Aimee couldn't cope in LA on their own, so their projects were put on hold. Ozzy's family came down to visit from Birmingham, and Louis came over from Ireland. The Newmans came, and Maryshe and her husband came straight from Yugoslavia after cutting short their holiday. Zakk flew in from California, so did Mark Hudson, Ozzy's writing partner, and our old friends Marsha and Peter Velasek came in from New York. And of course Tony would sit and talk to him for hours, like we all did, about the past, reminding him of things, trying to bring him back to consciousness. The staff shaved and washed him every day, but they couldn't wash his hair because of the neck, and so I continued to pick bits of blood and dirt out, and I would take a warm cloth and try to tidy him up with the end of it while I was stroking him and talking to him. Sometimes his eyes would open, and then they would put drops in and tape them over to close them again, to stop them drying up because he wasn't blinking.

Although there were always people around to call on, I was overwhelmed with a terrible feeling of emptiness. I have never felt so alone in my entire life. It was like, If my husband doesn't make it, this is my life without him.

On the eighth day they took him off the ventilator, but his breathing was very shallow. He wasn't getting enough oxygen in his blood, they said. So I sat there beside him, telling him, 'You've got to breathe, Ozzy.' Sometimes I must have sounded like a fucking midwife. 'Nice deep breaths, Ozzy. Breathe, just breathe.' While all the time he kept trying to pull the tubes out with his right arm, and the alarm was going off every time he pulled one free.

I was desperate that they shouldn't cut into his throat. Because Bobby had had a tracheotomy, and I saw what he went through.

But thank God he managed to get enough oxygen into his blood so it wasn't necessary.

Gradually things seemed to improve: the tape was now off his eyes and they had removed some of the tubes. Everything was going fine, they said. But when you're in a trauma unit, it can all turn within a second. He was groaning a lot, trying to pull out the tubes in his nose, which is how you're fed.

By the tenth day he was beginning to come round and saying the odd word – but you could see he had no idea where he was, and he was moaning because, for the first time, he was conscious of the pain.

On the eleventh day when I arrived I was greeted by a beaming nurse.

'We've got a surprise for you, Mrs Osbourne,' she said.

He was sitting up and the number of tubes going in and out of him had been halved. And I went over to kiss him. I had kissed him so often when he was lying unconscious, and I ached to see that lovely smile and his eyes light up.

He turned away. It wasn't that he didn't recognise me. He obviously recognised me, but he seemed to be angry with me, just from the look in his eyes. It was the weirdest thing and, in spite of myself, I felt very hurt.

I told him what had happened to him, that he'd had an accident, but he was going to be OK and that I loved him. There was a pause of a few seconds, perhaps fifteen, then, for the first time, he spoke coherently.

'You can go now,' he said.

'What do you mean, Dadda?'

'You can go home to your family.'

'Our family, you mean.'

He shook his head and turned his face away.

Over the next few days it became clear that he had been dreaming while he was unconscious, and it basically had been one long complex dream. Later he remembered it in incredible detail, and for months was convinced it was true.

As far as he believed, I had left him and gone off with a very wealthy man who owned a plane with a swimming pool in it, that he lived surrounded by guards with machine guns, and I was flying round the world with this wealthy man.

'But there is no wealthy man,' I insisted. 'You're the wealthy man.' But nothing I could say would convince him. The children tried, but it was no better; he just thought they were covering up. And it was so, so sad, to see him like this. The physical pain was now equalled by this terrible idea that we had abandoned him and were lying to him because we felt sorry for him. Nothing any of us said would get through. He thought he was in Ireland, which must have been related to Louis' wedding.

On the twelfth day I decided to take everyone up to London. It was 20 December, and we had done nothing as far as Christmas was concerned. Everything I had planned would be the same, only it wouldn't be at Welders but in a private room where Ozzy would be moved in a few days' time. It was attached to the main trauma unit, but was all glass so he could be monitored by the nurses, but he had a TV and his own lavatory and it was private. We had Bobby's family coming, and Robert as well as the Newmans as usual, but I wanted it to be Christmassy and fun, even though this would be the most difficult Christmas any of us had ever had to face.

'So I'm taking the Thomsons and the kids,' I told him, 'and we're going into town. I'll take everybody out this evening, then we'll stay in a hotel overnight but I'll be back to see you in the morning.'

He wasn't at all happy that we were going, but the children desperately needed a break and Ozzy was still spending most of the time sleeping anyway. And when he was awake, there was physiotherapy he was supposed to be doing to keep himself flexible.

When I got back home the following morning there was a call from the hospital: I had better get there quick because he was about to check out. *Check out?* The medical team had told me he had to stay in till March at least.

When I got to his room, he was in tears. 'You've got to get me out of here, Sharon,' he said, and looked so pathetic sitting there in this horrible metal collar, but I told him that he was in no fit state to leave.

'Look, Ozzy, they're moving you to a great room. Somewhere I can stay overnight, and we're fixing the room out now, and we've arranged Christmas lunch, and it's going to be just great.'

'I want to get out. I want to get out.'

'Ozzy, this is insane behaviour.'

'Get me the papers. I'm signing myself out.'

The hospital staff, me – all of us were at our wits' end. But Ozzy knows how these places work, and he knew that he had the right to sign himself out, and not me or anybody else had the power to stop him. What made it worse was that this behaviour was clearly manic. I tried to buy myself some time.

'At least give me a day to get a hospital bed in, and some nurses,' I said. Because how could I lift him, or take him to the bathroom, or get him into the shower? In hospital they'd been using a hoist and a bedpan. And he had to have physio every day. And he had such a massive amount of medication to take – I didn't want to be responsible for that. So I just begged and pleaded with him.

'Please let me at least get a nurse. Let me get the house ready. I mean, how am I going to get you upstairs? Please, Ozzy . . .'

He wouldn't have it. The kids were crying. Everyone knew that this was insane behaviour.

'You cannot come home, Ozzy. We cannot cope.'

'Get me the papers.'

I got on the phone. I could get a hospital bed the following day, and nurses, but not today.

His only concession was to bring a Zimmer frame back with him. Of course the whole journey was agony – it might have been only twenty minutes, but every bump made him wince with the pain – and then it took another twenty minutes to get him from the car into the bloody house. His bad arm was strapped to his chest, he had this horrific collar on and he couldn't sit normally because of his lungs. Everything was sore, everything was in agony, and there he was at home sitting on a sofa.

That night was the worst ever. Just getting him upstairs was a fucking nightmare. In the end it took four of them: Jack, Bobby's eldest son Kevin, Robert and David, who lives in the coach house. Then there was Maryshe, and David's wife Sharon standing behind him, just in case . . . I had to turn away. I was just, I can't watch this, I cannot fucking deal with this. Not only because I was worried that he was still acting so strange with me, but because it was Christmas and I wanted to make everything right for everyone. There were so many vulnerable people: the Thomson family who had just lost Bobby, Robert who had just lost his mum, not to mention Aimee, Kelly and Jack.

We tried three different beds in the house. He finally settled in the spare room, which has a Napoleonic bed with one side against the wall, and that night he insisted that I lie with him there, even though it was not much bigger than a big single. So I was lying against the wall, and he was on the edge, while Kelly was lying on the floor in case he rolled out. Every time Ozzy wanted to go to the bathroom, Kelly took him. 'Can't you just piss in a fucking cup or something?' I said. But no. I had to watch my nineteen-year-old daughter stagger across the room with her father hanging off her back. Then, when they got to the toilet, she would just hold him and look the other way. And I was like, What the fuck are we doing here?

'You are seriously sick, and you should be in hospital. Listen to me, Ozzy. I'm putting my hands up in the air and I'm saying, I am not responsible. I do not want to be a party to this. I cannot cope, I cannot fucking cope. Don't be so fucking selfish.' I was worn out.

The next day the hospital bed arrived and the nurses started. He was still pretty difficult, and still talking about Ireland and the wedding and some earthquake. And I was like, 'No, Ozzy, we didn't go to Ireland, Louis' wedding isn't until January. There was no earthquake, it never happened.' It was a big strain on everyone.

Christmas was not one of the best, but then it's an uphill battle with Ozzy anyway, and as soon as it was over the kids went back to LA, and I didn't blame them. 'Don't you worry,' I said. 'Just go.'

At the last minute I decided we needed something to cheer us up and so got in a caterer for a New Year's Eve party. There were only about thirty of us, a few of our good friends, the Newmans, my niece Gina and her husband Dean and their babies, Lynn, and my old flame Adrian, and I'm so glad I did. We had the best time. The mixture of people was perfect. Everyone knew each other, and no one person had to stay with Ozzy for too long, because everyone was trying to make him feel loved but he was being difficult, insisting on walking around with a stick and looking hideous, and we all had to suffer because you could see he was in agony.

I heard, 'For God's sake, Ozzy, sit down!' over and over again, but he took no notice. My husband can't sit still for two seconds at the best of times, and so being disabled like this was doing his head in. Even so, I think even Ozzy enjoyed it in the end, in his way. He certainly stayed up to see in the New Year. We stood at the window together, looking at the fireworks, and I held his hand and reminded him of where we had been just one year ago, telling ourselves and the world just how much we meant to each other. But he wasn't fully with it, and I kept wondering, when is he going to get clarity? When is he going to find the reality and realise that this is what's real, not the fantasy of the flying swimming pool? I don't know what time Ozzy went to bed that night, because by then I was legless. The catering company had made up a fruit punch and I had my head in the bowl it tasted so good, and for the first time in years and years and years I got very drunk. Finally a release. It was like, God, do I need this . . .

Telepictures were not happy that I had been away for longer than the agreed two-week Christmas break.

'Look,' I said. 'The show has hardly any more time to run, so let's just call it a day right now.' But no. They insisted I went back to LA to finish the fucking show, but it was a nightmare: Ozzy refused to stay in England without me but, because of his injury, no airline would take him for six weeks. In the end we had to charter a plane, and when I did get back to work, the first thing they told me was that they were not renewing my contract. I wasn't surprised.

One of my last guests was Simon Cowell. Simon is huge in America through his show *American Idol*, and the producers thought it might be fun to see the sparks fly between us, as he had been slagging us off, saying that Ozzy's accident was fabricated so we could get a No. 1 single, saying that Kelly was fat and couldn't sing, saying that *The Osbournes* was yesterday's news and that we were all nutters. Anything that's happening and popular, he always takes the opposite line. But that's Simon. It's his thing. I had never met him before. I can't say I warmed to him, but he was very open, admitted he was wrong and apologised. So there was nothing more I wanted from him.

I was late for the very last show. In fact, I had given up on the whole thing weeks before. It was like I was treading water, but I had to finish the commitment. I was just riding the contract out.

When they realised I wasn't in my dressing room, they started to fret.

'I'm sorry,' Melinda said when she answered the phone, 'but Sharon can't possibly make it today, she's in a closed-door meeting with Simon Cowell.' Then she switched on the privacy button. 'They're saying the audience is in, and smoke's coming out of their arses.'

'Tell them I want $200,000,' I told her, running some more hot water into the bath. 'Tell them I want gimlets served to me out of Manolo Blahnik shoes.' They didn't get the joke. I went in. My last line to camera was, 'I hope you've enjoyed the journey as much as we have.'

It ran a year but I worked out that with all the travel and promotion it was eighteen months of my life. Casey Paterson, the lovely, talented lady Telepictures said could never be the show runner because she didn't have the experience, now runs her own network. But I'm not blaming anyone; I had the forum and the show didn't work. They gave me a huge opportunity and I learnt a lot.

By the time the credits for the final *Sharon Osbourne Show* had run, I couldn't have cared less that it wasn't being renewed. Melinda's line about me being in a meeting with Simon Cowell was not so far removed from the truth. Shortly after our TV non-confrontation, his production company asked if I'd be interested in doing a talent show called *The X-Factor* in the UK. I had seen a couple of episodes of *Pop Idol* in England, and I had seen *American Idol* in the States, and on a professional level I had a lot of respect for Simon, but the money was very low.

'One time,' I said to him. 'I'll prove myself, but I will never work for this kind of money again.'

My life has always been extreme, even from birth. One parent Jewish, one Catholic. My weight: skinny to obese and back again. My life with my husband: a constant ricochet from joy to heartache. And then there was my life with my father, where it was either love or hate, feast or famine. Until now, I had rolled with the punches, but by the time Simon came to me with the *X-Factor* offer, I no longer had that option.

For twenty years I had lived in fear of the knock on the door, and on 17 October 2003 it had come.

Dana called to say that a letter had arrived from the California Franchise Tax Board, and she didn't understand it, she said. She is very meticulous and always knows where we are down to the last cent.

'What's to understand, Dana? Tax is tax.'

'But this is like a bill.'

'So?'

'Sharon, this is a bill for two million, four hundred and sixty-nine thousand, two hundred and twenty-one dollars and four cents, and I don't understand.'

'Two and a half million dollars? There must be some mistake, Dana. Just give them a call and sort it out.'

It wasn't a mistake. When it comes to tax there is no statute of limitations. If it had been my father's name on the bottom, they would just have to sing for it because he was penniless, an old man in a retirement home paid for by his daughter. But the signature at the bottom was not his; it was mine. And I remember that day so clearly. Batyu Patel, a faceless shadow in the doorway of my bungalow at the Howard Hughes house, a dark silhouette against the bright July sunlight pouring in from the courtyard; only the papers that he was waving in his hand showing up white.

'How can you not do this one last thing for your father?' he had said, having no idea what would happen years later.

And I had been so busy wrapping my final few ornaments in tissue paper, putting them in packing cases the removal company had brought, ornaments I never saw again, and I just wanted him to go. I just wanted him and everything to do with my father out of my life. Yet even as I signed, I had this feeling it would come back to haunt me. And now, twenty years later, it had. But I could never, ever have imagined it could be this much.

We hired lawyers to fight it. Spent even more thousands exploring this loophole and that loophole. But not one cent was deducted.

Fame comes at a price: if I had stayed quietly managing Ozzy, they might never have found me. But with *The Osbournes*, and then with my show, everything about me was out there. Sharon Osbourne was Don Arden's daughter. And in some office somewhere in downtown Los Angeles, they only had to put 'Sharon Arden' into Google to find out who I was now. Where I was now. There is no other explanation as to how they finally ran me to ground.

I didn't have the money. Nothing like the money. The money from *The Osbournes* had been split four ways and I gave my share to Aimee. To get these people off my back, Ozzy lent it to me. And now I have to pay it off. Ozzy would give me anything; he's not asking for anything back. But I just feel so guilty: my father again, coming to take Ozzy's money, and this time I am not going to let it happen. But to pay two and a half million, you have to earn three and a half million.

'If all goes well,' Simon Cowell had said, 'then there'll be a second series.' Now, for the first time since that phone call from Dana, there seemed to be light at the end of the tunnel. Not just one series, but two. But I needed big money.

21 April 2005, 5.30 p.m.
Doheny Road: my bedroom

'Sharon, call for you on line one.'

'Thanks, Howard.' I pick up the phone.

'You know what, Sharon? You are the most difficult person to get hold of.'

'Marsha!'

'We just wanted to say that Peter and I are thinking of Ozzy today. So do please give him our best love.'

I met Marsha in 1980 when there were very few women in the industry, but she is one of the greats, a very successful agent in New York, who was handling AC/DC, Def Leppard, Metallica, Neil Young, Bob Dylan, Elvis Costello, and we hit it off immediately. Not only did we have the music industry in common, but our children are the same age, and our husbands share the same sense of humour. Though as Peter is Croatian with an impenetrable accent, when Ozzy and he tell each other jokes, we swear that Ozzy can't understand him, and he can't understand Ozzy. Whenever we are all together, we always end up talking about sex. Because Ozzy and I have such an active sex life, Peter is always complaining that Marsha only wants to have sex on a Saturday morning before her run in the park, saying, 'You've got twenty minutes, Peter, so make the best of it.'

Throughout the years I've known her, Marsha and Peter have always been there for us. They flew over to England from New York to see Ozzy in hospital.

'Hey, I just read a thing on the internet about your Dr Kipper, and was wondering how that was all going.'

Dr David Kipper is a doctor who was recommended to us by a friend; as always it was about some groundbreaking way of getting Ozzy detoxed. He came into our lives three months before I was diagnosed as having cancer and he was very personable and had a great bedside manner with a creamy-sounding voice, and you felt so safe and reassured and calmed by him. He was very LA: he had the sun tan, the open-neck silk shirt, the Armani trousers, the Gucci loafers. I should have heard the warning bells when he started namedropping – everybody from movie directors to actors to rock stars. To listen to him you'd think he had personally saved half of Hollywood's rich and famous.

To cut a long story short, he put Ozzy on a drug – illegal at the time in California for detox – that was itself an opiate, which Ozzy became addicted to.

Soon it wasn't just Ozzy's detox he was dealing with. It was Ozzy's shaking, Ozzy's phobias, Ozzy's everything. He even put Ozzy on medication for his dyslexia. Then, once I was diagnosed with cancer, the prescriptions really started rolling out, both for me and for Ozzy, who basically had a breakdown. By that time he was taking forty-two pills and/or shots a day.

It's hard now to understand how we let ourselves be hoodwinked by this man. But we did. Perhaps because he was only ever a phone call away. In America doctors don't do house calls. He did. Kelly had only to fall over and hurt her leg and he would be there. We bought into this man wholesale, as a whole family. Like a drowning man, we were grasping at anything that seemed to offer a way out. In all, with Ozzy's various treatments, my treatments, the 24-hour nursing care he insisted I needed post my op, nurses that turned out to be useless, we paid that man $750,000 over the one year he was with us.

The *LA Times* won the Pulitzer prize with an investigation into his activities. He has denied all charges, and now it's just down to the slow-moving medical malpractice people. As far as we are concerned, Ozzy and I have decided to just let it go. There are plenty of others out there suing him, but we just don't have the energy to get involved. But I think of Dr Kipper, and probably will for the rest of my life, each time I look at a fucking fish.

21

X-Factor

Before *The X-Factor* I had never had much to do with the British press. I hadn't been well enough to do any promotion for *The Osbournes* in England – I couldn't risk picking up an infection on a long-haul flight, so when I flew over to see Ozzy after his accident, post my cancer, it was the first time I had been to Welders in two years. Although *The Osbournes* had been hugely successful in England, it was late night on Channel 4. *The X-Factor*, however, was ITV1, prime time, and it was a watershed for me: I was no longer thought of primarily as Ozzy's wife, I was now 'Sharon Osbourne, *X-Factor* Judge'.

Of the three judges on the show – Simon Cowell, Louis Walsh and me – I was very definitely the odd one out. Whereas they were both TV-talent-show veterans, I had never done anything like it before. I had never even worked in England. On every level I was flying blind. Luckily the people I found myself working with couldn't have been nicer and more welcoming. Although Louis and I had never met before, we hit it off immediately, and Kate Thornton, the presenter, is as spontaneous and natural as she appears on screen. She's very bright – the sort of person you know would make a success of anything she turned her hand to, and I instantly fell in love with her.

The success of the show was phenomenal and for the three months we were on air, it was as if *The X-Factor* owned Saturday nights. What's more, the British public seemed to take to me, not because I was shooting my mouth off this time, but because I wore my heart on my sleeve. I cared about these young people and wasn't ashamed to show it and would fight for those I believed in. When things didn't work out for them, I'd burst into tears on camera, often while they themselves were being wonderfully dignified and controlled. My regular outbursts of emotion were probably because I had the experience of being a mum and I knew that if it was my kid up there and some arsehole had destroyed their dream, I'd want to kill them. So many of them, especially the younger ones, would be literally trembling from the moment they stepped out onto that stage and my heart would melt.

Right from the start, Simon told me not to get emotionally involved, but I found it increasingly difficult not to, till it got to the point where I became so overprotective of the kids in my charge that if anyone said anything against them, I'd go insane.

However, as much as it felt right to fight for people I believed in, being diplomatic isn't my style and the sharp edge of my tongue was soon getting plenty of exercise. I found it extraordinary to see just how many people there were out there who thought they could sing and hadn't a fucking clue about how bad they really were. There was a set of twins who were so bad they were good, and when I refused to put them through to the next round they really let rip.

'What the fuck do you know?' they shouted. 'Your daughter can't sing, and neither can your husband', and I just cracked up.

I was like, Bring it on! I just loved it when people bounced back at me. I loved all that energy and for me it was home from home.

The whole experience was such an eye-opener. I was amazed at how little idea so many of them had of presenting themselves. One of the worst in the presentation area was the guy who ended up winning the contest. His name was Steve, and he turned up looking like he'd been in the pub all night: he hadn't shaved and generally looked scruffy with flip-flops, ill-fitting trousers and an old T-shirt. He had clearly made no effort what-soever. As for his voice, it was OK but a bit too 'smoothy' for my taste, and not suited at all for what he was singing, which was R&B. The first time we saw him, we couldn't make up our minds whether to put him through or not, so we said to come back the following day.

'And lay off the pop,' I added, as he walked off the stage. 'You look like you've been on the piss.' This did not go down well. As for the ten-o'clock shadow, it turned out this was his look. Some people can get away with it and some people can't. He couldn't. It was the start of an appalling relationship.

Steve was the typical guy you see performing on a cruise liner or in a pub and you go, 'This guy should have done something; he could have made it.' But in my view a white man from Essex is never going to make it as an R&B singer, and I told him so.

'But you see, Sharon,' he whined, 'I grew up listening to this music.'

'And I grew up seeing people play this music. My entire childhood, my entire life, I have seen the greats perform this music, and you are not one of them.'

Because I managed Ozzy, he thought all I knew about was heavy metal. But he had no clue who I was, what my back-ground was, nothing. And he was like an old gramophone record with the needle stuck in the groove: 'You see, Sharon, I grew up with this music.' I grew up seeing the Royal fucking Ballet. It didn't mean I could dance *Swan Lake*.

I had no respect for him and he had no respect for me. If he'd ended up in my group he'd have been out at the first opportunity, but at the mentoring stage I was given the under-24s to look after, so Steve, as an old-timer of thirty-six, belonged to Simon. But all the way through the contest – the elimination of this one and that one – our paths would cross, and I would always tell him variations of the same home truth: 'You ain't got it, you ain't got an ounce of soul in you.'

In my view, that was what we were there for: to tell the truth as we saw it. And if you're going to make it in show business, winning people over is part of the job. As far as I was concerned, Steve did the opposite. His arrogance behind the scenes made me sick.

As part of my mentoring team I was helped by two people I feel I have known for ever. As musical director, I brought in Mark Hudson, who has written and produced for everybody from Aerosmith to Bon Jovi and Celine to Cher. As stylist I brought in Ozzy's nephew, his sister Gillian's son, always known as Cousin Terry. Terry already had experience of reality TV as he was one of the hairdressers on *The Salon* on Channel 4, and he is really creative with a great personality, and Ozzy and I just adore him.

At each stage of the competition it got more and more emotionally demanding. I'd found it hard enough saying no to people in the first round, but as the weeks went by I could barely cope with dealing with the kids' emotions and dealing with my own. Because now these young people weren't strangers any more. It takes weeks and weeks for an artist to be signed to a record label, and we had to go through the same process of decision-making in a matter of days.

The schedule was horrendous for everybody involved. The kids never stopped working, day in, day out. They had the live show on the Saturday, and on Sunday morning they'd be up rehearsing the following week's song. If they couldn't keep up, they fell by the wayside. As for me, it took over my life for half a year. It totally consumed me; I allowed myself to get far too wrapped up in it all. Even my family were engulfed by it, with Ozzy and the kids watching at home every Saturday night.

I can't blame anybody but myself for what happened. Simon warned me again and again not to get emotionally involved. But I chose not to listen to him.

He would be the first to admit that it's been like a roller-coaster ride between us. Although I had always respected him professionally, at first I found him difficult to work with. But now I have got to know him, my view has totally changed. The truth is that we are very similar people, but now I would like to think that we are friends. He gave me the opportunity to come and work in England and for that I will always be grateful. But it nearly went very, very wrong.

It all came to a head on the last show. The kids in my group had all been eliminated, and it was down to a head-to-head between my bugbear Steve and a vocal group mentored by Louis, called G4.

So it's the rehearsal, and we've got music, orchestra, lights, pyro, the lot. We were going through the sound check and camera shots that were locked in. So Steve came on and did his thing and Louis made a comment, and then it was my turn to make a comment. 'Actually, Steve,' I said, 'you did really good tonight.'

And he goes, 'Yeah, yeah, yeah', and he's got that fuck-you expression on his face and he's rolling his eyes like a nine-year-old who's just been told not to talk back to the teacher.

'Just a minute, I said you did really good.'

'Yeah, yeah, yeah.'

He did it again. And suddenly I lost it. 'You disrespectful piece of shit,' I said. 'You are not good enough to fucking wash my underwear. You are a talentless, worthless piece of shit and I'm going to let everybody know about you, and that you are a fucking prick and a fake.'

Because what I most disliked about Steve was not his voice, it was his attitude. On camera he was all, 'Oh, I'm so glad to be here, I can't believe I got through . . . Winning is not what it's about . . .' And he was just like Uriah Heep, wringing his hands and going: 'I'm ever so 'umble.'

So anyway, there I was screaming and shouting, and Simon stood up and put his hands in the air as if to say, that's enough, stop it. Then one of the producers came running down from the control room. 'How dare you act this way in the studio,' she shouted. 'How dare you say these things?'

Well, I wasn't having that. 'Hey, excuse me. He's a grown man, he's thirty-six. Did you hear what he said? Who the fuck am I to sit here and take this shit from this pub singer? Because that's what he is. He's a pub singer.'

Nobody said a word. I walked back to the dressing room, and then called Ozzy to ask what he thought I should do.

'You have to be true to yourself, Sharon,' he said. 'You have to do what you want to do, and don't pretend.' And all the time I was waiting for the knock on the door, for someone to stand there and say, 'I think you two had better kiss and make up. Let's not take this on the set.' But it didn't happen. Nobody knocked. Nobody said or did anything.

So the studio is packed, and it's Saturday 11 December 2004, and it's the final. We've been on TV since September, but now it's just between Steve and G4. And Steve sings his first song, and Simon is up there standing next to him waiting for our comments. And I couldn't stop myself. I'd been planning to say what I had said in rehearsal, that tonight he'd done great. But I didn't.

'You're a fake,' I said. 'You come up as Mr Nice Guy and Mr Humble, but you're not. As far as your singing goes,' I continued, 'it's like what you said about your girlfriend, you're like a Volvo, you're reliable.' And I did the same after his second song. It just kept coming and coming and it was terrible. I should never have done it. I was meant to be a professional, and what I thought about him personally was neither here nor there. But I just heard myself explode. And then, one after the other, the audience started booing and hissing me, because good old Steve was very, very popular. If I had hoped to change the way people would vote, I got it completely wrong. Everybody loves the underdog, and now the bitch from hell had turned on him, slagging off poor old Steve the lovely pub singer who's been struggling for recognition all his life.

The night wasn't over. There was a half-hour break while the millions of votes came in from the viewers. As I made my way back to the dressing room, nobody talked to me, not a fucking soul. Just whispers and hissing as I went past, but I refused to be cowed.

Back in my dressing room I was greeted by white faces, people from my office saying things like, Oh God, Sharon, you've done it now. And I called Ozzy again, who was watching at home.

'Bloody hell, Shaz,' he said, 'what the hell did you just do?'

What I'd just done was wave goodbye to the chance of a second series.

This time the director, Richard Holloway, did come to the dressing room. 'Look,' he said. 'I think you ought to take it back.'

'How can I take it back, Richard? How can I say, "Oh, actually I didn't mean that. I forgive you for being a fucking hustling piece of shit." How can I do that? It would mean nothing.' And no one would have believed me anyway, least of all him, and we'd have had another fucking round of eye-rolling and smirking.

So we go back into the studio and the results come in and Steve has won, hands down. And it's the confetti and the pyro and everybody stands up and they're like, 'Yes! Steve has won!' So, of course, I stood up too, I had to. But I couldn't go near him. I wasn't about to be that much of a hypocrite. What was I going to do? Give him a kiss?

Finally came the after-show interviews that went out as *The X-tra Factor* on the satellite channel ITV2. So we went into the next-door studio and I was interviewed, as usual, about the result. And I said that, as far as my views about Steve were concerned, it was just my opinion, and good luck to him.

On paper, and in the tabloids, Steve had won. But in the long run, in the record industry where it counts, I think that Louis's group G4 could be said to be the ultimate *X-Factor* winners, because they have gone on to sell hundreds of thousands of records. They have a real career ahead of them, whereas Steve has yet to find his form.

Louis is a bit of a dark horse. Because he's very low key and unpretentious, people are inclined to underestimate his talent. But he is a great songs guy and has an encyclopaedic knowledge of music. He's managed the boy bands Boyzone and Westlife, and from *Pop Stars: The Rivals* he got Girls Aloud, who he won the show with, and who have gone on to be a very big group in Europe.

Until that night it had seemed that, as far as the British press were concerned, I could do no wrong. Over the previous months hardly a day had gone by without a picture of me appearing in some newspaper or magazine, and – as far as I can remember – the approach was always positive. The next morning, however, it was a different story. The Sunday papers slaughtered me. Simon was quoted as saying I was a loose cannon, and he didn't want people like that on his show. There wasn't a single voice saying, 'Well, actually she might just have had something there . . .' Not a one. They even suggested that it was because of my outburst that Steve had won at all. There they were wrong: I discovered afterwards that he had won at every stage, although none of us knew that at the time. But I was wrong in what I did. It was Steve's night, and not mine, and he won fairly.

As for Simon, there was no goodbye, no nothing. But Simon was right. I took it too far. I had taken it too personally. It was not my show. I was employed to do something, that was all. Next time I would do it different, I thought. In fact, there were a lot of things I would do different. All along I had been looking for perfection, the perfect combination: the look, the voice, the personality, the everything. But perfection comes along very rarely and, when it does, that's what makes you a superstar, and the qualities I was searching for are like gold dust. I had forgotten that this was a TV show. I had forgotten that to get the audience at home involved they had to have someone to warm to. Perfection wasn't what they wanted; it's people's imperfections that are the things that make you love them.

Now it looked as if I would never get the chance. I heard that Simon never wanted to see me again, never wanted to talk to me again, never wanted to work with me again, and I didn't blame him. And he wasn't, as I was, just somebody employed to do a professional job. *The X-Factor* was his idea, it was his baby.

21 April 2005, 6.30 p.m.
Hollywood Boulevard

My father always wanted to live in Hollywood and now he's going to die here. He's seventy-nine.

He's sitting in his chair beside the bed. On the table, among the photographs in silver frames, is a jug of cranberry juice mixed with water.

'Hi, Dadders. I've brought you lots of stuff. Biccies and cake. So, what's been going on?' My father has lost so much weight since he's been in here, and I worry about how they're looking after him, but they keep his room nice. I will pay for everything for my father but I cannot give him my time. I hardly ever come here. But I will have him taken care of. 'Did David come for St Patrick's Day? He did? And did you have a great time?'

'Sarah.'

'That's right. Sally. My nana.' We sit looking at family photographs together, the ones that were sent to me by Dixie when my mother died. There's one of us at the Astor Club; another one of my parents, standing in the pool house at the Howard Hughes house.

'You been watching the telly, Dad?'

'I won't . . . I won't be frock . . . I won't . . .'

'Don't worry, Dad. You just rest. Ooh, look. Here's a picture before you had a beard. When did you first grow a beard?'

'I've had one or two.'

You can still hear his Manchester accent. In fact it's stronger now than it ever was. One pronounced 'wan'.

'One of them pradas. Just take it to the bank. That fella.'

'What fella's that, Dad?'

'He's got a woman on this thing.'

'I think we need to get a rug for you, Dadders. Your room could do with a bit of cheering up.'

'That one, I think I was saying chillies. Yeah.'

'Have you spoken to Auntie Eileen?'

'Forget now.'

'Are they looking after you well?'

'Couldn't really say.'

'It's nice here, Dad.'

'Suppose so.'

'How's that bloke you were having problems with? Is he still a pain in the arse?'

'Yes. A know-all.'

'Do you remember when you lived in Prestwich?'

'Being scratch, she'll want to be, she'll want to be somebody and it's not very hard. You can't. Very hard. Yes.'

'Have a nice choccy biccie.'

'Must see her right.'

'I'll put on some music, shall I, Dadders?'

I walk over to the CD player, press play and pick up the empty box. Frank Sinatra's comeback album, *September of My Years*, recorded in 1965 when he was fifty.

The melody swells up: 'When I was twenty-one, it was a very good year . . . for city girls who lived up the stair . . . their chauffeurs would drive when I was thirty-five . . . but now the days grow short . . . it was a mess of good years.' And we dance.

22

Payback

Simon Cowell has become infamous for the way he looks: the high-waisted trousers and long-sleeved cashmere top are his trademark. Jewellery is my trademark, though. I will never know if it was this that triggered the theft on the night of 22 November 2004.

It was Sunday night, and we had just come back from David Furnish's birthday party at the Ivy, and we'd had a great time because David is so lovely with Ozzy, and he and Elton are such caring people. They're very committed to their friendships. They're not fly-by-night friends. But I was so wired and so strung out with *The X-Factor* that I had taken a couple of sleeping pills, so was out before my head hit the pillow.

Our bedroom at Welders is at the back of the house over-looking the garden, and from my bed I can see through my bathroom and then through another door to my dressing room. All three rooms run along the back of the house. My dressing room was originally another bedroom but I closed up the door from the landing long ago. So it's big. In the centre there's an island made up of drawers back to back, and that's where I would lay out my jewellery so it was easy for me to put outfits together. I had my pearls, my diamonds, my gold, my platinum, everything out, so I could construct my look.

The only way in is through the bedroom and then the bathroom, unless, of course, you choose to come in through a window.

At around four o'clock that morning, Ozzy got up for a wee. He must have been sleepwalking, because he has his own bathroom on the other side of our bedroom and he normally goes there. He's sleepwalked ever since he was a child. He can have complete conversations, he can even eat, but he's not awake. Aimee is the same.

So I'm fast asleep and Ozzy is in my bathroom having a wee, and out of the corner of his eye he sees something move in my dressing room. So he walks in and there's a man crouched down wearing a balaclava.

Ozzy didn't scream or shout because he was sleepwalking and probably thought it was a dream. But when the guy saw Ozzy, he made a dash for the window. But this window is narrow, and even though the guy must have been small he squirmed his way out feet first, so his head and upper body were still in the room and Ozzy got him in a headlock. Ozzy knows all about the neck and how vulnerable it is, and he says he could have snapped it like a straw. Having worked in a slaughterhouse, he said it would have been the easiest thing in the world, because the guy's feet must have been dangling out of the window looking for the rungs of the ladder and the weight of his body was resting in Ozzy's arms. But even in his half-conscious state, my husband decided he couldn't have a man's death on his conscience, even a thief. So basically he shoved him out of the window. It's a drop of about twelve feet onto a terrace with a few shrubs to break the fall.

The first I knew of it was when Ozzy came running in, screaming to me at the top of his voice: 'We've been robbed! Call the police!'

I sat straight up in bed like a jack knife.

'Call the police, Sharon, we've been robbed!'

But what with the pills I'd taken, I was so muzzy that I couldn't remember what country I was in. I asked Ozzy where we were, but he didn't seem to understand. He was in shock, still running round the bedroom naked. First I dialled 9 to get an outside line, because I thought I was in Doheny. Then I dialled 411, directory enquiries in America. Finally I got through, said we'd been robbed and to please send somebody around immediately. When I put the phone back on the bedside table, I saw that my ten-carat diamond ring and my wedding bands were gone. I called the police again: 'Please send a helicopter, this is serious.' I still had no idea what was going on.

And it was serious. When I checked my other jewellery, all my best pieces had been taken. The most heartbreaking was a 54-carat sapphire, which I always called the Swimming Pool, a huge ring. They stole my pearls, pearls the size of gobstoppers with a diamond clasp. The daisy necklace Ozzy bought me for our twentieth wedding anniversary from Van Cleef, two limited edition watches by Franck Muller – one of them alone was worth £100,000. And little things, like a pin a promoter had given me back in the seventies: a circle of diamonds round the initials ELO. It wasn't something I would ever wear, but it was my past. They took one of the first pieces of jewellery that Ozzy gave me, again a pin, with the initials S and A, the A in diamonds. I would never wear it, because of the A – but, again, it was my past. Most ridiculous of all, they took a ring that I had got for a photographic session, an enamel owl with a big diamond on its head. Except that it wasn't a diamond, it was a fake. And they took two pairs of fashion earrings – real stones, but not investment diamonds. They were probably worth about £10,000 each, but considering what else they were taking, this was like small change.

In fact, this bastard probably thought he was the one who'd been robbed when he saw how little there was in his swag bag. Some nights on *The X-Factor* I'd have a million pounds' worth of jewellery on, and it would be different pieces every week. What these criminals hadn't realised was that it wasn't mine, and that somewhere out of sight of the cameras were the security guys who had brought it. Guys who, once the show was over, took everything back to the vaults at Van Cleef or Tiffany or wherever. Because the jewellery was on loan. Just like for the Oscars.

When the police arrived all they found were the pictures caught on CCTV of a man coming in with a ladder and then running away.

Even when I realised the extent to which we'd been robbed, my main reaction was how dare you come into my house when you know that we're there. How dare you even try and fight with my husband. That man could have beaten us both to death, and if they ever did catch him I would get great satisfaction from doing him serious bodily harm.

The likelihood is that the perpetrators had done a dummy run a whole year earlier. Shortly after Christmas 2003, when Ozzy had only just come back from hospital, we found muddy footprints in the hall and a windowsill was dirty. And I thought, that's funny, so we went to the security cameras and rolled back the tape, and lo and behold there's a guy with a ladder and a bala-clava filmed coming onto our land and leaving. We did a complete inventory, but nothing was missing. Cilla Black, who lives about five miles away, had been badly robbed not long before, and the police said there was a gang of about ten of these people who were very dangerous, and for the next month the police were constantly at the house, waiting in the garden. But nothing. When we went back to LA, all the valuables in the house – silver and paintings – were put into a vault away from the property, which is what we have always done.

Then, about six months later, the police called to say that they'd caught this gang, and on one of their computers they'd found a layout of our land. So that seemed like the end of the story.

Two days after the robbery we offered a reward of £200,000 for information leading to a conviction. £200,000 is a shitload of money – nobody offers that much, the police said; they only offer £10,000 to find a murderer. We were coming up to Christmas, so it was a huge incentive to turn somebody in. But no one even came forward, which just proves, they said, that this was a professional operation. I know now that I'll never get any of it back and the way I'll deal with it – I suppose – is how I deal with everything negative in my life: just close it off. Blank it. Put up a shield. Not there. Gone.

It wasn't insured, because it wasn't in the safe. I will never replace it.

A month or so later, Ozzy and I were guests on *The Howard Stern Show* in New York, and he went on and on about what were we doing having jewellery worth that much money anyway. And I said to him, as I've said before, that it's nobody's business what I spend my money on. Some people buy property as investment – they can live in it, enjoy it, but they can also sell it. And that's how I buy jewellery. I love wearing jewellery, but I also buy for investment. I have my houses, I have my jewellery, I have antiques, I have pictures. I don't have a single stock or share. If I can't live in it, wear it, look at it or sit on it, I don't want it.

There are certain rules I stick to when buying jewellery. I never buy second-hand, because with old jewellery there is always a story behind it. Somebody may have died; it may have been stolen and caused heartache. Having lost so much jewellery in my life – sometimes literally lost, or stolen, or my father taking it – I know the heartache it can bring. And even if you buy at a respected auction house, they'll say it's the property of the grand duchess of fucking manure and she left it to her great-niece in her will, but it's all bollocks. I have one necklace that Ozzy bought me from a vintage jewellery shop, which has never got lost and never been stolen. I love it for what it represents, because he went out and he chose it and he bought it, but I never wear it. Because its unknown history makes me too sad.

I have had so much stolen and so much pawned that you would think I would just wash my hands of this shit. But I don't. I never seem to learn. It is pathetic, and I know it. It's my addiction: it started when I was young and it made me feel better about myself. Also it was a status symbol when I had no other. And then, when I was fat, my jewellery was a distraction from my arse.

Then it became the way I could get back at Ozzy for his bad behaviour. Because when he hurt me, so I would hurt him. I couldn't get to him in a physical way, so I got to him in a mental way. I used my brain and, because he has always been terrified of being poor, I knew the worst thing I could do was spend his money. I would go into Tiffany's or Van Cleef or wherever and I would spend, and they would simply send the bill to him. I would show him what I had bought, and he would look in horror. The amount I spent would depend on what he had done. There was a sliding scale. Sometimes, if he was drunk, I would lie about how much something cost because I'd be afraid of his reaction. But he'd find out the truth soon enough when the bill arrived. And he would always pay up. Because of guilt. It was like, touché. Him and me.

The first time it happened was before we got married and we were on tour with Motörhead in America, and there was this wretched groupie who was following the tour around. Not content with fucking all of Motörhead, she was now in bed with Ozzy. The door to our room was closed, but I just got another key from reception and found them. I got her by the hair and said, 'Fuck off out of here', I swiped Ozzy one, cleaned my teeth, got into bed and went to sleep. Next day I went shopping.

That was the pattern. Something would happen and I would spend. I never bought shit; I always bought good. If he ever dared say anything, I would reply, 'Listen. I don't pour it down my neck and piss it out. I don't cancel shows because I'm drunk and lose money that way.' No, I'd go out and spend it, and it made him mad, while I got the satisfaction of living with it or wearing it, and Fuck You. And so my collection of jewellery grew.

I didn't only *buy* jewellery, I also threw it away. When I was pregnant with Aimee, there was a band on at a festival Ozzy was doing, and he wanted them off. It wasn't our show so there was nothing I could do. But he went on and on and on, until I just couldn't take any more. So it was, 'Fuck you!'

'No, fuck you!'

'No, fuck you! I don't want to be married to you anyway!' And I pulled off my engagement ring and put it down the toilet. We were in the Beverly Wilshire, and I didn't realise it was one of those suction flushes. I was making a statement. I thought the ring would be sitting there in the bottom when the water had stopped whirling. But no. It was gone.

Before we were married, we were staying near Stafford on a visit to see Ozzy's children and we were just arguing. It was a Sunday.

'That's it,' he said, and started walking down the drive. And we had borrowed Colin's BMW, so I got in the car and told Pete to get in the passenger seat.

'What for?'

'I'm going to fucking kill him, that's what for!'

When Ozzy saw the car racing towards him, he started running across the lawn, and I followed him and when we drew parallel I began throwing things at him, because I wanted to hurt him. I threw my shoes, I threw Coke bottles, I wrenched off the rear-view mirror, and the car was lurching because I was half driving, half lugging these things out of the window. By this time we were out of the hotel grounds, and we got to the church just as the service was coming out and people were shaking hands with the vicar at the door, and Ozzy decided it was safety in numbers, so he tried to mingle in with the crowd. He couldn't fool me: I took the car up on the pavement and the crowd scattered. Hats and handbags in the air. All I could see was Pete's bright red-check jacket as we were doing whirlies on the village green, and then Pete said, 'Fuck this, I'm off', and he opened the door and rolled out.

We made it up, as we always did, but that night Ozzy couldn't sleep for thinking about the last things I'd thrown at him, because they were all I'd had left: seventeen gold bangles. So he walked back to the church and started desperately looking for these fucking bracelets in a yew hedge in the dark. He found about half of them.

The main sadness for me in the theft from Welders is that they stole the pieces I had planned to pass on to my daughters. When Ozzy and I renewed our vows I had two wedding bands made, one for Kelly and one for Aimee when I die, and now I don't have those heirlooms to pass on, or the Swimming Pool sapphire and the 10-carat diamond ring, which were specifically a nest egg for my girls. And if I'd caught the bastard and I'd had a gun,

I'd have shot him, because I will fight and fight for what is mine and never shed a tear. I hope he gets leprosy and his dick and his nose fall off.

---

21 April 2005, 7.30 p.m.
Doheny Road: in my bath

Everything is ready for this evening. The tables outside are ready to be laid, but I asked David to do nothing until Ozzy had gone into his meeting, and then he could get going on the barbecue. Ozzy is safely in his meeting, and the door is closed. And all the regular guys are there, all people in the industry, trying to help each other, one day at a time. For the first time today I can just close my eyes and dream.

After the MTV Awards in Australia we flew north to Queensland, to the Whitsunday Islands on the Great Barrier Reef. And for two days running we chartered a boat and headed off, away from people asking for pictures and autographs, to a beach with sand of pure white silica that crunched under your feet like new-fallen snow. And Jack went boulder climbing, and Kelly and Ozzy went snorkelling, and I lazed and read and swam in the blue, blue waters off Whitehaven beach. On the third day, instead of a motor cruiser, we got the guy to take us out in an old sailing boat to watch the sunset. It was a beautiful old boat, all brass and ropes, and once out of the little harbour, he stopped the engine and we all helped pull on these ropes to unfurl the sails. And so we sailed. Nobody talking very much, the only sound being the slap of the wooden boat against the water. There was nothing out there. Not another boat, not a house, nothing except the sea and the sky and other islands green with tropical forest. And as the sun slipped down behind the horizon, the sky turned to fire. And it was so beautiful.

The darkening shapes of the islands, the silence. For those ninety or so minutes we were on that boat, I didn't have a care in the world. Jack was at the wheel, and he looked so happy, Ozzy was sitting next to me, and I looked out and saw Kelly, her face glowing in the sun, and I knew that Aimee was safe with her friends in Sydney. I've been to beautiful places before, but I have never felt serenity like that in my entire life.

Epilogue

21 April 2005, 11.00 p.m.
Doheny Road, my bedroom

Today, 21 April 2005, my husband has been sober for one entire year, the longest since we first met thirty-five years ago. Since even longer, in fact. Ozzy had his first drink at eleven, and because he was insecure and lacking in self-esteem it was his support system, and anything like that gets worse and worse. For years he didn't want to change; he thought nothing was wrong. That was just the way life was. Ozzy came from a background where you left school, you got a job, got married, went to the pub, beat up the wife, had sex, and then the week began again. And it's been a tortuous ride for him, dealing with his demons. But every day it gets easier, though there are still times when he needs to be held, needs to be told it's worth hanging on for. And all I can do is be there for him when these black times come, which are not easy, not for him or for me.

The bed is covered with rose petals, velvety red curls, scattered across the white linen cover, which he must have done while I was taking a bath before the party. And now I'm finishing packing for Thailand, because we're leaving tomorrow morning, going first to New York where Kelly is performing. I won't stay up here long because Ozzy's downstairs talking to Aimee and her boyfriend. They're flying out early tomorrow and if I don't go down soon I will miss them. I didn't think Aimee would come, but she did. She's still weak, but her doctors say it will just take time. And Kelly sent her daddy the most beautiful letter in the world that made us both cry, about how proud she is of him for having made it through one whole year. And Jackie Boy phoned from Thailand, not too busy getting ready for the fight to forget what a big day it is for Ozzy. We're both so proud of our son. He's got himself straightened out and he's such a joy to have around. He is my rock, and I miss him so much.

It's quiet outside now. The clattering and murmur of the party voices have gone, just the sweet smell of jasmine floats in from the balcony through the open windows. It has been a perfect day, from the moment Ozzy woke me with a kiss and a rose he'd taken from the 365 that were waiting for him down in the hall.

Then, coming back from seeing my father, I spotted Simon Cowell of all people, gave him a toot, pulled up and we both got out of our very English cars, my Bentley, his Rolls-Royce. It was so strange – we'd last seen each other in an airless, smelly studio in Wembley in not-so-happy circumstances, and here we were stand-ing in the middle of a road heavy with the scent of jasmine being all 'darling, how lovely'. And I told Simon how the contract for the second series had arrived only this morning.

'Terrific,' he said, looking genuinely pleased. 'So, see you in May!' Only in Hollywood.

For Ozzy's surprise party, everything worked out great. If he realised what was going on, he didn't say so, though it's hard to imagine how he could have missed it, but when he's writing he's blind and deaf to everything else, so perhaps it just washed over him.

He has asked me to announce that this year will be his final Ozzfest. If anybody should make that announcement it has to be him, not me. But, oh God, I hope he doesn't change his mind. At first, after his accident, he said he wanted to stop touring altogether, but performing is the only drug Ozzy has left now, and for someone who has low self-worth, it has to make you feel better to see that sea of faces out there, loving you. He thinks he would like to get out of the business altogether and raise Poms. But much as he loves his little Poms, would it really be enough? I've waited for this moment for a long time now. Ozzy has spent his entire adult life touring, and for our entire marriage both of us have worked constantly. I just think it's time for us now.

I look at people like the Rolling Stones, and they're going out again this summer and I think, how can you go up on stage and shake your arse in tight trousers when you're sixty-plus thinking you're sexy? It's the same as Ozzy going up on stage and trying to be scary. He can't go up there and act scary any more, because he's not; Ozzy is the least scary person in the world. It's not giving up; it's that there are times when it's right to move on.

Ozzy has such a fertile mind, and the songs that he and Mark are coming up with for *Rasputin* are just brilliant. He has already made the progression to TV that no other rock star has done, and now he will do it in the musical theatre. Not like the Rod Stewart story or the Abba show or the Queen show, when it's just their music that's being recycled into a stage production. He is creating something entirely new, a rock musical, and he'll be accepted on a different level. But I also know that he's scared.

People don't see it, but Ozzy is so vulnerable. He has never valued himself, and it would make me sad to see how he would always be so nice to the young artists but would never approach his peers; he never thought he was worthy enough. He is constantly needy, and the last few years haven't made it any easier. All his life he'd been the main attraction, then suddenly his children were in the limelight, I was in the limelight, and he has found it very difficult, as anybody would.

His entire career people have shat on him. Not the fans, never the fans – they have always been amazingly loyal. But the business side of the industry. There are only a handful of people left today I have any time for. As for the rest, it would honestly not faze me if I never saw them again. I've paid my dues and now I tell it like it is. Nothing about it excites me: I've heard it, seen it, done it, before you were born. And as far as these guys are concerned, I'm not worth a wank. I don't play golf. I don't go watch the Lakers throw a ball up in the air and then go out and have a beer and a fucking lap dance. I don't kiss arse. Because that's the industry. I will not kiss anyone's arse.

The last hour before the party was strange. Dave was cooking for the five thousand and the garden was filling with Ozzy's surprise guests come to celebrate, but Ozzy was still in his meeting. By the time he'd finished, everyone was there, from his doctors, to people connected with AA, and other friends from Hollywood's sober community who have to stay anonymous. Jude Alcala was there, lanky as ever, and even dear old Pete Mertons with his wife and brand new baby looking good enough to eat, the most lovely little girl with big blue eyes.

There was a time when I desperately wanted more children. Ozzy still asks me every few days to have another one. We still could, but I don't want to take a child out and be told, 'Your grandchild is gorgeous!' I'm too selfish at this time of my life and I couldn't take the heartache of being a parent again. Because it is the hardest thing in the world. When these little people arrive, with all that joy and excitement, you have no idea that along with the joy will come heartache.

The sun goes down quickly in California. The temperature might feel like an English summer's evening but it's not like that, and by eight the light had gone from the sky and faces were lit by the fire-light and candles, and I wandered round the tables. Then David brought out the cake, somebody got up and started singing 'Happy Birthday', the candles were blown out and it was truly like Ozzy's birthday. The end of the first year of his new sober life.

My husband is still frightened. He still goes to his meetings every day, and gets nervous if he can't get to one. But he is a different person. For so long he thought that he couldn't write, saying things like, 'I've never done this straight, I need booze, I need this, I need that.' But now I say 'Just shut up. That's a crock of shit.' He doesn't need it. And he's beginning to know it himself. Recently we did *The Tonight Show with Jay Leno* and I hardly said a word. I purposely held back because he was coming out with all this great stuff and it was totally genius, one-liner after one-liner, and it was like Jay Leno was his straight man. And afterwards everyone was coming up to me and saying, 'Oh my God, Ozzy's amazing, whatever happened to Ozzy!' What's happened to Ozzy is that he's sober. There are no more chemicals to stand in the way of his extraordinary imagination, his humour, his everything.

I know it's hard for people to understand how, after all I have gone through with my husband, I am still here. I am here because I love him, and, apart from my children – who he gave me – Ozzy is the only person in my entire life who has ever loved me. Fat, thin, crazy, horrible, it doesn't matter. His love is unconditional. And when he doesn't have his demons on his shoulder, he is the sweetest, funniest, loveliest, most caring man in the world, and Ozzy's demons are getting weaker and weaker. He has matured so much and grown so much over the past year, and he's bettered his life. Now it's my turn to work to change my behaviour. For the last twenty-something years I have made all the decisions in our life together. I was holding his hand; now it's time for him to hold mine.

'Sharon?'

There he is now, coming up the stairs.

'Yeseeee!'

'What are you doing? We're all waiting for you.'

'I'm coming down. Just having a bit of a think.'

He wanders into the room.

'Nothing bad, eh, Shaz?'

'No, Ozzy. Nothing bad. I was just packing', and I smile at him, looking so worried, pushing a curtain of hair behind his ear, something I must have watched him do ten thousand million times. And he smiles back at me. A smile that could light up a room.

'I love you, Mama.'

'And I love you, Dadda. Now come over here and give us a kiss.'